I0057232

Wall Street Terms

Financial Education Is Your Best Investment

Published April 10, 2020

Revision 2.1

Financial Terms Dictionary

Copyright And Trademark Notices

Limits of Liability and Disclaimer of Warranties

The materials in this book are provided "as is" and without warranties of any kind either express or implied. The Author disclaims all warranties, express or implied, including, but not limited to, implied warranties of merchantability and fitness for a particular purpose.

The Author does not warrant that defects will be corrected, or that that the site or the server that makes this eBook available are free of viruses or other harmful components. The Author does not warrant or make any representations regarding the use or the results of the use of the materials in this book in terms of their correctness, accuracy, reliability, or otherwise. Applicable law may not allow the exclusion of implied warranties, so the above exclusion may not apply to you.

Under no circumstances, including, but not limited to, negligence, shall the Author be liable for any special or consequential damages that result from the use of, or the inability to use this eBook, even if the Author or his authorized representative has been advised of the possibility of such damages.

Applicable law may not allow the limitation or exclusion of liability or incidental or consequential damages, so the above limitation or exclusion may not apply to you. In no event shall the Author's total liability to you for all damages, losses, and causes of action (whether in contract, tort, including but not limited to, negligence or otherwise) exceed the amount paid by you, if any, for this eBook.

Facts and information are believed to be accurate at the time they were placed in this book. All data provided in this book is to be used for information purposes only. The information contained within is not intended to provide specific legal, financial or tax advice, or any other advice whatsoever, for any individual or company and should not be relied upon in that regard. The services described are only offered in jurisdictions where they may be legally offered. Information provided is not all-inclusive and is limited to information that is made available and such information should not be relied upon as all-inclusive or accurate.

You are advised to do your own due diligence when it comes to making business decisions and should use caution and seek the advice of qualified professionals. You should check with your accountant, lawyer, or professional advisor, before acting on this or any information. You may not consider any examples, documents, or other content in this eBook or otherwise provided by the Author to be the equivalent of professional advice.

The Author assumes no responsibility for any losses or damages resulting from your use of any link, information, or opportunity contained in this book or within any other information disclosed by the author in any form whatsoever.

About the Author

Thomas Herold is a successful entrepreneur, mediator, author, and personal development coach. He published over 20 books with over 200,000 copies distributed worldwide and the founder of seven online businesses.

For over ten years Thomas Herold has studied the monetary system and has experienced some profound insights on how money and wealth are related. After three years of successful investing in silver, he released 'Building Wealth with Silver - How to Profit From The Biggest Wealth Transfer in History' in 2012. One of the first books that illustrate in a remarkable, simple way the monetary system and its consequences.

He is the founder and CEO of the 'Financial Terms Dictionary' book series and website, which explains in detail and comprehensive form over 1000 financial terms. In his financial book series, he informs in detail and with practical examples all aspects of the financial sector. His educational materials are designed to help people get started with financial education.

In his 2018 released book 'The Money Deception', Mr. Herold provides the most sophisticated insight and shocking details about the current monetary system. Never before has the massive manipulation of money caused so much economic inequality in the world. In spite of these frightening facts, 'The Money Deception' also provides remarkable and simple solutions to create abundance for all people, and it's a must read if you want to survive the global monetary transformation that's underway right now.

In 2019 he released an entirely new financial book series explaining in detail and with practical examples over 1000 financial terms. The 'Herold Financial IQ Series' contains currently of 15 titles covering every category of the financial market.

For more information please visit:

Herold Financial IQ Series

Herold Financial IQ Series

There are 15 books in this financial terms series available. Click the link below to see an overview and available formats available on Amazon.

Financial IQ Series on Amazon

Table Of Contents

AAA Rating

AAA Rating refers to the maximum potential credit rating that a credit ratings bureau can award to an issuing entity's bonds. Such a credit rating represents a superb level of creditworthiness. It means that the issuing entity is easily capable of meeting its various financial obligations. The three major ratings agencies of Moody's, Standard & Poor's, and Fitch Ratings all utilize the AAA as their top credit rating which designates those bonds and issuers which have the highest possible level of credit quality.

It is not possible to completely eliminate the potential risk of a credit default from a bond issuer. Yet those entities which possess AAA rated bonds are believed to have the least possible chance of defaulting on their interest payments or principal repayments. Because of this, such bonds provide their investors with the smallest possible yields of any bonds that possess the same dates of maturity.

Thanks to the Global Financial Crisis of 2008, many companies and countries lost their coveted AAA rating. In fact, by the middle of 2009, there were only four remaining firms out of the entire list of S&P 500 companies that still held their treasured AAA rated credit. The story was the same with the gold standard credit rated nations of the world as well.

Before the Great Recession, a number of nations enjoyed the highly coveted AAA credit rating from all three of the big three ratings agencies. Once the dust had settled, only the following nine nations still held it including Australia, Canada, Denmark, Germany, Luxembourg, Norway, Singapore, Sweden, and Switzerland. Countries that had lost it included Austria, Finland, France, the United Kingdom, and the United States. The U.S. still had the AAA rated credit from Moody's and Fitch, while the United Kingdom still held it from Standard & Poor's (who even removed it from negative watch).

High credit ratings like the AAA rating provide significant benefits to a company or nation which carries them. It allows the issuer to borrow at a reduced interest rate and ultimate cost. These companies and countries are also able to borrow greater amounts of money when they possess the highest ratings. Lower costs of borrowing allow for nations and corporations to access opportunities through cheap and easy credit. A company might be able to buy out a competitor as it is able to cheaply borrow the money for the transaction costs of the relevant merger and acquisition.

Where companies are concerned, it is possible for them to enjoy the highest AAA rating on bonds which they issue as secured while having a lower credit rating on those which are unsecured. This is simply because secured bonds provide a particular asset that has been put up as collateral in case the issuer defaults on the interest or principal payments of the bond in question. The creditor has the right to seize the asset if the issuer ends up defaulting. Such bonds could carry the collateral of real estate, machinery, or other forms of equipment. Conversely, unsecured bonds only carry the backing of the issuer's capability of repaying the obligation. This is why the credit ratings for unsecured forms of bonds only rely on the income source of the issuer in question.

Since the Global Financial Crisis destroyed the highest creditworthiness of many a long-standing AAA rated nation, neither the world's largest debtor nor creditor nations possess the all-important AAA rating. For example, S&P argues that it will only deliver the AAA rating in the cases where an "extremely strong capacity to meet financial commitments" exists.

The euro zone was long a shining example of many nations which possessed unanimous AAA rated credit. After the Great Recession and Sovereign Debt Crisis ravaged Europe, only the two nations of Luxembourg and Germany still retain this three ratings agency unanimous AAA status.

Absorption Rate

Absorption rate is a term used in real estate. It represents the speed with which homes available in a real estate market are sold in a certain amount of time. Real estate professionals figure out this absorption rate by taking the number of houses that are available and dividing this by the average number of sales in a month. The result provides a useful number. It is the total number of months it will require before all of the homes on the market are sold.

It is important to note that this absorption rate does not consider any supplies of other houses that enter the real estate market. As such it is a snapshot of a fixed moment in time. Higher absorption rates will usually signify that the numbers of available houses will decrease quickly. This means that a homeowner would likely sell his or her house in a shorter time frame.

In historical context, when the rates of absorption rose over 20%, this has meant that the market was ideal for sellers. Homes would sell fast. When the absorption rate proved to be lower than 15%, this means that a buyer's market is in effect. Buyers are being pickier. This slows down the rate at which homes are being sold.

The absorption rate is easier to understand by looking at an example. In this scenario, a given city has 2,000 houses that are up for sale. If buyers came into the market and bought up 200 homes each month, then the home supply would be depleted in 10 months. This is simply figured by dividing the 2,000 houses by 200 homes bought each month.

When buyers purchase the 200 houses from the 2,000 houses total, it means the rate of absorption equals 10%. This number is derived by taking the 200 houses buyers purchase every month and dividing it by the total 2,000 houses for sale. It would mean that the market is optimal for buyers. Any homeowner who was hoping to sell a house would be aware that the market should half sell out over a period of five months.

There are a number of different individuals who work with this important figure. Real estate industry professionals are most interested in the number. Real estate brokers would put this number to use when they price houses. If a market showed signs of lower rates of absorption, the agents might have no choice but to lower the listing price in order to attract a buyer. In the opposite case, the market might exhibit a higher rate. This would allow the realtor to raise the home price without eliminating demand on the property.

Home builders also look at these absorption rates when they are thinking about building new properties. A higher rate is often interpreted by the construction industry as an optimal time to begin building new houses. When the conditions on the market show higher absorption, it means demand can likely support them developing additional properties. The opposite is true if there is less absorption. This tells them that demand is lower. Construction may pause in efforts to build new houses.

A last group that carefully studies the rates of absorption are the property appraisers. They think about these rates when they are considering the total value of a given property. In 2009, new appraisal rules came into effect. These mandated that every home value appraisal connected with a home loan had to take into account the active rate of absorption. The reasoning behind this was that home values should be less in times where lower absorption resulted in fewer and more drawn out sales at lower prices.

Agency Bonds

Agency bonds are those bonds that are actually issued by United States' government sponsored entities. This means that these bonds are not government guaranteed, as they are created by private companies. They are backed up implicitly by the United States government, since these organizations were created to permit some categories of individuals to have the ability to receive lower cost financing, in particular first time home buyers and students.

The biggest, best recognized names in Agency Bond issuers prove to be Sallie Mae, Freddie Mac, and Fannie Mae. These three large companies are different from government agencies in that they are not guaranteed by the United States' government's promise of full faith and credit. Instead, they are all privately held and run companies that are given government charters as a result of their critical activities that carry out government directed policies.

Agency bonds are used to raise money to help these companies offer farm loans, home loans, student loans, and international trade financing. As a result of the government deeming these activities to be significant enough to grant charters, the markets consider that the Federal Government will not permit these chartered firms to go under. This gives their agency bonds the implied government sponsored entity guarantee. As a result of this implicit guarantee, these agency bonds carry ratings and yields that are comparable to government issued debt.

As an example, Private Export Funding Corporation bonds prove to be backed up by actual collateral of United States government securities. Federal Farm Credit Banks' bonds are not, although it is a government sponsored entity. Despite the differences, the yield-to-maturity of the two bonds are 4.753% and 4.760% respectively. These two organizations' debt obligations are nearly priced the same, demonstrating once again the implicit guarantee in the government sponsored entity securities.

The issue of taxation is another important one to consider when you are looking at Agency Bonds. All agency bonds are taxable on Federal levels. Many are not taxed on state levels. This is critical if you are an investor who resides in a state that has its own taxes. The interest payments from the best known of these organizations like Freddie Mac and Fannie Mae can be taxed on a state level. The majority of others agency bonds avoid this taxation, making their rates more attractive for many investors.

The vast majority of all agency bonds outstanding, more than ninety percent, are issued by only the four largest government sponsored entities. By largest size, these are Federal Home Loan Banks, Federal Home Loan Mortgage Corporation, Federal National Mortgage Association, and Federal Farm Credit Banks. The Federal Home Loan Banks' and Federal Farm Credit Banks' agency bonds are not state income taxable.

Algorithmic Trading

Algorithmic trading has many names. Users also know it as black box trading and algo trading. This system of trading works with complicated and highly advanced mathematical formulas. It takes these models and engages in rapid decisions to execute transactions in various financial markets. This type of trading is only possible with super fast computers and programs. It combines these with the algorithms to come up with trading strategies that deliver the maximum returns.

There a variety of trading and investment strategies that can benefit from algorithmic trading. Some of these are inter-market spreads, speculation, market making, and arbitrage. Nowadays this style of trading is able to operate and automate trading and investment strategies by working on electronic platforms. This means that the programs themselves can carryout specific trading instructions. They can be set up to consider special scenarios like volume, price, and timing.

Bigger institutional investors who buy enormous amounts of shares are most likely to use algorithmic trading. These programs help them to gain the optimal price in the market without substantially impacting the price of the stock or making their buying costs higher.

Among the most popular types of algorithmic trading strategies are trading in advance of index fund re-balancing, scalping, arbitrage, and mean reversion. These are complex strategies that mostly require speed of discovery and instantaneous decision making to be effective.

Trading in advance of index fund re-balancing has to do with mutual funds. Pension funds and other retirement accounts are heavily invested in these vehicles. Because the underlying assets held in these funds constantly change, they must purchase or sell index funds to match. This algorithmic trading strategy looks for the points where the mutual funds are ready to re-balance. It then buys or sells first. In reality it makes money for the algorithmic traders at the expense of the mutual fund investors.

Scalpers look to make money on the bid versus ask spreads. If they trade the difference quickly enough repeatedly during the day, it can make them significant amounts of money. For it to work, the movement in the price of the stock has to be less than the spread of the security or stock in question. These kinds of movements happen anywhere from seconds to minutes. Only the quick decision making of the algorithm formulas is sufficient to maximize this strategy.

Arbitrage refers to finding the differences in pricing of two related entities. Global businesses utilize this effectively all the time. They can buy supplies for less or contract labor cheaper by getting it in different nations. It helps them to lower their expenses and boost their profits.

In algorithmic trading, arbitrage strategies work with examples like S&P 500 stocks versus S&P futures. These two markets for the securities or index will often encounter price differences. Stocks on NYSE or NASDAQ could move ahead of or behind the futures market for them. The powerful and fast algorithms are able to both track and trade such differences and profit as a result.

Mean reversion refers to coming up with the average for short term low and high prices on a security. The algorithms are able to compile such an average rapidly. When the price moves towards or away from this average mean, the programs can rapidly trade them as they move back towards it.

There are a few other strategies that algorithms are able to enhance. Some of these pertain to dark pools of capital and reducing their transaction costs. Dark pools are unregulated and off market trades created when institutional investors make their own private exchanges.

American Stock Exchange (AMEX)

The AMEX is the acronym for the American Stock Exchange. This exchange proves to be the third biggest such stock market in all of the United States when trading volume is considered, after the NYSE and the NASDAQ national exchanges. Located in the American financial center of New York, the AMEX carries around ten percent of every security that is listed within the United States. In the past, it had a much larger market share of traded securities.

The origins of the AMEX lie before it was called the American Stock Exchange. In 1953, the New York Curb Exchange became known as the AMEX. This exchange proved to be a mutual organization that the members owned. In decades past, the American Stock Exchange had an important position as a major competitor for the New York Stock Exchange. This role gradually fell to the rising NASDAQ stock exchange.

Back on the seventeenth of January in 2008, the NYSE Euronext exchange announced its intentions to buy out the American Stock Exchange in consideration of $260 million in NYSE stock. They completed the transaction on the first of October in 2008. NYSE originally intended to integrate the AMEX exchange into its Alternext European small cap exchange. They first renamed it the NYSE Alternext U.S. By March of 2009, NYSE had scrapped this plan and renamed it the NYSE Amex Equities exchange.

The overwhelming majority of AMEX trading these days is done in small cap company stocks, derivatives, and exchange traded funds. These are niches that the AMEX exchange carved out and maintained for itself despite the rising allure of the newer NASDAQ in the 1990's. The AMEX observes regular trading session hours running from 9:30 in the morning to 4:00 in the afternoon on Monday through Friday. The exchange is closed on Saturdays, Sundays, and all holidays that the exchange announces in advance.

Angel Investor

An Angel Investor refers to an accredited investor (with over a million dollars net worth) which invests funds into entrepreneurs and smaller startups. These special investors are commonly from the friends or family of the entrepreneur. This capital which they deliver is often in the form of a lump sum one-time payment to help get the business going or to keep it funded during the challenging early stages where they are still developing and beginning to market their products.

Another characteristic of such an Angel Investor is that they offer better terms to the startup than would a comparable bank or lender in the same scenario. This is principally because they believe in the entrepreneur they are backing more than the viability of the business itself. Such investors concentrate their efforts on assisting startups with successfully making their initial business steps. They are less concerned with the potential for profit they might make off of the fledgling company. This makes most Angel Investors the diametric opposite of the venture capitalists.

There are a variety of different names which such Angel Investors go by. These include angel funders, informal investors, private investors, business angels, and seed investors. Such wealthy individuals who choose to inject desperately needed startup capital into firms do so in exchange for either convertible debt or a stake in the company's equity. There are such investors who become involved through one of the various crowd funding platforms over the Internet, and others who join with networks of other Angel Investors in order to pool their resources to be more effective (as with an Angel Investor syndicate). Angel List is a popular and well respected site that puts together angels and entrepreneurs.

Using this phrase to describe noble investors originally came from Broadway Theater. It was here that wealthy patrons would contribute money in order to advance theatrical productions. This terminology Angel Investor was first utilized by William Wetzel of the University of New Hampshire. As founder of the Center for Venture Research, he backed an extensive study on the ways that entrepreneurs are able to bring in capital.

In order to be official Angel Investors, these individuals have to meet the definition set by the SEC Securities Exchange Commission for accredited investors. This means that the interested party must possess at least a million in net worth along with an annual income amounting to at least $200,000.

Most Angel Investors will actually deploy their own funds in their investments. This puts them in direct contrast with the venture capitalists which instead gather up a pool of money from many investors and then combine this into a fund which is strategically managed. In general the Angel Investors represent actual individuals. It is also possible for the entity offering the funding to be a limited liability company, trust, business or even an investment fund.

Those Angel Investors who actually seed the entrepreneurs' startups which ultimately fail will lose their entire investment. It helps to explain why angel investors who are professionals will always be on the hunt for a clearly defined exit strategy opportunity. This might be through an IPO Initial Public Offering or an acquisition.

In truth, successful angel investors boast of portfolios with an average success rate of from 20 percent to 30 percent. This may sound costly for entrepreneurs who are involved in early stage business startups. Finding alternative cheaper sources of financing like banks are not often viable options for these fledging companies. It means that angels are often the ideal funder or backer for those entrepreneurs who find themselves still in the financially struggling days of the early startup stages in their company.

Arbitrage

Arbitrage refers to the practice of taking advantage of the price imbalances sometimes arising in two or even more markets. People who work in foreign money exchange run their whole businesses on this model. As an example, they look for tourists who require a rapid exchange of their cash for the local currency. Tourists agree to accept this local money for a lower amount than the actual market rate, and the money changer gets to keep the spread created by the higher rate that he charges them for the local currency. This spread that the different rates create becomes his profit.

Many different scenarios allow for investors or businessmen to become involved in the arbitrage practice. Sometimes, one market is not aware of the existence of the second market, or it simply can not access it. Arbitrageurs, persons who avail themselves of arbitrage, are also able to benefit from the different liquidities present in various markets.

Arbitrage is typically employed to discuss opportunities with investments and money rather than price imbalances for goods. Because of arbitrageurs operating in various markets whenever they spot opportunities, the prices found in the higher market will commonly drop while the prices in the lower market will usually rise so that they meet somewhere around the middle of the price difference. The phrase efficiency of the market then deals with the rate of speed at which these differing prices converge towards each other.

There are people who make arbitrage their livelihood. Working in arbitrage offers the possibilities of lucrative gains and profits. It does not come free of risk though. The greatest danger is that the prices may change rapidly between the varying markets. As an example, the spreads could rapidly fluctuate in only the tiny amount of time that is necessary for the two transactions to take place. In instances where these prices are moving quickly, arbitrageurs may not only find that they missed the chance to realize the profit between the differences in the prices, but that in fact they lost money on the deal.

Examples of arbitrage in the financial markets abound. Convertible arbitrage is working with convertible bonds to realize arbitrage. The bond can be converted into stock of the issuer of the bond. Sometimes, the amounts of shares that the bond will convert to are worth more than the price of the bond. In this case, an arbitrageur will be able to make a profit by purchasing the bond, converting it into the stock shares, and then selling the stock on the exchange to realize the difference.

Relative value arbitrage is using options to acquire the underlying shares of stock. It might be that the option is less expensive relative to the shares of stock that it will purchase. If a stock trades at $200, and the option that permits you to buy a share of the stock for $120 is trading at only $50, then you could buy the option, exercise it for the shares, and sell it for $200. You would only have spent $170 per share on the purchase, and then realize a $30 per share profit.

Asset Allocation

Asset allocation involves diversifying an investor portfolio into a variety of different assets based on the appropriate level of risk. This procedure has investors divide up their investments between varying types of assets. Among these might be stocks, real estate, bonds, and cash.

The goal is to maximize the reward and risk balance using the investors' own goals and scenarios. This has become one of the critical ideas behind money management and financial planning today. There are several different types of asset allocation to consider. These are strategic, tactical, and dynamic.

In strategic asset allocation, the investor sets out target allocations for the desired different classes of assets. When the percentage balance deviates from the original set levels, it will involve the investor rebalancing the overall portfolio. The allocations will be reset to the original ones as they change significantly because of different returns that each class earns.

Strategic asset allocation sets these initial allocations up using a number of different considerations. Among these are the investor objectives, the intended time frame of investing, and the risk tolerance. These allocations can be changed in time as the different variables alter.

A good comparison to this form of allocating is a traditional buy and hold investment strategy. This form of strategic allocating of assets and the tactical allocation approach are both derived from modern portfolio theory. They seek diversification so that they can lower risk and boost the returns on portfolios.

Tactical asset allocating is more active than strategic forms of the discipline. Investors who follow tactical allocating will re-balance the asset percentages in different categories on a more regular basis. They will do this in an effort to benefit from market sectors that are stronger or poised for gains. They might also re-balance in an effort to capture anomalies in market pricing.

Tactical allocating is well suited to professional portfolio managers. They study the markets and look to find extra returns from scenarios that develop. This is still only considered to be a strategy that is moderately active. When the short term gains are attained, these managers go back to the original strategic asset balance of the portfolio.

Investors or managers who look for tactical asset allocators often choose ETF exchange traded funds or index funds for this purpose. The goal of these vehicles concentrates on asset classes rather than individual investments. This reduces the costs of rebalancing. The transaction costs of buying and selling index funds is far less than with many individual stocks or even several mutual funds.

For an individual investor, they allow them to pick a stock index fund, bond index fund, and money market fund. It is also possible to focus on sub-sectors within the bigger funds. There are foreign stocks, large cap stocks, individual sectors, and small cap stock funds or ETFs from which to choose.

When tactical allocating in sectors, investors can pick out those which they believe will perform strongly for either the near term or intermediate time frames. Those that believe health and technology will do well in upcoming months or even a few years might rebalance some of the portfolio into ETFs in those industry segments.

With dynamic asset allocation, investors are focused on re-balancing the portfolio to keep it near its long term goals of asset mix. This means that positions in assets classes that are outperforming have to be reduced. Those that are under-performing must then be increased with the proceeds from the outperforming assets. This restores the portfolio mix to the desired allocation. The reason investors would do this is to keep the original asset mix so that they can capture appropriate returns that meet or beat the target benchmark.

Asset Management

Asset Management refers to an organization, institution, or individual asset manager directing a client's securities, assets, and cash. It is commonly a financial services company that will do this, and especially an investment bank like Morgan Stanley, Barclays, UBS, Julius Baer, or Goldman Sachs. Such a financial institution will provide highly researched and sought after investment advice and a wide range of investment services. These would include both a variety of alternative and traditional investment product offerings. Many of these will not be available to the typical retail investor.

The financial institution will hold the account and usually offers credit cards, check writing privileges, debit cards, courtesy margin loans, and an automatic sweeping of any available cash balances into a money market fund. Brokerage services are naturally a key cornerstone of this service. Family offices and high net worth and ultra-high net worth individuals as well as institutions such as trust, pension, and insurance funds will typically be clients of asset management firms.

Because the associated investment minimums that such services demand are often in the millions of dollars, the services are typically only available to the accounts of financial intermediaries, major corporations, government entities, and wealthy families or individuals. Their products are many and vast but focus on real estate, fixed income, international investments, and commodities. Diversification is a key cornerstone to the services and investment products that good asset management offers its clients.

As these well-to-do individuals and institutions deposit their considerable sums of money into their accounts at the firm, the money is swept into a money market fund straight away. This provides a far greater return than mere checking accounts or even savings accounts offer customers. The account holders will often have the choice of either a non-FDIC backed fund (with correspondingly higher returns) or a Federal Deposit Insurance Company backed money market fund that naturally pays less since it is considered to be risk-free.

One of the principal advantages to these accounts is that these firms offer a true one-stop shop service for all of their financial needs. This includes the convenience of check writing privileges, debit and credit cards, lucrative private investments, and more all under a single roof. Both their investment and their banking needs will be serviced by the single institution instead of needing to maintain separate banking and brokerage accounts.

It was thanks to the passing of the Gramm-Leach-Bliley Act of 1997 that permitted the repealing of the Glass-Steagall Act. This Great Depression-era legislation had stopped financial institutions from providing both security and banking services to clients in an effort to protect the clients from the investment banks' rapacious greed and mis-investing of their funds.

It is always a helpful idea to look at a real-world example of the concept under discussion in order to better understand it. Consider the real-life case of investment bank Merrill Lynch, which was long the largest in the world until the Global Financial Crisis ended its near-century of successful independence and dominance in the field. Today they are a subsidiary of Bank of America.

Merrill provides its CMA Cash Management Account to meet the particular needs of its wealthy clients who want to pursue both investment and banking possibilities with only a single integrated account. This account provides customers with a personalized financial advisor as well. This financial advisor will deliver both advice and many investment options. Among these will be potentially highly lucrative IPO initial public offerings that Merrill often participates in, as well as foreign currency trades and even private investments.

The interest rates offered on such cash deposits will be tiered. This means that by linking together all deposit accounts, the eligible funds will aggregate together in order to qualify for the highest possible interest rate. The securities contained in this account will not be protected by the FDIC but instead by the umbrella of the SIPC Securities Investor Protection Corporation. SIPC will not save any owner's assets from the risk of decline or failure, but instead safeguards them from the collapse of the brokerage firm which holds them on the clients' behalves.

Back to the Merrill Lynch account example from above, the CMA account will include the ubiquitous check writing privileges and also global access to the investor's cash via any Bank of America-branded ATM automated teller machines, all without having to pay transaction fees for this convenient service. There will also be wire transfers, internal fund transfers, and bill payment services offered. The online app is called MyMerrill and it permits the account holders to have access to their accounts and engage in many of the account maintenance and management functions from their mobile device or lap top. Those accounts with over $250,000 in assets which are eligible will avoid the two fees - the annual $125 cost and the $25 assessment on every sub account the client holds.

Bailout

Bailouts prove to be the action of handing money or other capital to a company, individual, or nation that will likely go down without help. This is done in an effort to keep the entity from financial insolvency, bankruptcy, or total failure. Sometimes bankruptcies are pursued to permit an organization to fail without panic, so that fear and systemic failure does not become endemic, taking down other similar entities along the way.

Various different groups might qualify for urgent bailouts. Countries like Greece have been prime examples in the year 2010. Companies such as major banks and insurance outfits have been deemed too big to fail in the several years preceding 2010, during the height of the financial crisis and resulting Great Recession. Other industries have qualified as well, including car manufacturers, airlines, and vital transportation industries.

A good example of companies that receive preferential bailout treatment lies in the transportation industry. The Untied States government believes that transportation proves to be the underlying core of the nation's economic versatility, necessary to support the country's geopolitical power.

Because of this, the Federal Government works to safeguard the largest companies involved in transportation from failing with low interest rate loans and subsidies, which are a form of bailout. Oil companies, airlines, railroads, and trucking companies could all be considered to be a critical part of this industry. Such firms are considered to be too big and important to fail because their services prove to be nationally and constantly necessary to support the country's economy and thereby its eventual security.

Bailouts that are done in an emergency fashion typically prove to be full of controversy. In 2008 in the United States, intense and angry debates erupted regarding the failing banking and car manufacturing businesses. The camp standing against such bailouts looked at them as a means of passing the expensive bill for the failures over to the taxpayers.

Leaders of this group savagely denounced any monetary bailouts of the big three car makers and large banks, which they said all needed to be broken up as punishment for mismanagement. They criticized a new moral hazard that was being created by guaranteeing safety nets to other businesses. They similarly did not like the big central bureaucracy that arises from government agencies selecting the size and disposition of the bailouts. Finally, government bailouts of these groups were attacked as a form of corporate welfare that continues the cycle of more corporate irresponsibility.

The other camp argued that these bailouts were necessary evils, since the state of the American economy did not prove to be solid enough to suffer the failure of either the major banks or the car makers. With the car makers, fully three million jobs stood on the line. The banking industry had the argument of systemic failure of the financial system backing it up. No one on the side of the bailouts pretended to like having to engage in them, but they were said to be necessary nonetheless. In the end, such bailouts were issued to both major industries totaling in the trillions of dollars.

Bear Market

Bear markets are periods in which stock markets drop for an extended amount of time. These pullbacks typically run to twenty percent or even greater amounts of the underlying stock values. Bear markets are the direct opposites of bull markets, when prices rise for extended amounts of time.

Bear markets and their accompanying drastic drops in stock share prices are commonly caused by declining corporate profits. They can also result from the correction of a too highly valued stock market, where stock prices prove to be overextended and decline to more historically fair values. Bear markets commonly begin when investors become frightened by lower earnings or too high values for their stocks and begin selling them. When many investors sell their holdings at a single time, the prices drop, sometimes substantially. Declining prices lead still other investors to fear that their money that they have invested in the stock market will be lost too. This motivates them to sell out through fear. In this way, the vicious cycle down progresses.

There have been many instances of bear markets in the United States since the country began over two hundred years ago. Perhaps the greatest example of an extended bear market is that found in the 1970's. During these years, stocks traded down and then sideways for more than a full decade. These kinds of encounters keep potential buyers out of the markets. This only fuels the fire of the bear market and keeps it going, since only a few buyers are purchasing stocks. In this way, the selling continues, as sellers consistently outnumber buyers in the stock exchanges.

For long term investors, bear markets present terrific opportunities. A person who is buying stocks with the plan to keep them for tens of years will find in a bear market the optimal sale price point and time to purchase stocks. Though many individual investors become frenzied and sell their stocks continuously during a bear market, this is exactly the wrong time to sell them.

Bear markets provide savvy investors with the chance to seek out solid companies and fundamentals that should still be strong ten to twenty years in the future. Good companies will still do well in the coming years, even if their share prices fall twenty or forty percent with the overall market. A company like Gillette that makes razors will still have a viable and dependable market going years down the road, even if the stock is unfairly punished by a bear market. Making money in a bear market requires investors to understand that a company's underlying core business has to be distinguished from its short term share price. In the near term, a company's fundamentals and stock prices do not always have much in common.

This means that a discounted price on a good company in a bear market is much like a periodic clearance sale at a person's favorite store. The time to buy the products heavily is while they are greatly discounted. The stock market is much the same. History has demonstrated on a number of different occasions that the stock prices of good companies will rebound to more realistic and fair valuations given some time.

Bitcoin Cash

Bitcoin Cash refers to the first split from the legendary crypto-currency market leading Bitcoin block chain. On August 1st the splinter group created its new crypto-currency Bitcoin Cash. The developer of this rival to the original behemoth is Calin Culianu. He explains that there are two principle noteworthy changes to the new bitcoin. These are an increase in the size of the block chain to eight megabytes and a removal of the SegWit code change that could activate on the bitcoin block chain by the end of August.

There are many detractors from this first Bitcoin splinter group who refer to the new Bitcoin Cash as merely an "altcoin." This refers to a software fork which leads to a newer crypto-currency that has its own independent market. The splinter Bitcoin has already taken a severe beating on the crypto-currency markets by trading at only $461 to the real Bitcoin's hefty price tag of $2,568. This represents approximately an only 18 percent valuation against the original on the futures market. It reveals the still limited level of confidence in and support for this altcoin which it boasts from current Bitcoin backers.

What gives the Bitcoin Cash crypto-currency some legitimacy is that it will maintain the same transaction history as the real Bitcoin does all the way up to the point of the split. This means that current users of bitcoin would have it on the two block chains. The newer project will also allow for multiple implementations of the new software. The first software that has implemented the Bitcoin Cash protocol is Bitcoin ABC. The splinter group's ultimate goal is for many more such implementations in the future. In fact, developer Culianu is already working on Bitcoin Classic and Bitcoin Unlimited as future implementations which will boost the block size of the BTC. Their goal is to ensure that they are compatible with the original implementation of Bitcoin Cash.

While there are a few supporters who are eager to embrace the changes, the majority of Bitcoin mining pools, mining companies, developers, and users are uninterested. The leading firm that has enthusiastically embraced the new code is the Chinese-based mining company ViaBTC. They control a nearly four percent of all Bitcoin computing power today. ViaBTC even operates its own BTC exchange. It is the first one to list the new crypto-currency format and even has plans set to launch its own mining pool which is entirely dedicated to the new Bitcoin Cash.

Certainly the Bitcoin Cash has garnered much-needed support from those users who long to see an increase in the size of the block chain. This includes the developers from the new rivals Bitcoin Unlimited and Bitcoin Classic.

Many former supporters of the new rivals such as Bitmain and Bitcoin.com are hesitant to actually back the new breakaway efforts now that they have formally split off. They are still committed to the Segwit2x scaling proposal which is set to be implemented on the main Bitcoin by end of August.

In fact it was Bitmain that came up with the inspiration for Bitcoin Cash. Despite this, they announced that they will only switch over to the rivals if the conditions are right. They have left the door open to support both Segwit2x main BTC as well as the newer varieties going forward.

Meanwhile, Bitcoin.com has announced that it will permit its miners in the pool to decide if they want to mine the newer Bitcoin Cash tokens which go under the acronym of BCC. It will mine the traditional Bitcoin and its revised Segwit2x chain itself. Yet it threatened that it will support the rival forthwith should the block size increase planned by SegWit not materialize as scheduled.

Bitcoin Currency (BTC)

Bitcoin is the name of a new electronic currency. An unknown individual who called himself Satoshi Nakamoto created this currency in 2009. This world's first widespread virtual currency appeals to many individuals because there are no banks or governments involved in issuing, trading, spending, or processing the transactions. There are also no transaction fees involved. Owners do not have to provide their actual identity to use them.

Bitcoin users like that they are able to purchase goods and services completely anonymously. They also enjoy the inexpensive and simple to use international payment system. This exists because this currency is not heavily regulated nor tied to any single bank or nation. Small businesses tend to like Bitcoin since they do not have to pay any credit card usage fees.

Many speculators have purchased Bitcoins for investment. Booms and busts in this currency are all too common. Those who bought in to the crypto currency early made spectacular returns as the value skyrocketed with growing demand. Others lost fortunes as the price of the Bitcoins subsequently crashed in value.

There are several ways to obtain these Bitcoins. Users buy them on open marketplaces known as Bitcoin exchanges. Those who wish to have them can buy and sell it with a variety of different currencies. Mt. Gox was the largest Bitcoin marketplace until it spectacularly collapsed and went bankrupt. Many clients who held their Bitcoins at Mt. Gox lost most of their money there at the time.

Individuals also buy and sell Bitcoins by transferring them to each other and by paying with them. They can do this with their computers or mobile apps. This is much like sending cash with a digital service like PayPal.

A last way to obtain Bitcoins is by mining them. Mining is the way that individuals create new Bitcoins. They do this by utilizing computers to solve complicated math problems or puzzles. When such a puzzle is solved, 25 Bitcoins are awarded to the group which solves them.

Owners keep their Bitcoins in a digital wallet. This can be stored on a personal computer or in the cloud. A virtual wallet is much like an electronic bank account which permits owners to receive or send Bitcoins, to save their money, or to pay for their goods and services. These wallets do not receive the protection of FDIC insurance as do traditional bank accounts.

To users, Bitcoins are simply computer programs or mobile apps which give the owners the Bitcoin wallet. The payment system is easier to utilize than is a credit card or debit card purchase. An individual does not require a merchant account in order to receive the currency. All an individual has to do to make a payment is to put the payment amount and address of the recipient then click send.

An important fact about Bitcoin is that no one owns the actual network. Bitcoin users control the Bitcoin currency. Various developers work on the software to improve it. Users are able to decide which version or software they use it on, which prohibits developers from forcefully changing the operation. For the software to work properly, all Bitcoin users have to work with programs that abide by the same rules.

As with most new currencies Bitcoin is not without problems. When digital wallets are left in the cloud, some servers have been hacked and coins stolen. Bitcoin exchanges like Mt. Gox have failed. Other companies have disappeared with their clients' Bitcoins. When the wallets stay on a person's computer, they can be destroyed by viruses or accidentally deleted.

Increasing government regulation appears to be in the future of Bitcoin and other crypto currencies. Because of the anonymous nature of the currency, they have evolved into the preferred payment method for illegal activities such as drugs and smuggling. Governments are concerned about being able to trace these types of activities back to the users. They are also worried about not being able to tax transactions made in Bitcoin currency.

Blockchain

Blockchain refers to a technology that serves as a means of structuring and storing data. As such it is the ultimate foundation of the revolutionary crypto-currencies such as Bitcoin and Ether. The true breakthrough in coding capability permits participants to share digital ledgers back and forth over a computer network. Its genius and appeal lies in the fact that it does not require a central authority to run or oversee it. Since there is no meddling central authority like a central bank or boss to the system, no one party can interfere with the financial records.

In other words, the straight math makes sure that all the parties who participate are honest with each other. Blockchain is made up of concatenated transactions blocks. Nowadays, the technology has become so important and offers so many future possibilities for real world applications that over forty of the world's biggest and most important financial firms are experimenting with uses for it.

Blockchains are also public record ledgers of all transactions in a crypto-currency which have ever taken place. For this reason, the chain is always expanding as every new record adds additional completed blocks to it. These become a part of the blockchain via a chronological and linear fashioned order. Every participating node receives a copy of this blockchain as it is updated. Nodes are computers which share a Bitcoin network connection that utilizes the system to validate and relay such transactions which were performed in it. The chain comes as an auto download once a computer network joins up to the Bitcoin network. This chain maintains full information on all balances and appropriate addresses from the very first transaction ever all the way to the latest one which has been performed utilizing the block.

In the end, it is this blockchain that represents the primary technological advance offered by Bitcoin. It amounts to the proof and record of every transaction performed using the network. The blocks represent the current record in the chain that will ultimately record all or at least some of the recent transaction. After it is finished, this block will join the chain as part and parcel of the current and permanent database. Once a block is spoken for, a new block will become generated. Myriads of such blocks exist in the chain. They are linked one to another, much like a physical chain, in their correct chronological and linear order. Each block contains the hash of the prior block in it.

It is always helpful to consider a real world example to better understand a somewhat complex concept like this one. Traditional banking is a solid analogy. This blockchain is much like a complete history of banking records and transactions. Bitcoin transactions must be chronologically entered in the blockchain as real world banking transactions are at financial institutions. Such blocks are something like the statements recording individual bank accounts and banking transactions.

The protocol of Bitcoin is based upon all nodes in the system sharing the blockchain's database. A complete and unaltered copy of the chain will include records of all the transactions in Bitcoin which have ever been executed. This delivers useful insights into the quantity of value that a specific address owned at any time in the past.

The problem with the ever growing nature of the chain is that it has become so very large with over a decade of increasing size that synchronization and storage have become serious issues. These days, the average time of a new block appearing on the chain amounts to only ten minutes. Mining, the process of unlocking new BTC, is adding the majority of new blocks to the chain these days.

Bloomberg

Bloomberg is a multimedia news and financial data services provider company. It puts decision makers in touch with an enormous network of ideas, people, and information. Bloomberg rapidly deploys financial and business news, information, insight, and general news to people around the world.

The company provides important decision makers with the necessary edge through financial and business information intelligence. The company is named for New York billionaire businessman, philanthropist, and politician Michael Bloomberg.

Three other individuals founded Bloomberg L.P. alongside Michael Bloomberg. These were Thomas Secunda, Charles Zegar, and Duncan MacMillan. In less than ten years from the company's beginnings, it boasted more than 10,000 individual installations of the Bloomberg Professional service. This groundbreaking service delivered data, information, and analytics. That same first decade saw Bloomberg L.P. open up offices throughout the globe and launch their ubiquitous Bloomberg News.

In its second decade of existence, Bloomberg's subscriptions increased massively to 150,000. The company launched Bloomberg Tradebook so that individual traders were able to place stock trades directly via the Bloomberg Professional service. They also created Bloomberg.com that decade.

In the most recent decade, the company experienced an even more rapid pace of growth. Impressive technological ideas and innovation helped propel Bloomberg L.P. as the professional's information choice for news, data, and analytics. Subscriptions again doubled, increasing to more than 300,000. This was in part thanks to new and improved algorithms that helped finance and financial professionals to remain a step ahead of their industry competition.

Today Bloomberg.com covers markets, technology, politics, opinion, business week, and collectors' interests. Parts of the site require a paid subscription, while other portions of the news and financial data site remain free to users. Today the site has a global circulation with more than 980,000 subscribers living in 150 countries of the world.

Principle founder Michael Bloomberg has used the springboard of his international multimedia news and financial company to successfully launch himself into politics. He served as Mayor of New York City for three terms from 2002 to 2014. The billionaire founding businessman attended John Hopkins and Harvard, which he paid for with his own efforts. He worked his way to partner level at investment firm Salomon Brothers. It was the founding of his own self-titled company that brought Bloomberg to international fame.

This company remade the way that financial information became distributed around the world. In the process it turned him into a billionaire. Bloomberg constructed his company on the platform of a financial information computer. This revolutionized both the storage and consumption of securities and financial data. The company became so incredibly successful that it expanded into the global media business. In the process it opened up over 100 offices around the globe.

In the late 1990s, Michael Bloomberg used his among the greatest in the world fortunes to become a philanthropist. He funded countless endeavors centering on medical research, education, and the arts. In 1997, he published his own autobiography entitled Bloomberg by Bloomberg.

By 2002, Michael Bloomberg had won election as mayor of New York City as a Republican. He served the legally allowed two terms after winning re-election. In the midst of the 2008 global financial crisis and Great Recession, Bloomberg changed the city statutes to allow himself to run for a third consecutive term. Running as an independent, he won and served a controversial third term until the city had recovered from the devastation wrought by the terrible financial crisis.

Though he has mostly been known as a liberal Republican, in 2016 Michael Bloomberg decided to endorse democratic candidate for President Hillary Clinton over his long time republican candidate rival Donald Trump.

Blue Chip Stocks

A blue chip stock proves to be the nickname given to a stock that belongs to a firmly established company. Blue chip stock companies commonly feature no major outstanding liabilities and incredibly stable earnings track records. These blue chips are believed to be in excellent financial condition, and are commonly referred to as safe investments.

Blue chip company stocks feature many similarities with one another. On the one hand, they are all solidly established as a leader or the leader within their respective fields. They all pay reliable dividends to their shareholders, even if business is not as strong as is typical for them. On the other hand, for literally decades now, investors have thought highly of blue chip stocks in general. Blue chip stocks feature proven track records of solid growth and incredibly high market capitalization. Some examples of blue chip stocks are Coca-Cola, Wal-Mart, McDonald's, Berkshire Hathaway, IBM, Gillette, and Exxon-Mobile.

Blue chip stocks are occasionally also known as bell weather issues. The name blue chip came from casinos. In casinos, blue chips stand for the highest value chips out of all the various chip colors available.

The origin of the phrase Blue Chip Stock dates back to 1923/1924. At this time, Oliver Gingold of the Dow Jones coined the phrase one day. Dow Jones company history says that Gingold used the phrase for the first time when he stood beside a stock ticker at the firm that eventually became Merrill Lynch. After watching a few stocks trading at $200 to $250 each share and higher, Gingold reportedly said to Lucien Hooper from Hutton and Company that he would get back to his office so that he could "write about these blue chip stocks." Oliver Gingold's coined phrase stuck. It has been utilized to talk about successful stocks from that point forward.

Originally, Blue chip stocks were those that were expensively priced. Today they are more likely the ones that are the highest quality stocks and their associated companies. The financial channels and newspapers will regularly display the performance of blue chip stocks next to the major stock market averages such as the NYSE and the Dow Jones Industrial Average. This is why these blue chip stocks are also known as bell weather issues.

Bond Market

A bond market is a financial market where investors buy and sell bonds. In practice this is mostly handled electronically over computers nowadays. There are two principal types of bond markets. These are primary markets where companies are able to sell new debt and secondary markets where investors are able to purchase and resell these debt securities. Companies generally issues such debt as bonds. These markets also trade bills, notes, and commercial paper.

The goal of the bond markets is to help private companies and public entities obtain funding of a long term nature. This market has generally been the domain of the United States that dominates it. The U.S. comprises as much as 44% of this bond market on a global basis.

There are five primary bond markets according to SIFMA the Securities Industry and Financial Markets Association. These include the municipal, corporate, mortgage or asset backed, funding, and government or agency markets. The government bond market comprises a significant component of this market thanks to its massive liquidity and enormous size. Because of the stability of U.S. and some international government bonds, other bonds are often contrasted with them to help determine the amount of credit risk.

This is because government bond yields from countries with little risk like the U.S., Britain, or Germany are traditionally considered to be free of default risk. Other bonds denominated in these various currencies provide greater yields as the borrowers are more likely to default than these central governments.

Bond markets often serve a useful secondary function to reveal interest rate changes. This is because the values of bonds are inversely related to the interest rates which they pay. This helps investors to measure what the true cost of obtaining funding really is. Companies which are perceived to be riskier will have to pay higher interest rates on their bonds than companies believed to have strong and stable credit and repayment abilities. When companies or government entities are unable to make a partial or full payment on their bonds, this becomes a default.

When a company or a government needs to raise money and does not want to issue stock, it can sell bonds. These are contracts the issuers who are the borrowers make with investors who function as lenders. When investors purchase such instruments, they lend money to the issuing organization (company or government). The issuer of the bond promises to repay the original investment back along with interest in the future.

Bonds traded on these markets have many elements in common, whichever type of market they represent. All bonds have a face value. This is the amount of money which a bond would be valued at when it matures and the amount on which interest payments are based. They also have coupon rates that represent the interest rate which the issuer of the bond pays in its interest payments.

The coupon dates turn out to be the times when the issuer will pay its interest payments. Issue prices are the amounts for which the issuer sells the bond in the first place. The maturity date proves to be the exact date when the bond would be repaid. At this time, the issuer of the bond would pay the bond's face value to the bond holder.

Though a holder of a bond might keep it until maturity, this is often not the case. Many investors buy and sell them on the bond markets as their needs dictate. It is possible to sell a bond at a premium when the market value becomes greater than the original face value. Investors could also sell them at a discount to their original face value as the market price declines.

Brokers

Brokers are professional intermediaries that work on behalf of both a seller and a buyer. When brokers function as agents on behalf of only a buyer or seller, they become representatives and principal parties in any deal. Brokers should not be confused with agents, who instead work on the behalf of a single principal. In the financial world, there are stock brokers, commodity brokers, and option brokers.

Stock brokers are highly regulated broker professionals that sell and buy stock shares and related securities. They work on the part of investors who purchase and sell such securities. Stock brokers transact through either Agency Only Firms or market makers in a given security. These types of brokers are commonly employees of brokerage firms, such as Morgan Stanley, Prudential, or UBS.

Stock brokers are essential in stock transactions, since these exchanges of stocks can only occur between two individuals who are actual members of the exchange in question. A regular investor can not simply enter a stock exchange like the NASDAQ and ask to buy or sell a stock. This is the role that brokers fulfill.

Within the stock broker realm, three different kinds of broker services exist. One of these is advisory dealing, in which a broker makes recommendations to the client of what types of shares to purchase and sell, yet allows the investor to enact the ultimate decision. A second type is an execution only broker, who will simply transact the customer's specific buying and selling instructions. Finally, discretionary dealing involves brokers who learn all about the customer's goals in investing then carry out trades for the customer based on his or her interests.

These same functions are carried out by other financial market brokers as well. Commodities brokers deal in commodities contracts for clients in commodities such as gold, silver, wheat, and oil. Commodities contracts are comprised of options, futures, and financial derivatives. These commodities brokers act as middle men to an investor to transact buy and sell orders on such commodities exchanges as the New York Mercantile Exchange, Commodities Mercantile Exchange, and New York Board of

Trade.

Options brokers deal in options on stocks, commodities, or currencies, depending on what their area of specialty proves to be. They specialize in providing research, trading, and education on options to individual investor clients. Besides handling the main options that include straddles, option spreads, and covered calls, a number of options brokers facilitate trade in related fields that include ETF's, stocks, bonds, and mutual funds.

Brokers in the financial world are typically regulated by one oversight group or another. Stock brokers, for example, are licensed and overseen by the Securities Exchange Commission. They must pass an exam called the Series 7 in order to practice their trade as a stock broker. Commodities brokers, on the other hand, must obtain a Series 3 license from the Financial Industry Regulatory Authority. They are closely monitored by the Commodities Futures Trading Commission. Options brokers are monitored by the regulatory agency associated with the area of options that they trade.

Bull Market

A bull market is one in which an entire financial market or a select grouping of securities sees rising prices over an extended period of time. It is also used to describe a scenario in which prices are expected to rise. While the phrase bull market is most frequently utilized to address the stock markets, it can similarly reference any items that trade, such as sustained rising prices in commodities, currencies, or bonds. The opposite of a bull market is a bear market.

The simplest definition of a bull market is one that is rising. Bull markets are those that witness an increase in prices of market shares that is sustained for a period of time. In bull markets, investors show great confidence that this rising trend will only continue to exist over a longer term. When bull markets are in effect, a nation's economy remains strong and employment levels prove to be higher.

Bull markets show the characteristics of high investor confidence, general enthusiasm about the future, and anticipation that strong and successful results will continue to occur. Forecasting with any certainty when such bull market trends will wane is challenging. Much of the problem lies in attempting to decipher speculation's role and the psychological impacts of investors that can often have a major influence on the markets in general.

Bull markets in stocks commonly develop as an economic slow down is waning. They begin in advance of an economy demonstrating a convincing recovery. As investors' confidence levels grow, they show this by their buying and investing in a belief that stock prices will gain in the future. Bull markets generally turn out to be positive and winning scenarios for most investors.

The phrase bull market is derived from the animal world, as is its opposite concept of bear markets. Bulls attack their prey by using their horns in an upward thrust, as when markets are moving up. Bears on the other hand swipe their victims down with their paws, as when markets are falling down. When the trend is rising, the market is a bull market. When it is falling instead, it is called a bear market.

Examples of bull markets abound in both the United States and developing countries. Throughout most of the 1980's and 1990's, the U.S. stock markets rose in a long running bull market. Prices rose by nearly ten fold in that time period. The Dot Com bubble put an end to this bull market at the turn of the century.

Around the world, there have also been numerous bull markets in foreign stock exchanges. In India, the Bombay Stock Exchange, known as SENSEX, experienced a dramatic bull market for five years from mid 2003 to the first of 2008. In this time frame, the index ran from 2,900 points on up to 21,000 points.

Capital Appreciation

Capital appreciation refers to the increase in an asset's value. This gain is based on the increase in the market price of the asset. It primarily happens as the asset which an investor backed goes for a greater market price than the investor first paid for the asset in question. The part of the asset which is considered to be capital appreciating covers the entire market value which exceeds the cost basis, or original amount invested.

There are two principle sources of returns on investment. The largest of these is typically the capital appreciating component of the return. The other return source is from dividends or interest income. The total return of an investment results from the inclusion of both the appreciation of capital and the dividend return or interest income.

There are a wide variety of reasons why capital appreciation can occur in the first place. These differ from one asset class or market to the next, but the idea is the same. With financial assets like stocks or hard assets such as real estate, this can occur similarly.

Examples of this appreciation of capital abound. If a stock investor buys shares for $20 a piece while the stock provides a yearly dividend of $2, then the dividend yield is ten percent. A year after this, if the stock is trading at $30 and the investor obtained the $2 dividend, then the investor has enjoyed a return of $10 in capital appreciating since the stock increased from $20 to $30. The percent return of the stock price increase amounts to a capital appreciating level of 50 percent. With the $2 dividend return, the dividend yield is another ten percent. That makes the combined capital appreciation between the stock price increase and the dividend payout $12, or 60 percent. This stunning total return would please most any investor in the world.

A variety of different causes can lead to this appreciation of capital for a given asset. A generally rising trend can support the prices of the investment. These can come from such macroeconomic factors as impressive GDP growth or accommodative policies of the Federal Reserve in lowering their benchmark interest rates. It might also be something more basic having to do with the company that issued the stock itself. Stock prices could rise when the firm is outperforming the prior expectations of analysts. The real estate value of a house or other property could increase because it has good proximity to upcoming new developments like major roads, shopping centers, or good schools.

Mutual funds are another investment example which seeks out capital appreciation. The funds hunt for investments which will likely increase in value because of their undervalued but solid fundamentals or because they have earnings which outperform analysts' expectations. It is true that such investments often entail larger risks than those alternatives picked for income generation or preservation of capital, as with municipal bonds, government bonds, or high dividend paying stocks.

This is why those funds which focus on capital appreciation are deemed to be more appropriate for those investors who have a higher tolerance for risk. Growth funds are usually called capital appreciation investments since they pour their funds into company stocks which are rapidly expanding and boosting their shareholder values at the same time. They do employ capital appreciation as their primary investment strategy to meet the expectations of lifestyle and retirement investors.

Capital Gains

Capital gains refer to profits that arise when you sell a capital asset like real estate, stocks, and bonds. These proceeds must be above the purchase price to qualify as capital gains. A capital gain is also the resulting difference between a low buying price and a high selling price that leads to a financial gain for investors. The opposite of capital gains are capital losses, which result from selling such a capital asset at a price lower than for what you purchased it. Capital gains can pertain to investment income that is associated with tangible assets like financial investments of bonds and stocks and real estate. They may also result from the sale of intangible assets that include goodwill.

Capital gains are also one of the two principal types of investor income. The other is passive income. With capital gains' forms of income, large, one time amounts are realized on an asset or investment. There is no chance for the income to be continuous or periodic, as with passive income. In order to realize another capital gain, another asset must be purchased and acquired. As its value rises, it can also be sold to lock in another capital gain. Capital gain investments are generally larger amounts, though they only pay one time.

Capital gains have to be reported to the Internal Revenue Service, whether they belong to a business or an individual. These capital gains have to be designated as either short term gains or long term gains. This is decided by how long you hold the asset before choosing to sell it. When an asset with a gain is held longer than a year, the capital gain is long term. If it is held for a year or less time frame, such a capital gain proves to be short term.

When an individual or business' long term capital gains are greater than long term capital losses, net capital gains exist. This is true to the point that these gains are greater than net short term capital losses. Tax rates on these capital gains are lower than on other forms of income. Up to 2010's conclusion, the highest capital gains tax rates for the majority of investors proves to be fifteen percent. Those whose incomes are lower are taxed at a zero percent rate on their net capital gains.

When capital gains are negative, or are actually capital losses, the losses may be deducted form your tax return. This reduces other forms of income by as much as the yearly limit of $3,000. Additional capital losses can be carried over to future years when they exceed $3,000 in any given year, reducing income for tax purposes in the future. These capital gains and losses should be reported on the IRS' Schedule D for capital gains and losses.

Capital Inflow

Capital Inflow refers to money (in the form of investments) moving into a certain benefitting nation. The country which is the recipient of the inflow is best known as the host country. The source countries are the ones sending or investing the initial funds. Host nations often have a range of causes for attracting such capital inflows.

Direct foreign investment occurs when multinational corporations purchase literal tangible assets in the host country. This could come in the form of purchasing a local company outright or building a manufacturing plant locally. There could also be portfolio investment in the host nation's financial securities. This might include bonds and stocks which may be bought by international banks, foreign residents, insurance companies, pension funds, hedge funds, or other cross-border groups.

A third way that this occurs is when host governments are forced to borrow money off of international governments or foreign banks in order to pay their deficit on the balance of payments. It also occurs when domestic corporations or citizens elect to borrow from foreign banks. Finally inter-company transfers can finance investment and consumption in this category of capital inflow.

A last form of capital inflow happens when the host country has higher interest rates than the source nations' own corresponding rates. In this scenario, shorter term deposits will often flock to the banks' and money market instruments of the host nation. This could be straight up investment or speculation that the host national exchange rate will increase and so lead to a capital gain. This is the opposite of capital outflows. Outflows occur as funds move out of the host nation into other competing countries for the same reasons detailed above.

There are many beneficial effects to a country which receives capital inflows. As money comes into the host country via a business or stock purchase on the nation's stock market exchange, the recipient firm will deploy the funds either for startup purposes or to expand their existing business products and lines. This is really good for the companies which receive the funds. Such expansion of the companies in question then leads both job creation and employment growth in the host nation. Businesses will finally realize profits utilizing the original capital investment and the projects they subsequently fund with it. With these profits, the company is able to pay for additional expansion or investment in other projects and/or financial investments.

In the last few decades, foreigners have invested literally hundreds of billions worth of foreign capital into the United States economy. This has massively advantaged the American economy and workers (besides just creating countless jobs) as it boosted the international value of the dollar, lowered interest rates for American individuals and businesses, and grew the capital supply for loans which banks could make to residents and companies alike. With the onset of the catastrophic Global Financial Crisis from 2007-2009, the capital inflows to the United States dropped considerably. The subsequent Sovereign Debt Crisis in Europe dramatically decreased the capital inflow to Europe as well.

Years later by 2012, China finally surpassed the U.S. to capture the spot as the globe's greatest host of direct foreign investment . At the conclusion of 2012, the United States managed to recapture this coveted top spot. China had several reasons to steal the American thunder this way. The Chinese economy grew quicker than the United States as well as the other developed nations. Besides this, China has finally matured into a country that does not appear to be a high risk investment any longer. This has helped to draw in direct foreign investment by the hundreds of billions over the decades.

Capital Loss

Capital Loss refers to a type of loss that companies or individuals experience as one of their capital assets decreases by value. This includes a real estate or investment asset. The loss only becomes realized when the asset itself sells for less than the price for which it was originally purchased. Another way of looking at these capital losses is that they represent the difference from the asset's purchase price and the asset's selling price. In other words, for it to be a loss the selling price must be less than the original price. As an example, when investors purchase a home for $300,000 and then sell the same home six years later for only $260,000, they have taken a capital loss amounting to $40,000.

Where income taxes are concerned, capital losses often offset capital gains. Capital losses in fact reduce the personal or business income in a like dollar for dollar amount. When net losses are higher than $3,000, then the overage amount can not be applied. Instead, this amount higher than net $3,000 simply carries over against any other gains or taxable income to the following year when they will similarly offset capital gains and income. When losses are multiple thousands, they continue to carry forward as many years as it takes for them to be fully exhausted.

Both capital losses and capital gains will be reported using a Form 8949. This form helps taxpayers to determine if the sale dates allow for the transactions to be counted as long term or short term losses or gains. When such transactions are deemed to be short term gains, they become taxable by the individual's ordinary income tax rates. These ranged from only 10 percent to 39.6 percent as of 2015. This is why the shorter term losses when paired off against shorter term gains give significant tax advantages to higher income earning individuals. It benefits them when they have earned profits by selling off any asset or assets in under a year from original purchase point.

With longer term capital gains, investors become taxed by rates of zero percent, 15 percent, or 20 percent. This occurs when they take a gain which results from a position they possessed for over a year. Such capital gains also can only be offset by capital losses which they realize after holding the investments for over a year. It is also on form 8949 that these assets become reportable. Here investors list out both the gross proceeds from the sales and assets' cost basis. The two figures are compared to determine if the total sales equate to a loss, gain, or wash. Such losses become reported on Schedule D. Here the taxpayer is able to ascertain the amount that may be utilized to lower overall taxable income.

These wash sale rules can be confusing to individuals without an example. Consider an investor who dumps his IBM stock on the last day of November in order to realize a loss. The taxing authority of the Internal Revenue Service will disallow such a capital loss if the exact stock was bought again on the day of December 30th or before this. This is because investors have to wait at least 31 days before such a security can be repurchased then sold off once more in order to realize another loss.

Yet the regulation does not affect sales and re-buys of different mutual funds that possess similar positions and holdings. As an example, $10,000 worth of Vanguard Energy Fund shares may be entirely reinvested in the Fidelity Select Energy Portfolio at any point. This would not forfeit the investors' ability to recognize another loss even as they continue to own an equity portfolio (through the mutual fund) that is similar to their earlier mutual fund holdings.

Capital Outflow

Capital Outflow is a phenomenon where financial assets and money move away from a given nation. All countries of the world consider this to be a negative action. It typically occurs as a result of economic and/or political instability or at least the perception of it. Such asset flight results from domestically and especially foreign-based investors choosing to sell their stakes within a certain nation. They do this as they see potential weakness in the economy or political establishment of a country. They begin to feel that greater and safer opportunities for investment lie overseas.

When such Capital Outflows become too fast and great, it is a serious indicator that economic and political turmoil is present and a primary cause of the asset and capital flight. Many governments will begin to set limitations for capital choosing to exit. The connotation of such actions tends to warn still other investors who have not left that the condition of the host nation and economy is rapidly deteriorating.

Abnormal capital outflow creates increasingly severe pressure on the macroeconomics of a country and its economy. It tends to dissuade domestic and foreign investors alike from investing in the state and its companies. There are a range of valid explanations for why such capital flight actually occurs. Among them are unnaturally low national interest rates and growing political unrest.

It often helps to look at a real world example to better understand a difficult concept. Japan chose to decrease its interest rates to actual negative levels back in 2016. This applied to all government bonds and securities. They simultaneously began unprecedented aggressive stimulatory measures to boost the growth of the GDP Gross Domestic Product at the same time. The economic problems in Japan started after massive capital outflows from the island nation throughout the decade of the 1990s kicked off two long decades of sub-par stagnated growth in the country which formerly boasted the position of second greatest economy in the world.

Often times, governments impose severe restrictions on capital flight in a valiant effort to stop the fleeing money and financial assets. This is in an endeavor to shore up the capital markets and especially domestic banking institutions and system which can fail if all the money is simultaneously withdrawn. Too few bank deposits often cause banks to crater into insolvency when a great number of assets depart all at once. Subsequently, many banks find it difficult if not outright impossible to call back in existing issued loans in order to make good on customer withdrawal demands.

Consider the sad case study of Greece. Back in 2015, the government of the world's first democracy had no other choice than to instate a week long bank holiday. Wire transfers became restricted only to those recipients with Greek bank accounts. When such events occur in developing (or sometimes third world) countries, the weakness it institutes can create a vicious downward spiral that leads to domestic public panic and foreign investment fear and resistance.

There are also dramatic effects on exchange rates. The supply of a given country's currency rises dramatically as investors cash out of the state. Investors in China have periodically sold off the Yuan in order to obtain American dollars. This drives down the value of the Chinese Yuan, which has the additional side benefit of reducing the costs of Chinese exports while simultaneously boosting the costs to import foreign goods. It unfortunately also leads to inflation since import demand will fall while exported goods demand increases. During the second half of the year 2015, Chinese assets to the tune of $550 billion departed China looking for a higher ROI return on investment. This caused not only Chinese government fears but ensuing worldwide government worries.

Similarly Argentina suffered from sudden, unexpected, and runaway capital outflows back in the decade of the 1990s following a dramatic currency realignment. Their new fixed exchange rate created a resulting recession. The nation has now become the popular example and poster country for fledgling economies and the difficulties they all too often encounter in boosting their economic development.

Carl Icahn

Carl Icahn is a billionaire corporate raider, investor, hedge fund manager, and philanthropist. He earned a vast fortune operating as one of the infamous corporate raiders of Wall Street back in the 1980s. He is consistently ranked in the top 100 richest men, and he secured the spot of 43 on the Forbes' billionaire list for 2016.

Carl Icahn was born in 1936 in New York City. He started a financial career in 1961 working for Dreyfus & Co. as a broker. By 1968, he had been successful enough to get his uncle's financial help to secure a New York Stock Exchange seat. With this, he opened his own securities firm Icahn & Co. dedicated to options trading and arbitrage plays.

By the late 1970s, Carl Icahn had moved his efforts on to taking over a family owned appliance company Tappan. Once he was the majority share holder, he started a proxy battle to sell the company. His first successful corporate raid allowed him to sell the outfit to Electrolux for double the share prices. This was to be his first of many ventures that earned him a leading reputation among the corporate raiders throughout he 1980s.

Icahn would do this via a process called greenmail. He would threaten to gain control of major corporations like Viacom, Phillips Petroleum, RJR Nabisco, Texaco, and Marshall Field. He later sold his stocks and exited with substantial gains for he and his partners. His defenders say that he also made regular shareholders major money in the process. He became so good at this that his real life endeavors inspired the Wall Street 1987 blockbuster movie main character Gordon Gekko.

Not all of Carl Icahn's efforts succeeded. He tried to run some companies that he purchased. He met with success with American Car & Foundry Company, but lost money with the TWA (Trans World Airlines) bankruptcy and the failure with Time Warner. Though other Wall Street raiders such as Michael Milken and Ivan Boesky fell victim to scandal, Icahn avoided their mistakes and managed to carry his activist investing successfully through the 1990s and early 2000s. Even when he failed to take over RJR Nabisco, he still earned over $600 million in the battle.

Carl Icahn opened his first hedge fund in 2004. This failed to break up Time Warner or to gain control of Blockbuster. He had more success in selling companies such as Kerr-McGee and Mylan Laboratories. He took on the role of CEO of Icahn Capital LP, subsidiary company to his Icahn Enterprises in 2007. His fund closed to investments from outsiders in 2011. The year 2012 saw him acquire a major stake in Netflix. Though over 80 years old, he continues to capture headlines in dealings with Apple and eBay and a feud he went though publicly with Bill Ackman of Pershing Square Capital Management. In 2016, he held majority stakes in firms Tropicana Entertainment, XO Communications, and CVR Energy.

Besides being a tough negotiator and ruthless investor, Carl Icahn has also shown a more humanitarian side to the world. He has given substantially to medical research and education. Genomics has been a specialty interest of his. In 2012, he provided a $200 million donation to Mount Sinai School of Medicine. He also set up the Icahn Scholars Program to help bring over the top physician scientists to the school. He has also founded a number of homeless shelters and charter schools throughout the Bronx and New York City.

Cash Flow

Cash Flow is either an incoming revenue or outgoing expense stream that affects the value of any cash account over time. Inflows of cash, or positive cash flows, typically result from one of three possible activities, including operations, investing, or financing for businesses or individuals. Individuals are also able to realize positive cash flows from gifts or donations.

Negative cash flow is also called cash outflows. Outflows of cash happen because of either expenses or investments made. This is the case for both individuals' finances, as well as for those of businesses.

Where both individual finances and business corporate finances are concerned, positive cash flows are required to maintain solvency. Cash flows could be demonstrated because of a past transaction like selling a business product or a personal item or investment. They might also be projected into a future time for some consideration that a company or individual anticipates receiving and then possibly spending. No person or corporation can survive for long without cash flow.

Positive cash flow is essential for a variety of needs. Sufficient cash flow allows for money for you to pay your personal bills and creditors. It also allows a business to cover the costs of employee payroll, suppliers' bills, and creditors' payments in a timely fashion. When individuals and businesses lack sufficient cash on hand to maintain their budget or operations, then they are named insolvent. Lasting insolvency generally leads to personal or corporate bankruptcy.

For businesses, statements of cash flows are created by accountants. These demonstrate the quantity of cash that is created and utilized by a corporation in a certain time frame. Cash flows in this definition are calculated by totaling net income following taxes with non cash charges like depreciation. Cash flow is able to be assigned to either a business' entire operations or to one particular segment or project of the company. Cash flow is often considered to be an effective measurement of a business' ongoing financial strength.

Cash flows are also used by business and individuals to ascertain the value or return of a project or investment. The numbers of cash flows in to and out of such projects and investments are often utilized as inputs for indicators of performance like net present value and internal rate of return. A problem with a business' liquidity can also be determined by measuring the entire entity's cash flow.

Many individuals prefer investments that yield periodic positive cash flow over ones that pay only one time capital gains. High yielding dividend stocks, energy trusts, and real estate investment trusts are all examples of positive cash flow investments. Real estate properties can also be positive cash flow yielding investments when they provide greater amounts of rental income than their combined monthly mortgage payments, maintenance expenses, and property management upkeep costs and outflows total.

Chicago Board of Options Exchange (CBOE)

CBOE is the acronym for the Chicago Board of Options Exchange. The exchange arose in 1973. Since then it has grown to become the biggest options' market on the planet. As a market leader in technological innovation and creative financial products that are new and ground breaking, it has pushed the envelope on electronic forms of trading over the years. The Chicago Board concentrates its efforts on options contracts pertaining to indices, single stock equities, and interest rates. This exchange has such a broad and deep reach in options that it can claim to host a majority of the options traded around the globe. Industry insiders refer to this largest option exchange in the world as the "See-bo."

The CBOE has come an enormous distance since its very first trading day back in 1973. On that first day, the exchange offered 16 individual stocks and actually traded 911 contracts. The daily average volume nowadays is well in excess of a million contracts every market day. They trade these massive numbers of options primarily on single equity options, indices options, and options on ETF exchange traded funds and ETN exchange traded notes.

The market is the home for the volatility index options, which trade on this index investors affectionately call the VIX. This VIX is universally held to be the leading equity market volatility barometer in the globe. Besides this index, investors can also trade options on such internationally known and popular indices as the SPX S&P 500, the DJX Dow Jones 30 Industrials, the London FTSE, the MSCI, the NDX NASDAQ 100, and the RUT Russell 200 Index.

The exchange has counted itself a global leader and even pioneer in the purveying of stock indices options which are cash settled. Investors are able to take advantage of these tools in order to hedge their portfolio exposure and manage their risk. They can also gather regular premium income to help increase or stabilize the returns on their various portfolios. Every single trading day, literally billions of dollars in value of options transact through these ranges of popular and beloved indices.

The CBOE boasts creating the single stock options market all by itself, as well as the universe of ETF and ETN options. Investors throughout the world can utilize these exchange traded product and single stock options to hedge the positions they have in the stocks, manage their risk, and create additional income through writing covered calls.

Today's exchange provides the vast range of literally thousands of different publically exchange traded stocks, ETNs and ETFs with option tradability. By selling cash secured puts and covered calls, investors are able to boost their portfolio income and hedge their various literal stock positions. It is important to keep in mind that these particular financial products come with physical settlement when expiration occurs. This means that any options on single stock securities still held at expiration would be delivered. With the options on the various indices, the expiration settlement is cash-based.

CBOE worked to ensure that investors of all sizes could participate in these contracts. To that effect, they pioneered the concept of mini options. The exchange's website offers a full range of product details and contract specifications on the various mini options contracts, such as the ever popular Mini S&P 500 contract.

In other ground breaking product firsts, CBOE led the world with such innovative options ideas as weekly options that offer end of week expiration for precisely targeted strategies, quarterly and end of month options on the S&P 500, FLEX Options that permit investors to customize their options contract terms (including styles of exercise, exercise prices and dates), strategy benchmark indices like the PUT and BXM indices, and social media indices. With the Social Media Indexes, the Chicago Board of Options Exchange is partnering up with SMA Social Market Analytics to create a range of interesting indices based on such SMA data which allows for the CBOE-SMA Index Suite of products based on social media.

Collateralized Debt Obligations (CDO)

Collateralized Debt Obligations are one of the financial weapons of mass destruction that helped to derail the global financial system in the financial crisis of 2007-2010. They are literally securities that are supposed to be of investment grade. The backing of collateralized debt obligations proves to be pools of loans, bonds, and similar assets. These investments are rated by the main ratings agencies of Moody's, Standard and Poors, and Fitch rating companies.

The actual value of collateralized debt obligations comes from their asset backing. These asset backed securities' payments and values both derive from their portfolios of associated assets that are fixed income types of instruments. CDO's securities are divided into different classes of risk that are called tranches.

The senior most tranches are deemed to be the most secure forms of securities. Since principal and interest payments are given out according to the most senior securities first, the junior level tranches pay the higher coupon payments and interest rates to help reward investors who are willing to take on the greater levels of default risk that they assume.

The original CDO was only offered in 1987 by bankers for Imperial Savings Association that failed and became folded in to the Resolution Trust Corporation in 1990. This should have been a warning about collateralized debt obligations, but their popularity only grew apace during the following ten years. CDO's rapidly became the fastest expanding part of the synthetic asset backed securities market. There are several reasons for why this proved to be the case. The main one revolved around the returns of two to three percentage points greater than corporate bonds that possessed identical credit ratings.

CDO's also appealed to a larger number of investors and asset managers from investment trusts, unit trusts, and mutual funds, to insurance companies, investment banks, and private banks. Structured investment vehicles also made use of them to defray risk. CDO's popularity also had to do with the high profit margins that they made for their creators and sellers.

A number of different investors and economists have raised their voices against collateralized debt obligations, derivatives in general, and other asset backed securities. This includes both former IMF Head Economist Raghuram Rajan and legendary billionaire investor Warren Buffet. They have claimed that such instruments only increase and spread around the uncertainty and risk that surrounds these underlying assets' values to a larger and wider pool of owners instead of lessening the risk via diversification.

Though the majority of the investment world remained skeptical of their criticism, the credit crisis in 2007 and 2008 proved that these dissenters had merit to their views. It is now understood that the major credit rating agencies did not sufficiently take into account the massive risks that were associated with the CDO's and ABS's, such as a nationwide housing value collapse.

Because the value of collateralized debt obligations are forced to be valued according to mark to market accounting, where their values are immediately updated to the market value, they have declined dramatically in value on the banks' and others owners' balance sheets as their actual value on the market has plummeted.

Collateralized Mortgage Obligation (CMO)

Collateralized mortgage obligations are investments that contain home mortgages. These mortgages underlie the securities themselves. These CMO yields and results derive from the home mortgage loans' performance on which they are based. This is true with other mortgage backed securities as well.

Lenders sell these loans to an intermediary firm. Such an intermediary pools these loans together and issues certificates based on them. Investors are able to buy these certificates to earn the principal and interest payments from the mortgages. The payments these homeowners make go through the intermediary firm before finally reaching the investors who bought them.

The performance of collateralized mortgage obligations depends on the track record of the mortgage payers. What makes them different from other types of mortgage backed securities is that it is not only a single loan on which they are based. Rather they are categorized by groups of loans according to the payment period for the mortgages within the pool itself.

Issuers set up CMOs this way to try to reduce the effects of a mortgage being prepaid. This can often be a problem for investments based on only a single mortgage as owners refinance their loans and pay off the initial one on which the investment was based. With the CMOs, the risk of home owners defaulting is spread across a number of different mortgages and shared by many investors.

Tranches are the different categories within the mortgage pools on which the collateralized mortgage obligations are based. The tranches are often divided according to the mortgage repayment schedules of the loans. For each tranche, the issuer creates bonds with different interest rates and maturity dates. These CMO bonds can come with maturity dates of twenty, ten, five, and two years. The bondholders of each individual tranche receive the coupon or interest payments out of the mortgage pool. Principal payments accrue initially to those bonds in the first tranche which mature soonest.

The bonds on collateralized mortgage obligations turn out to be highly rated. This is especially the case when they are backed by GSE government mortgages and similar types of high grade loans. This means that the risk of default is low compared with other mortgage backed securities.

There are three types of groups who issue these CMOs. The FHLMC Federal Home Loan Mortgage Corporation issues many of them. Other GSE Government Sponsored Enterprises like Ginnie Mae provide them as well. There are also private companies which issue these CMOs. Many investors consider the ones issued by the government agencies to be less risky, but this is not necessarily the case. The government is not required to bail out the GSEs and their CMOs.

There are investors who choose to hold their CMO bonds until they mature. Others will re-sell or buy them using the secondary market. The prices for these investments on this market go up and down based on any changes in the interest rates.

The other most common type of mortgage backed securities besides these CMOs are pass through securities. Pass throughs are usually based on a single or few mortgages set up like a trust that collects and passes through the interest and principal repayments.

Collective Investment Fund (CIF)

A collective investment fund is a vehicles that manages a combined group of trust accounts. They are sometimes called collective investment trusts. Trust companies or banks operate these funds. The idea behind them is to pool together the funds and assets of organizations and individuals so that the managers can create bigger and better diversified portfolios.

Two types of these CIFs exist. A1 funds are combined together so that their operators can effectively reinvest or initially invest them. With A2 funds, trusts contribute assets that are not subject to any federal income taxes.

The main goal with a collective investment fund lies in utilizing superior economy of scale in order to reduce costs. The operators are able to combine together pensions and profit sharing funds to come up with a greater amount of assets. Banks then put these funds which are pooled together in a master trust account. The bank that controls the account then serves as executor or trustee of the CIF.

Banks that serve collective investment funds are the fiduciaries. This means that keep the legal title for the fund and all assets within it. The individuals or groups that participate in the CIF still own the results of the invested fund' assets. This makes them the beneficial owners of the relevant assets. Those who are participating within the fund do not actually own any individual assets that the CIF holds. They do maintain an interest in the aggregated assets of the fund.

Banks designed these collective investment funds so that they could improve their investment management tactics. They do this when they pull together a number of accounts' assets and merge them into a single fund with a common investment strategy. Pooling these assets into only one account allows the banks to dramatically reduce their administrative and operating costs for the fund. The investment strategy they come up with is structured to optimize the performance of the investments.

There are a number of different collective investment funds operating. Invesco Trust Company operates several of them. Examples of their funds are the Invesco Balanced Risk Commodity Trust and the Invesco Global

Opportunities Trust.

Though comptrollers use the name collective investment funds, other names sometimes refer to these vehicles. Generally applied names for them include common funds, common trust funds, comingled trusts, and collective trusts. An important characteristic of CIFs is that they are not regulated by the Investment Act of 1940 (as with mutual funds) or the SEC Securities Exchange Commission. Instead the OCC Office of the Comptroller of the Currency regulates and oversees them.

Mutual funds and collective investment funds are both pooled funds with an important distinction. These CIFs are not registered investment vehicles. Instead they exist in a class that is similar to hedge funds.

In 1927, the world's first collective fund began. Thanks to the stock market crash that occurred only two years later, CIFs became a scapegoat. They were believed to have contributed to the severe crash. This caused regulators to heavily restrict them. Banks could only provide them to trust clients or by utilizing employee benefit plans. They received a significant boost in the Pension Protection Act of 2006. This act chose them to be the standard option in defined contribution plans. Now 401(k) plans often feature them as an option for stable value.

Commercial Banks

Commercial banks are those financial institutions which offer a wide range of financial services to a variety of clients. Chief among these services are issuing loans and receiving deposits. The customers of such commercial financial institutions are able to avail themselves of a broad range of investment products that such banks offer. Included in these are certificates of deposit and savings accounts. Such banks issue a wide variety of loans which range from car loans and business loans to home equity loans and mortgages.

Banks which are commercial in nature deliver a range of financial products like checking accounts, savings accounts, and certificates of deposit. Customers of banks prefer these kinds of financial products since they are guaranteed by the FDIC Federal Deposit Insurance Corporation within the U.S.

In consideration for their funds' deposit, the commercial banks provide interest to their clients against their deposits. This is how these institutions realize profit--- they utilize the deposits of their customers to make loans that bring in higher interest rates than the ones they offer to their depositors. This spread from the amount the banks are paying out to the ones it is gathering back in becomes the net interest income of the commercial banks.

Such financial institutions do not all offer the same exact loan products to their various customers. They may specialize in several types or only a single kind of loan. These commercial banks are able to provide mortgages to purchase homes and home equity loans. In these cases, the houses provide the collateral to underlie the loans. Such financial institutions also provide auto loans with the vehicles as the loan collateral. The institutions similarly deliver personal loans, credit cards, and lines of credit to well-qualified borrowers.

Besides the interest such banks earn for their loans on the books, they can also create income through levying fees on their customers for banking services. This is common on products including checking and savings accounts, credit cards, and especially mortgage applications and originations.

There has been an evolution within the universe of commercial banks over the last two decades. Institutions that originally began as traditionally physical "brick and mortar" outlets complete with bank tellers, ATM's, bank vaults, and safe deposit boxes are still dominant. Yet a new and powerful challenger has arisen. This is the story of the commercial bank without physical branch locations.

Such virtual banks, or online only banks, lack physical branches. They force customers to do all of their transactions either over the Internet or by phone banking. The trade off for this accommodation is that these financial institutions deliver higher interest rates for accounts, deposits, and investments as their overheads are substantially lower. They also tend to charge significantly smaller and fewer fees. They can do this since they lack all of the associated costs which come with property taxes, rents, utilities, and additional staff salaries and benefits.

It is important to realize that the activities of commercial banking are vastly different than those of their colleagues in investment banking. With investment banking, the institutions engage in a number of stock and financial markets-related businesses. Among these are financial markets underwriting, performing tasks as intermediaries between the investors of and issuers of securities, fostering and participating in mergers and acquisitions and various kinds of corporate restructurings, and performing services as primary broker on behalf of institutional clients.

Other commercial banks boast investment banking divisions. This means that they are both involved in commercial banking and investment banking all at once. These include such well-known and enormous American financial institutions as JPMorgan Chase and Citibank and the multinational giant British banks like HSBC and Barclays. Other operations including Ally focus exclusively on the commercial banking segment of the industry.

Commercial Paper

Commercial paper proves to be a corporation-issued short term form of debt instrument which is unsecured. This paper is generally used to finance such things as inventories, accounts receivable, and other short term liabilities. The maturity dates for commercial paper vary, but they do not typically run any more than 270 days. Such paper instruments are generally issued at discounts to their face value. These discounts take into account the market interest rates that are effective when the company issues its paper.

Because commercial paper does not come with any underlying collateral, it turns out to be unsecured corporate debt. This means that only those companies that boast debt ratings which are highest quality will be able to find takers easily. Other companies must float their paper debt issues at greater discounts. This makes the funds come at a higher cost. Large organizations issue these paper instruments in significant denominations of typically $100,000 or higher. The most usual buyers of these paper instruments are banks and financial institutions, other companies, money market funds, and wealthy investors.

Commercial paper offers significant advantages for the corporations who utilize it. One of the biggest is that they do not have to register these offerings with the SEC Securities and Exchange Commission if the paper reaches maturity within 270 days or before nine months pass. This makes it a cost effective and quick way to obtain finance. While companies do have up to 270 days before the SEC is involved, typical maturity time frames for this paper only average around 30 days.

There are some restrictions to the use of commercial paper. It's funds can only be utilized for current assets and inventories. They may not be employed to purchase fixed assets like new facilities or plants unless the SEC is involved.

The financial crisis that began to erupt in 2007 involved the commercial paper market in a significant way. When investors had fears that major companies like Lehman brothers had problems with their liquidity and financial condition, markets for commercial paper seized up. Companies lost their access to funding which was affordable and simple to obtain.

This market freezing also led to money market funds "breaking the buck." As major investors in these paper instruments, the funds suffered from the suspect health of firms whose issued paper caused their own fund values to drop below the standard $1. Up to this point, money market funds had been considered risk free for investors. Government backing and guarantees were required to restore order and functionality to these markets.

A company might need additional short time frame funds in order to pay for Christmas holiday season additional inventory. The company could issue paper for $20 million in needs at $20.2 million face value. This means investors will provide it with $20 million in funding and receive $200,000 as interest when the paper matures. It would amount to a 1% interest rate. If the paper is not redeemed at its initial maturity, the interest rate would adjust the amount of principal and interest the paper would return appropriately based on the number of days it remained outstanding.

Commodities Futures Trading Commission (CFTC)

The CFTC is the regulatory agency whose acronym stands for the Commodities Futures Trading Commission. This group arose as a direct result of the Congressionally enacted Commodity Futures Trading Commission Act of 1974. Since that time, the group has carried the responsibility of regulating both the commodity options and futures markets. Their goals range from protecting investors from manipulative endeavors of firms to promoting fair, efficient, and competitive futures markets to stopping fraud and other abusive trading practices.

This regulatory group with vast powers is a fully independent agency under the umbrella of the United States' government. Besides their core objectives listed above, they seek to use their considerable powers to safeguard against systemic risk and to encourage transparent and financially viable markets. Following the Global Financial Crisis of 2007-2009 they have been working towards greater transparency and more stringent regulation of the swaps market, a multiple trillion dollar enterprise. The Dodd Frank Wall Street Reform and Consumer Protection Act of 2010 gives them this authority and ability to transition into this additional role as safe guardian of the swaps markets.

Five different committees comprise the CFTC. Each of these governing groups reports to a commissioner. The President of the United States appoints these commissioners directly which the Senate must then approve. The areas of concentration for the five committees include global markets, technology, agriculture, energy and environmental markets, and cooperation with the SEC Securities Exchange Commission. Each committee is made up of people with backgrounds in and connections to various industries and their interests. This includes the commodities exchanges, the futures exchanges, traders, the environment, and consumers.

The history of regulation of these futures and commodities markets stretches back nearly a century. While these contracts have been trading in the United States for longer than 150 years, they have only been Federally regulated from the 1920s. The original Congressional act that gave the government the authority to regulate and monitor these high stakes and leveraged markets was the Grain Futures Act of 1922. This authority was expanded by the Commodity Exchange Act of 1936.

With the advent of technological advances in the 1970s, the futures and commodity contracts trading has rapidly grown well beyond the original agricultural and other physical types of commodities. It now spans a dizzying range of financial instruments. Among these are the securities of foreign (and American) governments, foreign currencies, and foreign and American stock indices, and even individual company shares. Because of this rapid and spiraling expansion into countless other arenas, Congress decided to act to ensure that the oversight functions of these markets were adequate to handle the vast array of new activity.

They passed the Commodity Futures Trading Commission Act of 1974 in order to establish the CFTC. This new agency took the place of the U.S. Department of Agriculture and its Commodity Exchange Authority with regards to regulating both commodity futures and options exchanges and markets throughout the U.S. This new Act enabled vast changes to the old simple powers which the Commodity Exchange Act of 1936 had granted.

When their original mandate expired around the year 2000, Congress updated it with the Commodity Futures Modernization Act of 2000. This act mandated that the CFTC and the SEC begin to establish a combined regulatory authority for the relatively new single stock futures. These financial instruments had started trading in November of 2002. By 2003, such swaps had massively and exponentially expanded from the time when they had been originally introduced in the latter years of the 1970s.

As with the SEC, the CFTC does not exercise direct regulatory control for individual companies in the commodity and futures markets and their corporate financial soundness. The exception to this general rule pertains to huge swap participants and the now-regulated swap dealers. For these organizations, the CFTC actually sets the minimum capital standards as mandated by the Dodd-Frank Act.

Since 2014, the Commodities Futures Trading Commission has also gained oversight over the DCM designated contract markets. This includes the derivatives clearing organizations, swap execution facilities, swap dealers, swap data repository, commodity pool operators, and futures commission merchants, as well as other intermediary groups. This regulatory body also coordinates its efforts with major international counterparts, such as the British regulatory group the Financial Conduct Authority that oversees the London Metal Exchange.

Commodity Broker

A commodity broker commonly is an individual who makes commodity trades for his or her customers. The term also refers to the brokerage company that manages the trades for whom this broker works. This is an oversimplification as there are several different kinds of brokers. Where the CFTC Commodities and Futures Trading Commission is concerned, there are FCM Futures Commission Merchants, IB Introducing Brokers, and AP Associated Persons who are the individuals at the various commodity broker firms.

Commodity brokers do interesting jobs. They are involved in facilitating trades done in the commodity markets on behalf of the typical investor. The main other way to place such trades is by having one's own seat on the commodities exchange or by trading in the open outcry commodity pits. For the majority of people interested in trading these markets, they will be required to utilize the broker in some fashion to place their trades.

The commodity brokers themselves have one of two ways they can route their clients' trades through to the exchanges. They may have their company's floor traders who can place the trade literally on the exchange floor. Otherwise they will possess a special direct link trading platform that will allow them to place and then execute the trades via the electronic system on the various exchanges.

The commodity exchanges depend on these commodity brokers to gather in the business and clients for them. This is because they are unable to do so directly thanks to the governing rules on the way brokers carry out their business. The exchanges find it much simpler to carry out trade with only several dozens of brokerage firms than they do with literally hundreds of thousands of different customers trying to place their particular trades at the exchange directly.

Besides this valuable introducing service which the commodity broker provides, a great number of individual investors and traders need the brokers to offer them both recommendations and general position trading advice. This is because the commodities markets are often hard to comprehend in the beginning. Without the services and assistance of a good commodity broker, many investors would simply never engage in commodities trading ultimately.

Until the 1990s, the realm of commodities trading was limited to only the commodity pits at the various exchanges. The majority of the different orders came in from what was called a full-service commodity broker. The customers would first call their introducing brokers to make them aware of a trade they wished to enter. Next this broker would write up the order and place a timestamp on it. They immediately called their FCM clearing firm which takes their orders. The broker would articulate the exact trade from the ticket which their customer had phoned in to them.

The clearing firm was receiving calls at a special phone bank directly on the floor of the relevant exchange. A clerk would be taking down the order. The clerk would then write up a ticket to hand off to one of the floor brokers. These individuals stood in the trading pits and physically filled the order. The floor broker would then hand back the ticket to a runner who would run it back to the clerk. Finally the clerk would phone the introducing broker back and provide the trade confirmation and fill price. After the broker received his confirmation information, he would contact the original client back to provide the fill price and other information.

This form of manual trading via the telephone has all but disappeared in the past two decades. Now clients simply log on to the trading platform which their broker provided. They enter the trade information and hit buy or sell using their mouse. Such orders instantly route and match up at the relevant exchange's trading platform so that the confirmation on a market order is no more than one to two seconds away. This has made the trading process far more efficient, less expensive, and faster. Other traders insist on working with the full-service broker model still so they have a professional with whom they can talk about the various trading strategies and possibilities.

Commodity Exchange (COMEX)

The COMEX Commodity Exchange is the wholly owned subsidiary of the Chicago Mercantile Group that is responsible for both precious metals and base metals futures and options on futures trading. This once independent exchange is where the speculators, hedging companies, and traders all come to participate in trading FTSE 100 London exchange index options, along with precious metals silver and gold futures and options on futures, and industrial metals futures such as copper, aluminum, lead, and zinc futures.

For the first more than half a century of its existence, the Commodity Exchange proved to be an individually owned and run commodities futures exchange. COMEX arose in New York back in 1933 in the depths of the Great Depression. Through ups and downs in the markets, this exchange endured.

On December 31st of 1974, the Commodity Exchange launched its gold futures contract. This was the date when Americans regained the right to own gold again after a more than 40 year hiatus. This made it the biggest and most important center around the globe for gold futures and options. COMEX next launched options trading based on their gold futures in 1982 to cement their place in the world futures market and history. Silver has also been traded on the exchange since the 1970s.

COMEX merged with rival exchange NYMEX in 1994 to form the two still separately run exchanges under the listing of NYMEX Holdings, Inc. They did not obtain their publicly traded listing on the New York Stock Exchange until November 17th of 2006 when it began to trade under the ticker symbol of NMX. This new entity did not maintain its independence for long.

By March of 2008 the Chicago Mercantile Exchange Group of Chicago had conclusively committed to an agreement to purchase all of NYMEX holdings at a combined stock and cash offering that totaled $11.2 billion. The deal successfully completed in August of 2008.

From this point forward, the once independent and then jointly held NYMEX and COMEX exchanges continued their existence as Designated Contract

Markets of the CME Group. As such, they joined the two sister exchanges of the organization, the Chicago Mercantile Exchange and the Chicago Board of Trade. All four of these exchanges together make up the DCMs of the CME Group.

COMEX still maintains its separate identity under the CME Group. The precious metals trade is what it is best known for today. This precious metals complex volume that it transacts both monthly and annually is so large that it is greater than the volume of all competing futures exchanges in the world combined.

Commodities Exchange brings in participation from around the globe. A substantial number of the traders from East Asia, Europe, and the Middle East remain at their offices until the daily closure of COMEX.

This fact provides the Commodities Exchange with unparalleled liquidity almost around the clock. This more or less explains why it has been so very successful for the past near century despite intense competition in a constantly changing global trading environment. The hours that it trades continue to reflect the global participation. This is why the Commodities Exchange has opened ever earlier in order to meet the needs of the Asian, Middle Eastern, and European overseas trading clientele base.

Electronic trading on COMEX starts from the night previously from 4pm until the following morning at 7am. The regular trading session occurs from 8:20am through to 2:30pm. This means that COMEX is open for 21 hours per trading day from Monday to Thursday. Sunday electronic hours begin from 7pm EST. The group publishes both exchange open interest and volume every trading day.

Commodity Trading Adviser

Commodity Trading Adviser refers to either a firm or alternatively an individual that delivers personalized advice on the purchasing and selling of futures contracts, foreign exchange contracts, or options on futures. For individuals to be commodity trading advisers, they will have to have a CTA registration which is required by the NFA National Futures Association regulatory organization with oversight on the futures industry. The NFA proves to be the self-regulating organization of the commodities trading industry.

These CTAs work and receive their compensation based on commissions in exchange for their advice on the prospects and value of futures trading on options on futures, futures contracts, swaps, and off exchange retail Forex contracts.

Such Commodity Trading Advisers function much as do their stock market counterparts the financial advisors. The difference of course pertains to the delivering advice relevant to commodities trading, hence the CTA designation. Getting this CTA registration means that the applicant must pass proficiency exams such as the Series 3 National Commodity Futures Exam. There are other proofs of proficiency besides this particular exam as well.

One of these is registration with the National Futures Association. The CTA designation would not be required in cases where the adviser is providing advice to no more than 15 individuals in the last 12 months. Of course the individual or company would not be able to herald itself in front of the public as a CTA if they were not actually registered as such.

Such firms and individuals might be involved in many different industries or professions covered by the CEA Commodity Exchange Act or be otherwise registered. So long as this given advice on commodities investing proves to be only incidental to the main business of the firm or professional, then it is generally alright. This also applies if the advice they are dispensing does not require knowledge or is not specifically targeted to the commodity account of the customer in question.

As far as requirements go, the Commodity Trading Adviser designation will always be required for the principals involved in the commodity trading company along with all employees who receive the order from or provide the advice to the clients. This CTA will need to be registered in order to provide advice on all types of commodity investments. This includes everything from futures contracts, to options on futures, to swaps, to forwards, to Forex off-exchange contracts.

Such investments made in commodities typically require that a high degree of leverage be deployed. This argues for a greater level of expertise in order to safely trade such instruments and simultaneously avoid the possibility of taking major losses. It was in the late 1970s when the regulations surrounding commodity trading advisors began to arise as retail investors suddenly gained access to commodity market investing. It was then that the CFTC Commodity Futures Trading Commission began to expand its powers as well as the regulations it maintained surrounding being CTA registered little by little.

CTA funds should not be confused with simple CTA registration. These funds are usually hedge funds which employ futures contracts in order to attain their investing objectives. These CTA funds utilize a range of different trading strategies in order to attain said objectives. These might include such things as trend following and systematic trading. The best fund managers will actively manage the investments relying on a raft of strategies including fundamental and technical analyses, discretionary strategies, and trend following plus systematic trading together.

Convertible Bond

A convertible bond is like a hybrid between a stock and a bond. Corporations issue these bonds which the bondholders may choose to convert into shares of the underlying company stock whenever they decide. Such a bond usually pays better yields than do shares of common stocks. Their yields are also typically less than regular corporate bonds pay.

Convertible bonds provide income to their investors just as traditional corporate bonds do. These convertibles also possess the unique ability to gain in price if the stock of the issuing company does well. The reasoning behind this is straightforward. Because the bond has the ability to be directly converted into stock shares, the security's value will only gain as the stock shares themselves actually rise on the market.

When the stock performs poorly, the investors do not have the ability to convert the convertible bond into shares. They only gain the yield as a return on the investment in this case. The advantage these bonds have over the company stock in these deteriorating conditions is significant.

The value of the convertible instrument will only drop to its par value as long as the company that issues it does not go bankrupt. This is because on the specified maturity date, investors will obtain back their original principal. It is quite correct to say that these types of bonds typically have far less downside potential than do shares of common stocks.

There are disadvantages as well as advantages to these convertible bonds. Should the issuer of the bond file for bankruptcy, investors in these kinds of bonds possess a lower priority claim on the assets of the corporation than do those who invested in debt which was not convertible. Should the issuer default or not make an interest or principal payment according to schedule, the convertibles will likely suffer more than a regular corporate bond would. This is the flip side to the higher potential to appreciate which convertibles famously possess. It is a good reason that individuals who choose to invest in single convertible securities should engage in significant and extended research on the issuer's credit.

It is also important to note that the majority of these convertible bonds can be called. This gives the issuer the right to call away the bonds at a set share price. It limits the maximum gain an investor can realize even if the stock significantly outperforms. This means that a convertible security will rarely offer the identical unlimited gain possibilities which common stocks can.

If investors are determined to do the necessary research on an individual company, they can purchase a convertible bond from a broker. For better convertible diversification, there are numerous mutual funds which invest in only convertible securities. These funds are provided by a variety of major mutual fund companies.

Some of the biggest are Franklin Convertible Securities, Vanguard Convertible Securities, Fidelity Convertible Securities, and Calamos Convertible A. Several ETF exchange traded funds provide a similar convertible diversification with lower service charges. Among these are the SPDR Barclays Capital Convertible Bond ETF and the PowerShares Convertible Securities Portfolio.

It is important to know that the bigger convertible securities portfolios such as the ETFs track have a tendency to match the performance of the stock market quite closely in time. This makes them similar to a high dividend equity fund. Such investments do offer possible upside and diversification when measured against typical holdings of bonds. They do not really offer much in the way of diversification for individuals who already keep most of their investment dollars in stocks.

Corporate Banking

Corporate Banking refers to the banking services for businesses. It relates specifically to those accounts that apply to corporate clients. The United States initially employed the term to separate it from the branch of banking activity known as investment banking following the congressionally passed Glass-Steagall Act of 1933. This act separated out the two different activities for more than half a century.

In the 1990s, Congress repealed this act and once again allowed for investment banking and corporate banking to be combined jointly under a single roof. Most banks jumped at the chance to become involved in both activities once again. Where the majority of banks are concerned, this banking for corporate customers proves to be a mainstay profit center. At the same time, this largest originator of customer loans also turns out to be the continuous source of routine write offs for loans that have not repaid. In fact, combing investment and retail banking again led to the root causes of the Global Financial Crisis.

The divisions of banks which handle corporate banking commonly help a large variety of customers. This might range from international multinational conglomerates with billions in revenues and offices around the world on down to medium-sized regional businesses that boast several million in income to small family run companies in only a single city. These commercial banks provide a significant range of services and products to companies and corporations, as well as other smaller financial institutions.

Treasury and cash management operations are a first key service. Corporations utilize these services to convert currency and manage their daily cash and working capital. There are also credit products and loans, often the largest segment of the corporate banking world. It is also among the greatest single sources of both risk and profit for the corporate banks. There will also be commercial real estate services offered involving portfolio evaluation, real asset analysis, equity and debt structuring.

Besides this, many such banks will provide trade finance such as bill collecting, letters of credit, and factoring. Equipment lending is another important arena as the commercial banks will structure specifically tailored loans as well as leases for a wide variety of different types of equipment which companies may need for various industries. Finally, employer services deliver group retirement plans and payroll services. They offer these through special subsidiaries of the bank.

The commercial banks will also offer to cross-provide a range of useful services through their investment banking divisions. These include securities underwriting and asset management.

Commercial banks prove to be crucially important to both national and global economies. Commercial institutions provide the loans which help businesses to expand and hire additional staff members. It is the fuel that allows the economy to grow larger. In the wake of the Global Financial Crisis of 2007 to 2009, banks suddenly stopped lending money to companies and corporations alike.

It led to an almost complete freeze in the worldwide lending and banking activities necessary to keep companies operating. This meant that the recession which ensued proved to be the most devastating and deep one since the Great Depression of the 1930s and early 1940s. The global economy suffered the total shock of a near-death experience. It woke up the global regulators and forced them to renew their regulatory focus on the biggest international banks which have since been considered to be "too big to fail" thanks to their critical importance to the global financial system.

The largest commercial banks in the United States (as of 2017) are JPMorgan Chase, Bank of America, Citigroup, Wells Fargo, and U.S. Bancorp. This contrasts with the largest American banks overall which include Bank of America, Wells Fargo, JPMorgan Chase, Citigroup, and U.S. Bancorp.

Corporate Bonds

Corporate bonds are debt securities that a company issues and sells to investors. Such corporate bonds are generally backed by the company's ability to repay the loan. This money is anticipated to result from successful operations in the future time periods. With some corporate bonds, the physical assets of a company can be offered as bond collateral to ease investors' minds and any concerns about repayment.

Corporate bonds are also known as debt financing. These bonds provide a significant capital source for a great number of businesses. Other sources of capital for the companies include lines of credit, bank loans, and equity issues like stock shares. For a business to be capable of achieving coupon rates that are favorable to them by issuing their debt to members of the public, a corporation will have to provide a series of consistent earnings reports and to show considerable earnings potential. As a general rule, the better a corporation's quality of credit is believed to be, the simpler it is for them to offer debt at lower rates and float greater amounts of such debt.

Such corporate bonds are always issued in $1,000 face value blocks. Practically all of them come with a standardized structure for coupon payments. Some corporate bonds include what is known as a call provision. These provisions permit the corporation that issues them to recall the bonds early if interest rates change significantly. Every call provision will be specific to the given bond.

These types of corporate bonds are deemed to be of greater risk than are government issued bonds. Because of this perceived additional risk, the interest rates almost always turn out to be higher with corporate bonds. This is true for companies whose credit is rated as among the best.

Regarding tax issues of corporate bonds, these are pretty straight forward. The majority of corporate bonds prove to be taxable, assuming that their terms are for longer than a single year. To avoid taxes until the end, some bonds come with zero coupons and redemption values that are high, meaning that taxes are deferred as capital gains until the end of the bond term. Such corporate debts that come due in under a year are generally referred to as commercial paper.

Corporate bonds are commonly listed on the major exchanges and ECN's like MarketAxess and Bonds.com. Even though these bonds are carried on the major exchanges, their trading does not mostly take place on them. Instead, the overwhelming majority of such bonds trading occurs in over the counter and dealer based markets.

Among the various types of corporate bonds are secured debt, unsecured debt, senior debt, and subordinated debt. Secured debts have assets underlying them. Senior debts provide the strongest claims on the corporation's assets if the venture defaults on its debt obligations. The higher up an investor's bond is in the firm's capital structure, the greater their claim will ultimately be in such an unfortunate scenario as default or bankruptcy.

Credit Default Swaps

A credit default swap, or CDS, is a contract exchange that transfers between two parties the exposure of credit to fixed income products. Two parties are involved in this exchange. The purchaser of a credit default swap obtains protection for credit. The seller of this credit default swap actually guarantees the product's credit worthiness. In this process, the default risk moves from the owner of the fixed income security over to the party that sells the swap.

In these CDS transfers, the purchaser of the protection gives a series of fees or payments to the seller. This is also known as the spread of the Credit Default Swap. The party selling the protection gets paid off in exchange for this, assuming that a loan or bond type of credit instrument suffers from a negative credit event.

In the most basic forms, Credit Default Swaps prove to be two party contracts arranged between sellers and buyers of credit protection. These Credit Default Swaps will address a reference obligor or reference entity. These are typically governments or companies. The party being referenced is not involved in the contract as a party or even necessarily aware of its existence. The purchaser of such protection then pays pre defined quarterly premiums, or the spread, to the party who is selling the protection.

Should the entity that is referenced then default, the seller of the protection pays the face value of the instrument to the buyer of the protection against a physical transfer of the bond. Such settlements can also be accomplished by auction or in cash. Defaults in Credit Default Swaps are called credit events. These defaults might include a bankruptcy, restructuring of the referenced entity, or a failure to make payment.

Credit Default Swaps are much like insurance on credit. The difference between them and such insurance lies in the fact that a CDS is not regulated like life insurance or casualty insurance is. Besides this, investors are capable of purchasing or selling this type of protection without having any such debt of the entity that is referenced. Resulting naked credit default swaps permit investors to engage in speculation on issues of debt and credit worthiness of entities that are referenced. These naked Credit Default

Swaps actually make up the majority of the CDS market.

The majority of Credit Default Swaps prove to be in the ten to twenty million dollar range. They typically have maturities ranging from one to ten years. The Credit Default Swap market is mostly unregulated and turns out to be the largest financial market on earth.

These CDS products were actually created in the early part of the 1990's. The market for them grew dramatically beginning in 2003. By the conclusion of 2007, the total amount of them in existence proved to be an astonishing $62.2 trillion dollars. This amount declined to $38.6 trillion in the wake of the financial crisis at the conclusion of 2008. Since then, it has been growing alarmingly again. Critics of Credit Default Swaps have consistently referred to them as financial weapons of mass destruction, capable of blowing up the financial system and world economies in the process.

Credit Derivatives

Credit derivatives refer to bilateral contracts which are privately held. These contracts permit the holders to manage their credit risk exposure. Such derivatives turn out to be financial assets. Examples of the better-known ones in the derivatives universe are swaps, forward contracts, and options. The price of these is necessarily based upon the credit risk of economic entities like governments, companies, or private investors. This means that banks which are worried about one of their customers not being capable of repaying their loan are able to purchase protection against such a potential loss in default. They do this by keeping the loan on their books at the same time as they transfer the credit risk off to a third party more commonly referred to as the "counter party."

Such credit derivatives are only one of numerous different kinds of financial instruments available to investors and financial institutions today. With these derivatives, they are merely instruments whose existence derives from underlying financial instruments. The value which underlies them comes from a stock or other asset.

Two different principal forms of derivatives exist. These are calls and puts. Calls provide the right but not obligation to purchase a stock for a pre-set price called the strike price. Puts deliver the right but not obligation to sell particular stocks for pre-arranged strike prices. With either calls or puts, investors are obtaining insurance in case a stock price rises or falls. This makes every form of derivative product an insurance vehicle and particularly these credit derivative examples.

Numerous credit derivatives exist on the markets today. Among these are CDO Collateralized Debt Obligations, CDS Credit Default Swamps, credit default swap options, total return swaps, and credit spread forwards. Banks are allowed to utilize these complicated instruments in order to completely take away their default risk from even an entire loan portfolio. The financial institutions or banks pay a premium, or upfront fee, for this accommodation.

Considering a concrete example helps to make the credit derivatives concept clearer. Plants R Us borrows $200,000 off of a bank with a ten year repayment term. Because Plants R Us shows a poor credit history, they are forced to buy the bank a credit derivative in order to be able to receive the loan. The bank accepts this product which will permit them to transfer all of the default risk to a third counter party. This means that the counter party would be forced to deliver all unpaid interest and principal on the loan in the event that Plants R Us defaults on the said loan. For this guarantee, Plants R Us pays an annual fee to the counter party for their assumed risk. Should the Plants R Us not default on the loan, then the counterparty firm keeps the entire fee. This makes it a win-win-win situation for all three parties. The bank is protected against a default by Plants R Us, which gets to have its loan. The counter party collects the yearly fee. All parties gain and benefit from the arrangement.

Credit derivatives' values vary widely depending on several factors. These include the borrower's credit quality as well as the counter party's credit quality. The biggest concern comes down to the credit quality of the third party - counter party. If the counter party defaults or is otherwise unable to honor their commitments specified in the derivatives contract, then the financial institution will not get its payment for the loan principal and interest. The counter party would naturally no longer receive its annual premium payments any longer either. This is why the quality of credit for the counter party is so much more critical than is the credit quality of the borrower (Plants R Us in the example).

Credit Ratings Agencies

Credit Ratings Agencies are those companies whose purpose is to consider and report on the financial strength which firms and government agencies demonstrate. They report on national as well as international corporations and agencies in this capacity. Their reports are most interested in the ability of the entities in question to fulfill their obligations for both principal and interest repayments of their bonds and other kinds of debts. Besides this, the various ratings agencies carefully examine and review the conditions and terms on every debt issue.

The end result of the agencies' work is to release a credit rating on both the debt issues in particular and the debt issuers more generally. When they agencies have high confidence that the issuer will be able to meet their debt servicing of principal and interest as promised, they will issue a high credit rating. When the opposite is true, the credit rating will be lower. It is entirely possible for a particular issue of debt to receive a differing credit rating from the issuer. This heavily depends on the particular terms of the issuer.

The impacts of these debt issue ratings are enormous in the industry and for the specific issuers in question. Those debt issues that obtain the best credit ratings will receive the most attractive interest rates from the credit markets. This is because the confidence of investors in an entity's capability of making their various payment obligations comes down to the credit ratings agencies review, analyses and especially ratings. Since the interest rates which investors demand for a specific debt issue will be inversely correlated to the borrower's particular creditworthiness, weaker borrowers will have to pay more while the stronger ones will enjoy paying less.

In this way, the credit ratings agencies act on behalf of businesses in much the same capacity as the consumer credit bureaus do for individual consumers. Such credit scores which the credit bureaus develop for individual people will greatly impact the interest rates at which individuals are able to borrow money.

The downside to these credit ratings agencies and their work is that they have been made the scapegoat for company and government defaults in recent years. Their research quality in particular has been the target of heavy criticism from observers and analysts who point out companies which they rated highly suddenly collapsed. Governments in Europe on which they provided high credit ratings defaulted or almost defaulted on their debts, as with Greece in particular.

This caused third party observers to argue that the various credit ratings agencies are actually poor at financial forecasting, at uncovering growing and negative trends for the debt issuers they follow, and also are overly late in revising down their ratings. Besides this, critics point to the many conflicts of interest of the ratings agencies. This is because the debt issuers are able to pick out and pay the ratings agencies for the reviews of their bonds. In a survey conducted in 2008, 11 percent of the various investment professionals surveyed by the CFA Institute responded that they had observed personally instances where the major ratings agencies had actually upgraded their given ratings on bonds when they were pressured by the debt issuers in question.

There are only three firms today which dominate the space, and this is part of the problem. The Wall Street Journal provided the ratings shares of the big 3 agencies in their 2011 report. Of the 2.8 million ratings they issue collectively (with the other seven minor agencies), S&P 500 controls the greatest market share with 42.2 percent. Moody's holds 36.9 percent of the market. Fitch rounds out the top three with 17.9 percent.

The article claimed that fully 95 percent of all revenues in this industry were earned by the big three. Only 2.9 percent of the ratings issued came from the other seven firms. The other seven credit ratings agencies were A.M. Best, DBRS, Japan Credit Rating Agency, Rating and Investment Info., Egan-Jones Ratings, Morningstar Credit Ratings, and Kroll Bond Rating Agency.

Between the top two issuers Moody's and Standard & Poor's, they provide ratings for roughly 80 percent of all municipal and corporate bond issues. They are typically regarded as a level higher than Fitch. One particular example speaks volumes. While Egan-Jones had downgraded the U.S. Federal government debt to the second highest rating years earlier, it was ignored largely by the markets and world. When Standard & Poor's took the same action by downgrading the Federal government of the United States debt to AA+ on August 5th of 2011, this shook the world bond, currency, and stock markets. It demonstrates the clout S&P and Moody's especially enjoy over all of their various credit ratings agencies rivals.

Crypto Currency

A crypto currency turns out to be a virtual currency. These alternative currencies deploy cryptography as a means of security. It makes them extremely hard to counterfeit since this security feature is complex. An element that consistently defines the various crypto currencies and simultaneously endears them to users is their independent nature. They cannot be issued nor controlled by any of the global central banks or world monetary authorities. The theory is that this makes it difficult (if not outright impossible) for governments to manipulate or control such currencies.

Unfortunately for the governments of the world, this somewhat anonymous characteristic of the global crypto currencies also makes them an ideal vehicle for illegal and otherwise unethical activities. Among these are drug dealing, tax evading, and money laundering carried on around the world.

The world's original (and still leading) crypto currency proved to be Bitcoin. This was the first of the alternative currencies that caught on with the general and investing public. A mysterious individual or group of individuals who go only by the pseudonym of Satoshi Nakamoto created and launched Bitcoin back in 2009. These BTC (as they are abbreviated) must be mined in a tedious process which involves solving complex computer algorithmic problems. There is a maximum limit of 21 million to the total number of BTC which may be created. As of September of 2015, already 14.6 million of these Bitcoins had been mined and were circulating. The success of Bitcoin has been so vast that other competing crypto currencies have been spawned over the years.

The greatest and most successful of these is Ethereum, or Ether tokens. Others that have appeared include Litecoin, PPCoin, and Namecoin. These descendants of Bitcoin are often referred to as altcoins. This name is a derivative of the phrase bitcoin alternative. All of these crypto currencies have at least one thing in common. They all rely on a decentralized control. This stands out in direct contrast to the centralized banking systems of the mainstream traditional currencies.

There are a number of advantages and also some disadvantages to the major crypto currencies and this ground breaking technology. On the positive side, the crypto currencies enable simpler, cheaper, faster transfers of funds between one party and another in a commercial transaction. The transfers of funds occur utilizing both private and public keys to provide greater security.

The transfers happen with the lowest of possible processing and transaction costs. This has disrupted traditional banking and finance significantly. Individuals who transact in a crypto currency are able to side step the hefty middle man fee of financial institutions such as banks with their wire transfer costs, or with money transfer services like Western Union and Money Gram. These last two services charge upwards of ten percent transfer fees.

The great brilliance of Bitcoin and the other major crypto currencies lies in their block chain technology which acts as storage for the transaction ledger online. In fact all transactions in the BTC technology and currency which have ever happened are maintained in the block chain ledger database. Major banks like JP Morgan Chase have already invested heavily in initiatives to reduce the transaction costs of payment processing and transfers utilizing especially the up and coming Ethereum crypto currency.

This does not mean that there are not downsides to the crypto currencies. As they lack a central offline repository, the balance of an online wallet can be completely wiped out by either the invasion of hackers who steal it or the advent of a single computer crash if owners do not backup their holdings with data copies. There is also the negative of the wildly gyrating volatility in the currencies, which can easily swing up or down by even ten or twenty percent in a single trading session or week. There have also been more than 40 instances of online hacking theft of the various Bitcoin exchanges and companies in the short decade of Bitcoin history.

Currency Trading

Currency trading is speculating on the largest financial market on earth. Despite the fact that this is the world's largest, most liquid, and most impressive market, many individual traders do not know much about it. This is mostly because until Internet trading became popular, access to these markets was limited.

Only the large banks, multinational businesses, and shadowy hedge funds were able to trade them. Today the currency markets trade 24 hours per day, 6 days per week. This several trillion dollar market trades on every continent. Trillions of dollars per day change hands in the foreign exchange marketplace. All of this combines to make currency trading markets the most easily accessed on earth.

This speculative currency trading is not the main reason that the Forex, or Foreign Exchange, markets exist. They were set up to help big international companies change currencies from one kind to another. Many of these corporations need to trade currency constantly to pay for such costs as international goods and services payments, payroll, and acquisitions overseas.

Despite the origins of these currency markets, only around 20% of the total market volume comes from these company trades. An incredible 80% of the daily trades in the currency markets are from speculative currency trading hedge funds, large banks, and individual investors who want to take a position on one of the major currency pairs.

Currency traders are able to engage in these markets without many of the constraints that plague the stock markets. If individuals believe that the GBP/USD pair will drop dramatically, they are able to short sell as much of the currency pair as they desire. There are no uptick rules with currency trading. There are similarly no position size limits in currency trading.

Traders could buy tens of billions of any currency pair if they had the money to cover the trade. There are also no rules on insider trading with this type of currency trading. It does not exist. Economic data in Europe is routinely leaked several days ahead of the official release date.

Another way that currency markets are different from stock markets is that there are no commissions in foreign exchange markets. All currency companies are dealers. These dealers take on the counterparty currency in any trade. They earn their money with the spreads between the bid, the cost to buy the currency pair, and the ask, the cost to sell it.

Currency trading is always done in pairs. When a trader enters such a trade, the person is long one currency in the pair and short the other currency. Selling 100,000 GBP/USD means that the trader has sold the British Pounds and bought the U.S. dollars. This means that the trader is long dollars and short pounds.

Currency valuations are expressed in pips, or percentages in point. These pips prove to be the littlest trade increment in the foreign exchange pairs. This makes one pip equal to one-one hundredth of a percent. In all pairs except the Japanese Yen, these prices are quoted out to the fourth decimal point. This means that EUR/USD would be quoted in terms of 1.1595.

There are many different minor currency pairs on the market. The majority of foreign exchange dealers only allow individuals to trade the most seven widely traded and liquid pairs. These include the four major pairs of Euro/Dollar, British Pound/Dollar, Dollar/Swiss Franc, and Dollar Japanese Yen. The other three pairs allowed are the three commodity currency pairs of New Zealand Dollar/Dollar, Australian Dollar/Dollar, and Dollar/Canadian Dollar.

Currency trading is typically done in margin type accounts. The leverage is typically 100:1 on most of the major currency pairs. This means that currency traders are able to control 100,000 of a currency pair with only $1,000 of the base unit currency.

Custodian Bank

A custodian bank is a special financial institution that carries the responsibility for protecting the financial assets of individuals or companies. These institutions can also be called simply custodians. Such outfits serve as a third party check that protects the assets they are guarding against the fund managers and any illegal activities they may pursue.

Congress established these custodian banks with the Investment Company Act of 1940 in order to protect investors. Thanks to this particular legislation, investment companies must adhere to specific stringent listing requirements and must be registered with the Securities and Exchange Commission.

The custodian bank performs a number of activities in their primary function of watching over the financial assets of businesses and individuals. They settle sales and purchases of bonds and equities and physically protect the certificates of these assets. These institutions also gather information about and income from such assets. When the assets are stocks this means dividends. When the instruments are bonds, they collect the interest from the coupons. The custodians also disperse information they gather, pertaining to yearly general meetings and shareholder voting. They handle any foreign exchange transfers as necessary and manage all cash transactions. Finally, custodians deliver routine reports on their various activities to the customers.

Custodians banks provide reports on every trade or deal which they transact on behalf of the clients. They must be consistently delivered. Along with these reports they furnish information on the companies whose assets they hold besides information on general meetings. When a custodian is holding foreign shares or bonds, they will also have to change currencies as necessary. This is the case when the fund manager buys or sells foreign currency assets. It is also necessary when companies pay out dividends or bonds receive interest with these overseas financial instruments. Custodian banks are a critical component of the modern investment environment. Without them to carry out these functions, all of the important financial record keeping and housekeeping items would be neglected.

Not all custodian banks are national operations in the United States. A number of the major international financial institutions offer these services around the globe. These are called global custodians. Such international outfits use their own branches in the various countries in which they operate to manage the accounts and assets for their customers. In other cases, they may employ other custodians to assist them with these services. In these types of situations, the customer assets will be held by pension funds.

There are also local custodian banks whose job is to handle the ADR American Depository Receipts. These stock certificates are from foreign based companies that wish to offer their securities to the American stock markets. There are a number of international and large national American banks that participate as these local custodians. Among them are BNP Paribas, PFPC (a subsidiary of PNC Financial Services Group), Brown Brothers Harriman and Company, Kaupthing Bank, Citigroup, Northern Trust, Credit Suisse, RBC Dexia, Societe Generale, State Street Corp., German Bank AG, Goldman Sachs, HSBC, The Bank of New York Mellon, UBS AG, Union Bank of California, JPMorgan Chase Bank, and TO Bank NV.

Day Trading

Day Trading is the stock market strategy of purchasing and selling a given stock all in the say day. This form of trading is completely different from long term investing or even momentum or swing trading, which involves time frames of several days to several weeks. Day traders often try to make money on small movements in the stock price. In these cases they are attempting to leverage bigger amounts of investment capital to capture these lesser price movements in indexes or stocks that are extremely liquid.

Day trading can provide profits that allow individuals to make a living at it. It also can be an easy way for traders to lose money if they do not stick to a carefully designed strategy or if they have no experience in it. There are a variety of strategies that these day traders follow. These include selection, entry, and exit policies.

Entry strategies are critical for day traders. These traders first have to find a stock which works well for the day trading concept. Stocks with both liquidity and volatility are the best candidates. When a stock has liquidity, it is easy to get in and get out of the stock with small spreads and little slippage. Spreads represent the distance between a stock's bid and ask price. Slippage is the variance between a stock's actual trading price and the anticipated trading price.

Volatility proves to be the best way to measure the range of the daily price movements. It is in this daily volatility range that day traders work. For day traders, greater volatility can mean the chance to make higher profits or lose more money.

After day traders pick out the right kind of stock, they have to learn the best ways to find good entry points into the stock. Three tools that they utilize in this task are Level II quotes, daily candlestick charts, and actual time news services. Level II quotes show the orders as they occur. Daily candlestick charts give traders price action analysis. Actual time news service is critical since these companies release it directly as the news happens. This kind of news makes stocks move.

Daily and intraday candlestick charts provide a variety of useful information to day traders. They are able to see the volume of the stock and whether it is decreasing or increasing in picture form. The candlesticks can also form patterns like dojis and engulfing patterns that provide insight to these traders. Candlestick patterns may also provide useful elements of technical analysis such as triangle shapes and trend lines of a stock.

The entry strategies that day traders utilize are based on the identical tools that longer term traders employ. A key difference surrounds the proper time to exit the trade. Day traders are looking for the point where the interest in the stock in question decreases. They see this using their Level II volume tools.

Exit strategies are the other main component of a day trading policy. Traders using leverage trade on margin. Margin is borrowed money from the stock broker that multiplies potential gains and losses. Using margin means that a trader has a greater vulnerability to dramatic price movements in the stock than would a longer term trader not using margin. This is why day traders must use stop losses. These exit orders allow traders to sell out of a stock position and limit the losses.

The two different types of stop losses that day traders employ are physical and mental. Physical stop losses are more precise and disciplined. Traders program them to sell the stock at a particular price level that fits the loss the trader is prepared to take.

Mental stop losses are those points where the trader feels his or her reasons for entering have been invalidated. The trader would simply give a sell order at market price to close out of the position immediately. The problem with mental stop losses is that it is too easy for emotions to get involved and for the trader to continue to hold on to the position hoping that it will turn around. This can magnify losses when traders fall into this trap. Day traders should never risk more in a single than they can afford to lose both mentally and financially.

Debt to Equity

Debt to Equity refers to a ratio that is extremely important and often scrutinized in the world of business. It is the amount of longer term debt on the balance sheet of a corporation as related to and divided by the company equity. Long term debt for a company means money that it will not be expected to pay back in the coming 12 months. Both are critical factors in effective balance sheet analysis.

This ratio tells an analyst or investor a great deal about a company and the amount of debt it is carrying compared to its true net worth. This is accomplished by gathering together all of the company liabilities and then dividing this amount up by the shareholder equity. The end result which comes back in dividing the total debt by the equity proves to be the percentage of the firm which is leveraged (or more accurately stated---indebted).

Over time, the acceptable and average amount of debt to equity has varied significantly in the corporate world. Today it heavily depends on both the state of the economy, the industry in which the company operates, and the all-around feelings of society concerning credit and debt. If all else is equal, any firm with a debt to equity ratio in excess of 40 percent to 50 percent should be more careful about the risk hidden within its balance sheet and books. These could lead to a liquidity crisis at some point in the future.

When analysts consider the working capital of the company and find that both it and the current ratios of the firm are dramatically low, then this is a glaring sign of significant financial weakness in a corporation. This is why an analyst or investor truly needs to adjust any current profitability numbers to the economic cycle at hand. Many investors have lost fortunes over the years because the plugged in peak earnings at the height of an economic boom as their base case scenario metric for a firm's ability to pay back its various debt obligations.

There is no good reason to fall for this age old trap after all. All that is required to avoid it is to predict that the economy may fall off a proverbial cliff at any point and time. Then consider if the cash flow would be sufficient to cover the liabilities without the corporation being hurt and hampered by a lack of money for critical daily, monthly, and yearly expenses on items such as plant, property, and equipment.

The truth is that debt and elevated debt to equity ratios is not necessarily a bad thing. Many businesses are quite adept at earning a greater return on their capital than the cost of the interest which they incur in borrowing the money. This would make it extremely profitable to borrow money in such cases. It allows such firms to boost their earnings and profitability for one thing. The real key element is that the company management clearly understands the level of debt which will represent a danger level for smart and forward thinking stewardship of their company. Leverage cuts both ways. It dramatically boosts returns when it is working well for a firm, and it similarly can even totally wipe out a company if things turn on the firm in an economic recession or even economic depression.

Investors especially need to be careful in buying corporate bonds in such environments. Bonds issued in the lower interest rate environments of today will suffer drastically when the interest rates invariably rise higher, especially if this is quick and unexpected. This will lead to less profitability for the firm when the bonds have to be financed again. If the management did not wisely prepare for such an issue well in advance, then the company will truly have been mismanaged during the golden boom days and will suffer needlessly during the inevitable bust economic times.

Depository Bank

A Depository Bank refers to a facility like an office, building, or even warehouse that acts as a depository for safeguarding and storage purposes. This might be a bank, a vault, an organization, or even a financial institution which inventories and helps with the act of trading securities. The term also pertains to any depository institution which takes in financial deposits from their clients.

These depository institutions deliver financial services to both business and personal customers. These do not have to be cash-based only. They could be stocks and bonds certificates. The institution will inventory the securities. They often keep them in an electronic format called book-entry form. They might also hold physical paper certificates or dematerialized virtually-based certificates as well.

Depository banks carry the primary function in this regard of transferring stock shares ownership from the seller of an investment to the buyer as the trade becomes executed. They also assist with reducing paperwork needed to execute trades. They also increase the speed at which the transfer process will be completed. These depositories also get rid of any risk in maintaining physical format securities and keeping them from loss, theft, damage, fraud, or delay in actual delivery.

There are other depository services these institutions carry out for their clients. These include savings and checking accounts and also transferring funds electronically via debit cards and online banking. They also handle electronically submitted payments as part of these services. Customers surrender their cash to these banks and financial institutions under the core belief that the firm will simply hold on to them and then return them as the customer requests the money back upon demand.
In reality, the banks cheerfully take the clients' money and then pay them interest on this money slowly over time. As they hold the customers' money, they loan it out to other businesses and individuals as business loans and mortgages. They do this with the goal and hope of generating a higher amount of interest on the money than the amount which they pay out to their customers as interest.

In the field of depository institutions are three different types. These are commercial banks, savings institutions, and credit unions. All of them count on deposits from their clients in order to obtain their primary sources of funding. The Federal Deposit Insurance Corporation insures these consumer accounts up to a limit of $250,000 per account in case of bank failure.

Commercial banks prove to be for profit enterprises that represent the biggest of the depository institutions. These often times mega-banks provide a vast array of services to businesses and consumers in the form of commercial and consumer lending, checking and savings accounts, certificates of deposit, investment products, and credit cards. Their goals in accepting inbound deposits are to offer them back out to still other clients in the form of real estate loans, commercial loans, and mortgage loans.

With savings institutions, these are also for profit ventures called savings and loan institutions. They concentrate their efforts mostly on consumer mortgage lending although they do also provide commercial loans and consumer credit cards. The customers deposit their money in an account. This purchases shares within the firm. In one fiscal year, savings institutions might approve 710 real estate loans, 250,000 personal and automobile loans, and 75,000 mortgage loans. They then collect interest on all of these various loans, a portion of which pays the interest on their clients' deposits.

Credit Unions are quite different from the above two previous types. They are not for profit groups which instead concentrate their efforts on customer service. The customers bring in their deposits to the account. This is much like purchasing shares within the credit union in question. The earnings of the credit union become distributed back to the customers as dividends on a regular basis.

Derivative

In the financial world, derivatives are agreements between two different parties that contain values that are dependent on the price movements of an asset, as anticipated in the future, to which they are linked.

This asset, which might be a currency, stock price, or other element is referred to as the underlying. Derivatives are also alternative investments and financial instruments, of which they are numerous kinds. The most common forms of derivatives are futures, swaps, and options.

Investors use derivatives for many different activities. These include for gaining leverage on an investment so that when a small movement occurs in the value of the underlying, they can realize a great gain in the derivative value.

They may also be employed for speculation to profit from, assuming that the underlying asset value goes in the direction that they anticipate. Businesses might similarly hedge their risks in an underlying through opening a derivative contract that moves conversely to their position in the underlying, canceling all or part of the risk in the process. Investors similarly are capable of gaining exposure to an underlying that does not have a tradable instrument associated with it, like with a weather derivative.

Investors can also utilize derivatives to give themselves the ability to create options in which the derivative value is associated with a particular event or condition being met.

Derivatives principally remain a means of offering hedging insurance, allowing one party to lessen their risk exposure while the other reduces a different kind of risk exposure. Derivatives examples of transferring risk are helpful to consider. Millers and wheat farmers might create a derivative by signing a futures contract. This could specify a certain dollar value of money in exchange for a particular quantity of wheat to be exchanged at a future time. In this case, the two parties have actually diminished their risk for the future. The miller is not exposed to possible shortages of wheat, while the farmer is saved from the possible variances in price.

Risk is not completely eliminated in this example since the derivative contract will not cover events that the contract does not mention in particular, like weather conditions. There is similarly a danger that one of the parties will default on their part of the contract. To mitigate these problems, clearing houses insure many futures contracts, although not every such derivative is insured for the risk of counter party default.

Another way of looking at derivatives in this example is that while they reduce one form of risk, they actually present another one. The miller and farmer both pick up another risk by signing off on this contract. For the farmer, the danger lies in the fact that although he is saved from declines in the price of wheat, he is also exposed to the possibility that wheat prices will rise above the set amount in the contract, costing him extra income that he might have obtained. The miller also picks up a risk that the cost of wheat will drop below the amount that he has locked in with this contract.

Distressed Assets

Distressed assets are assets that a company or individual has been forced to place for sale at a significant discount to the acquired or actual value. This usually happens as the owner has no choice but to sell the asset to raise cash. Several different reasons might exist for why this is the case. These include excessive debt levels, bankruptcy, and regulatory requirements. Even debt can be put on sale at an amount that is lower than its face value. When this happens, it is known as distressed debt.

Although there are various types of distressed assets offered for sale, among the most common in the wake of 2007-2010's financial crisis and Great Recession are non performing loans on houses or foreclosures on mortgaged properties. Investors of all sizes are able to take advantage of such distressed assets in property by availing themselves of a homeowner's lack of ability to meet the mandatory mortgage payments or of his or her critical requirements for cash. In situations like this, such homeowners will consent much of the time to selling the property for a substantial discount in order to achieve a fast sale.

In the past, banks dealt with such distressed asset mortgages almost entirely themselves. As a result of the American banks still repairing their heavily damaged balance sheets from the countless write offs and over leveraging that they engaged in over the past five to ten years, they can not keep up any longer with the enormous number of foreclosures on their books. This leaves them with little choice but to have to sell some of their mortgage property asserts at massive discounts to actual value in order to be able to create quick cash flow.

The end result is that distressed assets can present a potentially profitable investment opportunity for you. The still ongoing crisis in global liquidity and credit has banks selling mortgages to individual, as well as to large, investors at significant discounts. Such discounts to perceived value would never occur in the days of normalized conditions in the mortgage and credit market place.

This means that investors are currently able to purchase distressed home assets with discounts amounting to as much as 72.5%. With as little as

$100,000, smaller investors are able to get involved with this efficient and potentially lucrative investment strategy. Professional management teams are available to help small investors realize appropriate exit strategies whose goal is to generate an impressive 20% return on investment per year.

Purchasing distressed assets such as homes in mortgage payment trouble can offer ethical options and benefits as well. Investors are able to restructure the debt and payments of the home owner in such a way that distressed home owners are able to afford the new payments. This lets the troubled home owners stay in their houses so long as the investor owns the mortgage and the home owner is able to work with the newly arranged payment schedule.

Distressed assets of companies include many different types of assets. These might be commercial office buildings, commercial jets, and even factories and equipment sold at substantial discounts to real value. Many times, other corporations are able to acquire these distressed assets for their own uses at fantastic prices.

Diversifying

Diversifying refers to the means of effectively lowering your investing risk by putting your money into a wide range of various assets. A truly well diversified portfolio offers the benefits of lower amounts of risk than those that are simply invested into one or two asset classes or kinds of investments.

Everyone should engage in some amount of diversification, even if the individual proves to be one who is tolerant of risk. Those individuals who really fear the present day economic uncertainties and very real amounts of risk in the market place will perform better forms of diversification into more asset groups.

Mainstream diversification is always recommended by financial experts because of the common example of not placing all of your investment eggs into just a single basket. If you do have all eggs in the one basket and then drop the basket along the way, then they can all break. The idea is that by placing each egg into its own individual basket, the odds of breaking all of the eggs declines significantly, even if one or several of them do get broken themselves.

Portfolios that have not engaged in diversifying might have only one or two corporations' stocks in them. This proves to be a dangerous investment strategy, since no matter how good a company looks on paper, its stock could decline to as low as zero literally over night. The past few years of the financial collapse have taught many investors the extremely painful lesson that even once blue chip financial companies' stock can decline to practically nothing as they spectacularly collapse.

Any financial expert will confidently state that portfolios made up of a dozen or two dozen varying stocks will have far less chance of plummeting. This becomes even more the case when you pick out stocks from a variety of types, industries, and market capitalization sizes of corporations. Better diversifying in stocks would include some companies that are based in other countries. Diversifying does not simply stop with stocks. It steers investors into bonds, mutual funds, and money market funds as well. Though all of these different investments diversify you, they still leave you mostly exposed to the one currency of the U.S. dollar.

More thorough diversifying will put at least a portion of your investments into assets whose values are not solely expressed in terms of only the American currency. This would include commodities, such as gold, silver, oil, and platinum in particular. Foreign currencies, such as the Euro, Pound, or Swiss Franc are another fantastic means of diversifying, and they can be acquired on the world FOREX exchange in currency accounts.

Real estate, including commercial properties, residential properties, vacation homes, or even real estate investment funds, offers another way to diversify away from U.S. dollar based financial investments such as stocks, bonds, mutual funds, and money market accounts. The strongest diversifying advice is to have at least three to seven completely different investment class vehicles, preferably one or more of which is not denominated in only U.S. dollars.

Dividend

Dividends represent portions of a company's earnings that are returned to the investors in the company's stock. These are typically paid out in cash that is either deposited into the investors' brokerage accounts or can be reinvested directly into the company's stock. As an example of a dividend, every share of Phillip Morris pays around 4.5% dividends on the stock price each year.

Investing in dividend paying stocks is a particular passive income investment strategy that is also a cash flow investment. This passive, or cash flow, income means that you collect income just from holding these stock investments. This kind of strategy entails building up a group of blue chip company stocks that pay large dividend yields which add money to your account usually four times per year, on a quarterly basis. Investors in dividends tremendously enjoy watching these routine deposits in cash arrive in either their bank account, brokerage account, or the mail.

Dividend investors who understand this type of investment are looking for a number of different elements in the stocks that they buy. Such dividend stocks should include a high dividend yield. To qualify as high yields, most value investors prefer to see ones that pay more than do the interest rate yields on U.S. Treasuries. Dividend yields can be easily determined. All that you have to do is to take the amount of the dividend and divide it by the price of the stock. So a stock that offers a $2 dividend and costs $40 is paying a five percent dividend yield.

Dividend paying stocks should also feature high dividend coverage. This coverage simply refers to the safety of a dividend, or how likely it is to be reduced or even eliminated. Companies that earn their profits from a large array of businesses are more likely to be able to continue paying their dividends than are companies that make all of their money off of a single business that could be threatened.

A more tangible way of expressing the coverage lies in how many times the dividend total dollar amount is covered by the corporation's total earnings. A company with fifty million dollars in profits that pays twenty million in dividends has its dividend covered by two and a half times. Should their profits drop by ten percent or more, they will have no trouble still paying the same dividend amount to shareholders. The dividend payout ratio is another way of measuring this. On the above example it would be forty percent. Dividend investors prefer to see no more than sixty percent of profits given out as dividends, as this could signify that the company lacks future opportunities for growth and expansion.

Qualified dividends are a third element that dividend investors are looking for in their dividend paying stocks. This simply means that stocks that are kept for less than a year do not benefit from lower tax rates on dividends. Since the government is attempting to convince you to become a longer term investor, you should take advantage of these lower tax rates by only buying stocks with qualified dividends that you have held for a full year and more.

Dividend Reinvestment Plans

Dividend Reinvestment Plans are also known by their acronyms as DRIPs or even DRPs. These plans come from corporations and companies which permit their investors to take their cash dividends in the form of reinvesting options. Generally this amounts to the investors acquiring extra fractional shares or additional whole shares. It occurs on the payment date of the dividend. DRIPs are intelligent means of growing the actual value in an investment holding.

The majority of these Dividend Reinvestment Plans allow their own investors to purchase these shares directly from the company. This provides them with a commission-free buy in usually offered at a substantial price discount to the present price of the shares on the stock market exchange. The majority of them will not accept reinvestments for under $10.

These Dividend Reinvestment Plans allow their shareholders to continuously invest in differing amounts over the span of longer-term timeframe investments in publically traded companies. Stake holders are able to buy either whole shares or even fractional shares through such dividend reinvestments in the best-known, most-famous public companies for only $10 or more at a single time.

Choosing this option means that investors forego their quarterly dividend payment check. The DRIP operating entity could be a transfer agent, company itself, or brokerage company. They will utilize the money from the dividend check to buy extra shares on behalf of the investor in question in the relevant company.

When the corporations directly operate their own Dividend Reinvestment Plans, they will appoint particular times throughout the year when they will permit the DRIP program buy in of additional shares from the company stakeholders. This is generally on a quarterly basis. The corporations in question never wade into secondary markets on exchanges to buy the shares then resell them to their investors. Instead the shares proffered through the DRIP come out of the companies' treasury reserve shares.

It is also important to note that such Dividend Reinvestment Plans shares issued directly by the company in question may not ever be resold on the stock market exchanges. Investors who wish to cash out of them will be forced to resell them back to the corporation which originally issued these for the present price on the stock market. When DRIPs run by brokerage companies are involved, the firm will just buy the shares for the investors who are acquiring them out of the secondary markets then tally such share into the brokerage account. In this case, these shares may be finally resold in the secondary market where they were originally acquired.

For those companies which do not directly offer their own share holders Dividend Reinvestment Plans, these can simply be established via a brokerage company. This is because a great number of the stock brokers permit their customers to reinvest such dividend payments directly into the stock shares which they already hold within their accounts. It is important that though such dividends do not come directly to the shareholders bank accounts, the IRS still requires that they be reported on a tax return like taxable income.

Many companies actually provide some significant incentives to take dividends from their DRIPs. They might provide a substantial discount of anywhere from one to ten percent from the present market share price. This can amount to a major savings when it is added to the lack of commissions on the trade.

Longer term advantages center on the miracle of compounded reinvestments on the returns. As the dividends become higher, the stake holders will receive an ever higher amount for every share they possess. This will then allow them to buy a still greater quantity of additional shares at each dividend payment. In a longer time frame, this will significantly boost the aggregate returns of the stock investment. This can really work to the advantage of the investors if the share price goes down and they gain the ability to cost average down with their DRIP share purchases. It offers them the possibility of significant gains from their reduced cost basis.

Companies like these DRIPs because they do not have to pay out as much capital when they are able to simply issue reserve shares from their treasury in lieu of cash dividend payouts. It also increases the loyalty of the shareholders, who will more likely hold on to the shares even when there are declines in the price of the share or the overall stock market.

Dividend Stocks

Dividend Stocks refer to stocks that pay especially generous and predictable shares of the corporate earnings out to their share holders. They are especially important for those investors who require dependable continuous streams of income off of their investment portfolios, such as retirees. This is why the optimal stock portfolio for those who are officially retired includes a strong and diverse mixture of industry-leading corporations which provide consistent, generous dividend yields.

These Dividend Stocks are famous for paying out significant stock dividends as a distribution on their earnings. They may pay this in the form of additional shares or as cash, depending on the wishes of the share holder in question. Sometimes the company will declare a stock dividend instead of a cash dividend, removing the ability of the shareholder to choose the form in which the dividend actually pays. When dividends become payable strictly as more stock, they are also known as stock splits.

For the companies that declare regular cash dividends of these Dividend Stocks, with each share stake holders have, they receive a set portion of the earnings from the corporation. This is literally being paid for simply owning the stock shares.

Consider a real world example to better understand how these Dividend Stocks work out in practice. Gillette, the world famous market leader in the shaving razors industry, may pay a dividend of $4 on an annual basis. Typically these dividends will be paid practically on a quarterly basis. This means four times each year Gillette would provide a $1 payout for each share of stock which the stake holders possess. If an investor owned 100 shares, he or she would receive four checks per year of $100 each check at approximately the conclusion of each quarter.

Most dividends from these Dividend Stocks come out in cash. Investors have the option to have them reinvested into additional company stock shares. Sometimes the corporation will provide a more advantageous reinvestment price than the current market prices to encourage such reinvesting of dividends in the company stock. These plans are called DRIPS (Dividend Re Investment Plans).

There are also occasional special dividends offered on an only one-time basis. They could be provided if the company wins a large and lucrative lawsuit, liquidates its share of an investment and receives a windfall payout, or sells part of the business to another firm for cash. These dividends can be made in cash, property, or stock share dividends.

There are several important dates with which Dividend Stocks' investors need to be familiar. These are declaration date, date of record, ex-dividend date, and payment date. Declaration date is the calendar day when the company's Board of Directors announces a dividend payout. This is the point where the firm adds a liability for the dividend payout to its company books. This means that it owes money (or shares) to the stake holders. This date will be the one when they announce both the date of record as well as the dividend payment date.

The date of record is the one where the corporation will review the appropriate records to determine who is holding the shares and is thus eligible for the dividends. Only holders of record will receive the dividend payment. The ex-dividend date is the day after which any investors who wish to receive dividends must own the shares. Only stake holders who possess shares on the day before the ex-dividend date get paid. Finally dividends are literally doled out on the payment date.

While most stock companies will pay out dividends on either a quarterly or half yearly basis, real estate investment trusts are structured differently. They pay out their dividends on an every-month basis as they receive monthly income from their various commercial, industrial, and/or residential properties.

Dividend Yield

Dividend yield refers to the payout of dividend price ratio on a given company's stock. It is simply determined by taking the yearly dividend payment total and dividing it by the cost for each share. This dividend yield is commonly given out as a percentage. The reciprocal of dividend yield proves to be the price to dividend ratio.

Dividend yields vary depending on whether a stock is a preferred stock or a common stock. With preferred shares, these dividend yields are outlined specifically in the stock's prospectus. A company will generally call such a preferred class of stock by the name first given to it, which included the yield based on this initial price. This might be a five percent preferred share. Since the pricing of preferred stock shares go up and down with the dictates of the market, the current yield will vary with the changes in price.

Preferred share holders have a variety of yields that they can figure up. These depend on the eventual disposition of their preferred share security. Besides the current yield formula of amount of dividend per price of preferred share, there are present value yields and a yield to maturity. These other yields only apply to those investors who purchase preferred stock shares after they have been issued or who choose to hold them until the reach the stated maturity date.

Preferred share dividends are almost always higher than the dividend yields on common stock shares.

Common stock shares have a dividend yield that differs entirely. With such common shares, the dividend amount is not guaranteed, and could vary from one quarter to the next. These dividends that are given to you, the common stock holder, are determined by the company's management. As such, they depend on the earnings of the company for the given quarter.

With common stocks, you can not be assured that dividends will be paid in the future that match dividends paid previously, or that these dividends will be paid period. Since it proves to be so challenging to correctly predict future dividends, the figures used in determining dividend yields are the present dividend yields. This means that the present dividend yield is always determined by dividing the most current full year's dividend by the present share price.

Dividend yields can have a major impact on how much money a stock makes for its owners over time. Dr. Jeremy Siegel is a well respected professor of investments who has determined conclusively with his research that ninety-nine percent of all after inflation gains that investors realize with stocks come from only dividends that are reinvested. Reinvestment of dividends means that the dividend yield amounts are simply taken and used to purchase more shares of the stock, instead of paying them out as cash to the share holder's account. This allows for investors to compound the number of shares that they own in a company over time.

Dow Jones

Dow Jones is an international and American news company based in the United States. Wall Street Journal co-editor Charles Dow and Edward Jones co-founded the company with fellow reporter Charles Bergstresser back in 1882. The independent history of Dow Jones & Company continued under the Bancroft Family from the 1920s all the way until 2007. At this point, an extensive takeover struggle ensued. In the end, News Corp. took over the company which it has owned and run as a subsidiary since 2007.

The company had been most famous for its continuous publication of stock market indices such as the Dow Jones Industrial Average and the Dow Jones Transportation Average. Besides this, it publishes a number of important financial publications such as its flagship product The Wall Street Journal along with Market Watch, Barron's, Financial News, and Factiva. It has run the Dow Jones Newswire service for decades. This is one of the biggest and most prestigious newswire services in the world.

The Wall Street Journal continues to be a leading daily newspaper that the company publishes in both print and online editions. It covers financial, business, international, and national news and topics throughout the world. They started publishing this gold standard of newspapers on July 8th, 1889.

Today there are 12 different versions of it they produce in nine separate languages. These include English, Japanese, Chinese, Spanish, German, Portuguese, Turkish, Korean, and Bahasa. The Journal has won 35 Pulitzer Prizes for its excellent and world leading journalism.

In 2010, News Corp. sold off the Dow Jones Indexes subsidiary. The CME Group bought it and continues running it. Since then, the company has concentrated its efforts on its publications of financial news and on delivering information and financial news and tools to companies involved in finance.

The company continues its efforts in the arena of publishing and data provision today. It calls itself the ultimate source for business data and news. The company boasts journalism that continues to be award winning, cutting edged technology, and sophisticated data capabilities. They combine these in order to provide news and financial tools and insights that move the world financial markets. Their efforts also help key players to make crucial decisions and major companies and individuals to run their businesses.

The company has expanded from its humble roots as niche news agency provider in a basement on Wall Street to become the global powerhouse of information and news that it is now. It claims that the reason for its success and long lasting appeal comes from a combination of factors. These include their constant commitment to accuracy, innovation and depth, and years of experience. It helps them to keep their efforts firmly focused on their future endeavors.

Dow Jones today calls itself the modern day portal to intelligence. They have state of the art data and information feeds. Their research is performed by experts in the field. The firm utilizes leading and creative technologies and solutions that are fully integrated. Their staff reporters practice journalism that consistently wins awards.

The company's delivery systems and apps can be fully customized to work on a variety of platforms. This helps them to get the important financial and news information gathered, written, and published. Thanks to their leading technologies, they can get it to their customers wherever they are and whenever they require it.

The Dow indices continue to be benchmarks for the overall stock market as a whole. The DJIA includes the thirty leading companies that represent the major U.S. based enterprises. These are no longer primarily industrial in nature as they were when Charles Dow and Edward Jones put their names on them.

Dow Jones Industrial Average (DJIA)

The Dow Jones Industrial Average, commonly referred to by its acronym DJIA, is also many times called the Dow 30, the Dow Jones, the Dow, or even just the Industrial Average. It proves to be the second oldest stock market index in the Untied States after the Dow Jones Transportation Average. The Dow Jones Industrial Average came into being when Charles Dow, the co founder of Dow Jones and Company worked with a business colleague Edward Jones, a statistician, to come up with an index that monitors the industrial sector. This index demonstrates the daily stock market trading session progress of thirty of the largest companies that are publicly traded within the U.S.

Ironically, most of the present day thirty companies listed in this index no longer have much or even anything to do with the historical definition of heavy industry. The components in the average are weighted by price and scaled in order to adjust for the impacts of stock splits and varying other forms of adjustments. This means that the total value that you see in the daily representation of the Dow Jones does not prove to be the true average of the different company stock prices.

Instead, it is the total of such company prices that are added up and then divided by a special divisor. This divisor is a number that is adjusted any time one of the company stocks underlying it pays a dividend or engages in a stock split. In this way, the index presents a constant value that is not altered by the external factors of the component stocks.

The Dow Jones Industrial Average remains one of the most heavily followed and carefully watched indices in the American stock market, along with peers the S&P 500 Index, the NASDAQ composite, and the Russell 2000 Index. The founder Dow intended for the index to monitor the American industrial sector's actual performance. Even so, the index is constantly affected by much more than simply the economic and corporate reports issued. It responds to both foreign and domestic incidents and political episodes like terrorism and war, as well as any natural disasters that might cause economic damage.

The Dow Jones Industrial Average's thirty components simultaneously trade on either the New York Stock Exchange Euronext or the NASDAQ OMX, which are the two largest American stock market outfits. Derivatives based on Dow components trade via the Chicago Board Options Exchange, as well as with the Chicago Mercantile Exchange Group. The latter is the largest futures exchange outfit on earth, and it presently owns fully ninety percent of the Dow Jones founded indexing business, along with this Industrial Average.

Investors who are interested in gaining the ability to track the progress of the Dow Jones Industrial average have several choices. There are index funds that buy the components of the index so that you do not have to own all thirty companies yourself. You might also invest in the Dow 30 by purchasing shares of the Exchange Traded Fund known as the Diamonds ETF. This trades under the AMEX exchange via the symbol DIA. Finally, you could by options and futures contracts based on the performance of the Dow Jones Average on the Chicago Board of Trade.

Earnings Per Share (EPS)

Earnings per share refer to the given total of earnings that a company has for every share of the firm's stock that is outstanding. There are several formulas for calculating earnings per share. These depend on which segment of earnings are being considered. The FASB, or Financial Accounting Standards Board, makes corporations report such earnings per share on their income statement for all of the major components of such statements including discontinued operations, continuing operations, extraordinary items, and net income.

To figure up the basic net earnings per share formula, you only have to divide the profit for the year by the average number of common shares of stock. With discontinued operations, it is only a matter of taking the discontinued operations income and dividing it by the average number of common stock shares outstanding. Continuing operations earnings per share equal the continuing operations income over the average number of common shares. Extraordinary items works with the income from extraordinary items and divides it by the weighted average number of common shares.

Besides the basic earnings per share numbers, there are three different types of earnings per share. Last year's earning per share are the Trailing EPS. These are the only completely known earnings for a company. The Current earnings per share are the ones for this year. These are partially projections in the end until the last quarterly numbers are released. Finally, Forward earnings per share are earnings numbers for the future. These are entirely based on predictions.

Earnings per share calculations do not take into account preferred dividends on categories besides net income and continued operations. Such continuing operations and even net income earnings per share calculations turn out to be more complex as preferred share dividends are taken off of the top of net income before the earnings per share is actually calculated. Since preferred stock shares have the right to income payments ahead of common stock payments, any money that is given out as preferred dividends is cash which can not be considered to be potentially available for giving out to every share of the commonly held stock.

Preferred dividends for the present year are generally the only ones that are taken off of such income. There is a prevalent exception to this. If preferred shares prove to be cumulative then this means that dividends for the entire year are taken off, regardless of if they have been declared yet or not. Dividends that the company is behind on paying are not contemplated when the earnings per share is calculated.

Earnings per share as a financial measuring stick for a company are extremely important. In theory, this forms the underlying basis for the value of the stock in question. Another critical measurement of stock price is price to earnings value, also known as the PE ratio. This PE ratio is determined by taking the earnings per share and dividing them into the price of the stock. Earnings per share are useful in measuring up one corporation against another one, if they are involved in the same business segment or industry. They do not tell you if the stock is a good buy or not. They also do not reveal what the overall market thinks about the company. This is where the PE ratio is more useful.

Energy Commodities

The term energy commodities refers to a variety of coal, oil, and gasoline derived products. These include such energy sources as coal, Brent Sea Oil, gasoline, heating oil, and natural gas. These energy resources prove to be essential in daily life. This makes consumers most aware of such commodities. Besides being among the most heavily used, they are also typically among those which are most widely traded.

These energy commodities find use in so many industrial applications that they maintain a strong investment appeal. Their prices have the ability to rise substantially over shorter time frames when demand picks up or supply drops. Energy is also a major component in inflation indices around the world, which makes investments in energy an effective hedge against rising prices. Higher oil and gasoline costs translate to higher prices in general throughout the U.S. and world economies.

Investors who are interested in investing in these different types of energy commodities have a variety of choices of investment vehicle and commodities. There are Exchange Traded Funds and Notes (ETFs and ETNs), futures and options contracts, and energy sector company stocks from which to choose.

Brent Sea Oil turns out to be the major oil benchmark in the world. It is the one to which around two-third of worldwide oil trade is tied and is especially relied upon in the EMEA region (Europe, Middle East, and Africa). This indicator represents a sweet form of crude oil, though it is not as sweet as the American benchmark WTI (West Texas Intermediate) crude oil. Brent oil is used to produce gasoline and mid purity distillates like diesel and kerosene. Crude oil finds applications in a wide range or consumer products that underpin modern day life, including plastics. Crude must first be refined in order to be turned into most useful products like gasoline or heating oil.

Coal is responsible for providing the energy for half of all the electricity generated on earth. It is usually obtained through open pit mining or via underground shaft mining. Major coal deposits exist in the Midwestern and Eastern United States as well as regions of Russia and China. Coal is principally utilized in generating electricity. Almost 40% of all energy production in the world comes from coal. In the last few years, coal has become less important in developed countries and more critical in developing nations like China who need cheap fuel. It is also useful for steel production because of the incredibly hot temperatures it produces which are critical for creating the purest steel.

Gasoline proves to be among the most critical of the energy commodities, especially for the American transportation industry. The American market makes up over 40% of all demand for gasoline. Emerging markets are utilizing an increasingly larger share of this energy resource.

Heating Oil finds its main uses in boilers and furnaces as the fuel source for warming businesses and homes. It is most heavily employed in places in the Northeastern United States and the United Kingdom and Ireland. Natural gas can be hard to access in some of these markets or too expensive to use in places where it is very cold.

Natural Gas is among the most important fuels for generating power. It is particularly popular in the cooling and heating systems throughout the United States. Natural gas powers either steam or gas turbines to create electricity. It is increasingly preferred over oil and coal as it is a much cleaner energy source that produces fewer greenhouse gas emissions. It has been made more practical for transporting thanks to LNG Liquid Natural Gas terminals that work with a CNG Compressed Natural Gas form.

Equities

Equities are another name for stocks and similar types of investments. Stocks turn out to be financial instruments that represent ownership, or equity position, within a given corporation. As such, they give an owner a stake in a representative share of the company's profits and assets. Such ownership in a given firm is determined by taking the total numbers of shares in the company's equities that the individual owns, and dividing it by the actual number of shares that exist.

The majority of these equities similarly give voting rights that provide representative votes in some decisions that the company makes. Not every company issues equities; only corporations engage in the practice, while limited partnerships and sole proprietorships do not. Equities can be further divided into smaller categories based on the market capitalization, or size, of the company in question.

Because they often yield greater returns over significant periods of time, they are typically characterized by higher amounts of risk than are bonds and money market funds. Because of these unique potential returns and associated risks, equities are generally considered to be their own class of assets that are utilized to a degree in putting together investment portfolios with proper diversification. Many different kinds of equities exist, including domestic equities, emerging market equities, developed market equities, and Real Estate Investment Trusts.

Domestic Equities prove to be those stocks for the publicly traded corporations that principally conduct their business in the same country in which the investor lives. When a person holds such equities, they receive their share of dividends that the corporation pays. Equities come with a higher degree of risk than do bonds, as bond holders have a greater claim on a corporation's assets should liquidation follow bankruptcy. Equity holders are commonly wiped out in such liquidation.

Emerging Market Equities are equities in corporations that are based in countries that are still developing their economies. Included in these are China, Brazil, and India. These nations feature economies that are commonly volatile and lack many protections for investors, like auditing and laws or monitoring of securities that are found in the industrialized countries.

Developed Market Equities are equities in firms that work primarily outside of an investor's home country but still in an industrialized country. For Americans, this mostly translates to European country companies, as well as those in places such as Japan, Australia, and New Zealand. Such companies and economies in these nations prove to be more stable than those in developing countries.

Real Estate Investment Trusts, also known as REIT's, are equity funds that invest in residential and commercial real estate. Because they receive lease and rent payments off of their investments, these typically pay greater percentage returns in dividends. These higher distributions mean that REIT's are much like a combination of fixed income and typical equity investments. This means that they commonly feature greater risk along with better anticipated returns than do the majority of fixed income investments.

Equity Financing

Equity Financing refers to raising capital via selling shares within the enterprise itself. This comes down to selling an ownership stake in the corporation in order to come up with much needed funds for business enterprises. This type of financing could cover a wide array of different activities in both scope and scale. It might be only several thousand dollars which an entrepreneur raises from his family and friends. It could also be enormous IPOs initial public offerings that amount to literally billions of dollars and come from such household favorite names as Facebook and Google.

The phrase is most often applied to mega financing of major public companies which are listed on a stock exchange. This could also cover financing of private companies too. Equity financing is more or less the opposite to debt financing. In debt financing, funds will be borrowed form a business to be paid back at a later date and time.

There is more to Equity Financing than only selling common shares of stock. It might also involve other forms of equity (such as preferred stock) or even semi equity instruments like convertible stock shares or equity units which come with either warrants or common shares. Startup companies that evolve into highly successful firms often go through a few rounds of such Equity Financing as they grow and mature. These startups commonly attract varying types of investors at the different points in their growth. They will often rely on differing equity instruments for the various financing needs which arise throughout the newer company's history.

Consider an example to better understand the concept. Venture capitalists and angel investors are two different investors who are commonly the initial investors in startup companies. They generally prefer convertible preferred shares of stock instead of common shares of stock for their early rounds of funding. This is because those convertible shares offer a much higher possibility for upside potential as well as a little bit of downside protection.

After the firm has expanded enough to think about going public, they might begin to sell common shares of stock equity to retail and institutional investors. It might be that later they decide they require additional capital.

At this point, they might go out for secondary equity financing. This could include rights offerings or even offering various equity units which include warrants to sweeten the deal.

Financing via equity has rules and regulations which govern it. National securities regulators such as the SEC Securities Exchange Commission have the jurisdictional authority. This is intended to safeguard the investing public from any unscrupulous practices and operators who simply trick investors out of their funds then vanish. This is why such equity financing will usually come alongside a prospectus or at least an offering memorandum.

These provide a huge amount of useful information which assists the investors in taking highly informed decisions on the merits of the company and its financing offers. This data will usually cover the activities of the firm, provide information on the directors and other officers, explain the uses for the financing proceeds, offer financial statement disclosure, and revel the various risk factors.

The appetite which investors display for the various equity financing offerings heavily depends on the equity markets status as well as the financial market demand. When there are steady equity financing deals in the works, this represents an evidence of high investor confidence. Too many financing deals might mean that optimism is exuberant and a top in the market is coming.

When the Initial Public Offerings of dot coms and technology firms touched incredibly high record levels at the end of the 1990's, the writing was already on the wall. From 2000 through 2002, NASDAQ crashed and burned in a slow motion but extremely painful train wreck from which it needed more than a decade to recover. The speed and frequency of equity financing fell off substantially after this sustained correction in the markets because investors quickly became risk averse in the wake of the massive market selloff.

Equity Securities

Equity securities prove to be those asset classes which feature shares of stock in a given corporation. Investors hold these as reported by a company's official balance sheet. Corporations issue such securities in an effort to raise business capital via the financial markets. They use this money for significant company life events, such as for product development, merger and acquisition activity, or internal expansion. The funds are seldom for daily operating needs.

When investors buy equity securities, they gain a partial stake in the underlying firm. This is a primary alternative to turning to the bond markets to borrow money in taking on debt via the publicly traded bond markets. When a company first issues such equity securities, this is called an IPO initial public offering. Companies often raise enormous amounts of cash in this means, since investors are always hunting for new stock issues that will enable them to possess a part of a new and exciting opportunity.

The total number of shares that an IPO released varies wildly. It comes down to the amounts which the companies obtain permission to issue in their financial documents which they file with the regulatory overseer for their area. Corporations are allowed to sell a specific amount of stock shares in a given price range on the actual IPO day. After these shares have been dealt out to the public via the financial markets, the price of their equity will go up and down on the stock markets every trading day. This movement all depends on the perception of investors and the accompanying demand for the shares on any given day.

It is not common for such a firm to issue its entire inventory of available stock shares in a single offering. Rather than do this, they commonly reserve a certain quantity of shares to be issued at a later date in a second offering. This is called a follow on offering or secondary offering. The management of a company would elect to do this as they know they will likely need to raise fresh additional capital in the future in order to pay for hoped for expansionary plans.

When corporations continue to issue out their equity securities via the financial exchanges there is a downoido for the existing shareholders and company investors. As additional shares are available to be bought, the pre-existing stake holders have their equity stake diluted as a percentage of the total. As an example, a major share holder could possess a huge quantity of shares that equate to fully 10 percent of all outstanding company shares which can be traded. Should the company choose to boost the total number of shares which are tradable, the equity of the shareholders will immediately drop in terms of the percentage ownership of all available shares.

The main alternative to issuing equity securities lies in issuing debt securities These publicly issued bonds offered via the bond markets by a company (or even government) raise money by taking on debt which must be repaid one day, known as the maturity date. Investors who buy debt instruments like these become de facto creditors of the bond issuing entities. The main disadvantage to such issuance in debt is that the company issuing has to provide continuous interest payments to the bond holders throughout the life of the bond contract. The company is able to maintain its ownership in itself in exchange for this trade off of interest payments.

EUREX Exchange

EUREX is a state of the art options and futures exchange which Deutsche Borse of Germany jointly operated with SWX the Swiss Exchange until 2012. At this point, Deutsche Borse acquired the remaining shares of the EUREX exchange from SWX. The exchange operates offices in nine global locations including in Frankfurt, London, Chicago, Zurich, and Paris.

This international exchange specializes in providing trading on derivatives based in Europe. As such, it turns out to be the biggest European options and futures market. Products across nine asset classes trade on the exchange. These range from Swiss and German debt instruments to individual stock and stock indexes of European companies and exchanges.

EUREX clearing handles the clearing of every transaction carried out on the exchange. In this way, it serves as a multi asset class clearing central counterparty for the considerable product range. It also clears products that trade over the counter.

The exchange itself has become enormous. The Futures Industry Association said in its 2015 annual survey that the EUREX exchange holds the position of third biggest derivatives exchange based on the volume of contracts it trades. Its headquarters is located in Eschborn, Germany near Frankfurt, the financial capital of Germany. The operators of the exchange are the EUREX Frankfurt AG and EUREX Zürich AG. Both publicly traded companies are now entirely owned by Deutsche Börse, the German stock exchange operator.

The EUREX Exchange offered something almost unique when it began functioning in 1998. In both the United States and Great Britain, open outcry trading still dominated markets. EUREX came along as among the first exchanges in the world to provide a trading platform which was completely electronic instead of the more traditional pit or open outcry trading so prevalent at that time. Using this method of trading, buyers and sellers perform transactions via remote locations that are connected by the electronic network and trading platform.

The exchange launched its present day platform the T7 trading architecture in 2013. This system advanced the electronic trading of derivatives significantly. Deutsche Börse Group developed it. Using this dependable system, over 7,700 different traders operating in more than 35 countries are connected so that they can trade in excess of seven million contracts each market day.

The EUREX Exchange won several major impressive awards for 2016. *Global Capital* presented it with the "European Exchange of the Year" honor for the second year in a row. It received this nod for its broad range of products that hedge risk throughout nine alternative and traditional asset classes, as well as for its impressive offerings of equity index products and volatility derivatives. *Financial News* also honored EUREX with the 2016 Best Derivatives Trading Platform. This is also its second consecutive year to win this award.

EUREX gradually enabled Deutsche Börse to wrest control of the Bund German bonds futures trading away from London. Up till the late 1990s, the London Financial Futures Exchange dominated trading in this segment. This back and forth struggle for control of this important market became known as the "Battle of the Bund."

Exchange Traded Funds (ETF)

These ETF's prove to be stock market exchange traded investment funds that work very much like stocks. Exchange Traded Funds contain instruments like commodities, stocks, and bonds. They trade for around the identical net asset value as the assets that they contain throughout the course of a day. The majority of ETF's actually follow the value of an index like the Dow Jones Industrial or the S&P 500. Since their creation in 1993, ETF's have evolved into the most beloved kind of exchange traded instruments.

The first Exchange Traded Fund particular to countries proved to be a joint venture of MSCI, Funds Distributor, and BGI. This first product finally turned into the iShares name that is accepted and recognized all over earth today. In the first fifteen years, such ETF's were index funds that simply followed indexes. The United States Securities and Exchange Commission began allowing firms to establish actively managed ETF's back in 2008.

Exchange Traded Funds provide a number of terrific advantages for smaller investors. Among these are elements like simple and effective diversification, index funds tax practicality, and expense ratios that remain very low. While doing all of this, they also offer the appeal of familiarity for you who trade stocks. This includes such comfortable and helpful options as limit orders, options, and short selling the ETF's. Since it is so inexpensive to purchase, hold, and sell these ETF's, many investors in ETF shares choose to keep them over a longer time frame for purposes of diversification and asset allocation. Still other investors trade in and out of these instruments regularly in order to participate in their strategies for market timing investing.

Exchange Traded Funds boast of many advantages. On the one hand, they provide great flexibility in buying and selling. It is easy for you to sell and buy them at the actual market price any time during a trading day, in contrast to mutual funds that you can only acquire at a trading day's conclusion. Since they are companies that trade like stocks, you can buy them in margin accounts and sell them short, meaning that they can be used for hedging purposes too. ETF's also allow limit orders and stop loss orders, which are helpful for assuring entry prices and protecting profits or safeguarding from losses.

ETF's also provide lower costs for traders. This results from the majority of ETF's not being actively managed. Also, ETF's do not spend large amounts of money on distribution, marketing, and accounting costs. The majority of them do not have the fees associated with most mutual funds either.

ETF's are among the greatest vehicles for diversifying portfolios quickly and easily. As an example, with only one set of shares, you can "own" the entire S&P 500 index. ETF's will give you exposure to country specific indexes, international markets, commodities, and even bond indexes.

ETF's have two other advantages. They are both transparent and tax efficient. Transparent in this regard means that they are clear in their portfolio holdings and are priced all day long. They are tax efficient as they do not create many capital gains, since they are not in the business of buying and selling their underlying indexes. They also are not required to sell their holding in order to meet redemptions of investors.

Expense Ratio

Expense ratio relates to the costs that a mutual fund incurs as it trades and does normal business. Typical mutual fund expense ratios include a number of different costs. Among these are management fees, transaction costs, custody costs, marketing fees, legal expenses, and transfer agent fees.

Management fees comprise those charges that the fund pays to the company which handles the portfolio management. They invest the fund's money as per the direction of the mutual fund board of directors. Management costs are typically the largest single portion of the mutual fund's expenses.

These fees commonly range from as little as .5% to as much as 2%. Lower fees are usually more advantageous for investors. This is because every dollar that goes to the management of the fund is not increasing the share holders' wealth. Some mutual fund types charge a higher amount in fees. International or global mutual funds will usually cost more than simple domestic market mutual funds. They justify these greater charges by the difficulty of managing an international portfolio.

Transaction costs include the fees that the fund pays to stock brokers. These are negotiated to extremely low rates such as a penny per share or even lower thanks to the enormous volumes that mutual funds trade. Those funds that are constantly purchasing and selling investments create significantly greater transacting costs for themselves and their investors. Higher turnover rates like this also can lead to larger capital gains taxes and other costs.

The investment holdings of a mutual fund must be kept by a custodian bank. This creates custody costs where these banks register the bonds, stocks, and other investments for the fund. Some of the banks do this electronically and others keep actual stock certificates in their vault storage.

Custodian banks also collect interest and dividend payments, maintain accounting for the various positions so gain/loss info is readily available to management, and handle stock splits and other transaction issues. These custodian costs prove to be a less significant percentage of expense ratios for the mutual funds.

Marketing fees for mutual funds come out of the money that the investors pool. This money is utilized to advertise the fund so they can raise additional investment dollars. More money in the fund means more management fees for the portfolio managers. These 12b-1 marketing fees are money that does not benefit an investor after the fund exceeds $100 million in net assets. A very small number of brokers actually refund such fees to their investors.

There are some legal expenses that mutual funds must incur in the course of normal operating business. These include for paperwork they are required by law to file for regulators like the SEC, specific licenses, incorporation, and other legal procedures. The majority of funds count such costs as a small amount of their overall expense ratio.

Transfer agent costs cover the expenses that arise when a shareholder cashes out or buys into the fund. Transfer agents must handle various account statements, paperwork, and money in the process. These agents take care of all the mundane daily paperwork for purchases, redemptions, and processing which keep the fund and other capital markets working.

There are various other costs that are not included in the mutual fund expense ratio but many experts feel should be. These include mutual fund sales loads. These fees are simply commissions that go into the pocket of the institution, company, or stockbroker that persuaded you to buy the mutual fund in the first place. Because of these and other high costs of many mutual fund expense ratios, some people prefer low cost index funds that involve very low management costs.

Fed Funds Rate

Fed Funds Rate refers to the most key interest rate benchmark in the United States. Such a benchmark rate is the one which the banks charge one another in order to borrow money from each other overnight. The Federal Reserve similarly deploys this rate as a tool in order to meaningfully impact monetary policy within the country. This is not the only benchmark rate in America today, yet it has no rival for importance.

The way the Federal Reserve is able to influence banks with it is somewhat complicated. The commercial banks must maintain a minimum level of money either in cash funds or with their particular regional branch of the Federal Reserve on deposit. The idea behind this is that it allows banks to meet customer withdrawals from their current accounts, including both checking and savings.

Sensible banks hold more than this bare minimum. They keep an excess of the reserves that the regulations and rules pertaining to the banking universe require. These are appropriately referred to as excess reserves. It is such excess reserves that the Fed Funds Rate directly affects.

As the better prepared banks keep plenty of excess reserves available, they are able to overnight loan out to the less prepared banks so that they can end business day operations at their legally required minimum obligation. This unsecured overnight loan occurs at the Fed Funds Rate. It represents the effective rate that the lending bank will charge the borrowing bank.

In nearly all cases, this Fed Funds Rate proves to be the lowest practical interest rate in the nation. Since the financial crisis, it has remained at slightly higher than zero percent. The Federal Reserve began increasing it with their first rate hike in December of 2015, both slowly and gradually.

This rate matters for more reasons than just the price at which a lending bank will charge a borrowing bank to utilize its excess reserves. The reason is that the Federal Reserve is able to set their monetary policy with the rate. As an example, they might decide they need to cut the effective rate of unemployment in the U.S. This is one of their two reasons for existing (along with keeping inflation low). In order to increase employment opportunities, the Fed will push down the Fed Funds Rate through purchasing securities off of commercial banks. As bank reserves go up, the price for them declines. This is their means for pushing down the federal funds rate.

A lower Fed Funds Rate means that banks try to find better opportunities to engage their excess reserves. They might do this by loaning out the money to individuals who seek to purchase a house. They could also lend the cash to companies interested in expanding their business. Either of these actions will boost the economy in some meaningful way. A more active economy will create more jobs and drive down the unemployment rate.

Besides this, the banks also employ the Fed Funds Rate as their basing benchmark from which they determine their other key interest rates. Once the Federal Reserve boosted their federal funds rate target back in December of 2016 as an example, each of the main banks in the country instantly increased their prime loan lending rates. These represent those rates which they offer to their best customers who are extremely creditworthy. The best customers are usually the large and economically powerful MNC multinational corporations.

This means that the effective Fed Funds Rate is not simply the one that the banks are paying each other when they borrow excess reserves from one another. Instead, it has a dramatic and literal connection to the rate of interest any individual will pay for a car loan, home equity loan or line of credit, and mortgage. It also impacts the price that companies will pay to build and grow their business using bank loans.

Federal Trade Commission (FTC)

The FTC Federal Trade Commission proves to be the agency responsible for protecting the American consumers. They strive to stop tricky, fraudulent, and unfair practices in business in the nation's marketplaces. They also disburse valuable information to consumers that helps them to recognize, stop, and sidestep these frauds.

The FTC accepts consumer complaints by phone, email, their website, and through the mail. They take these complaints and enter them into a database that is called the Consumer Sentinel Network. This secure online tool is utilized for investigation purposes by literally hundreds of criminal and civil agencies for law enforcement throughout the United States and overseas.

What the FTC would like to do is to stop these types of deceptive and non-competitive business dealings before they hurt consumers. They are also attempting to improve consumer opportunities so that they are better informed about and comprehend the nature of competition. The agency attempts to perform all of these tasks without putting too many burdens and restrictions on businesses activities that are legitimate.

Congress created the FTC back in 1914. Originally its mandate lay in stopping unfair means of competition in trade and business caused by the trusts. They were a part of the government's stated goal to bust up these trusts. Congress has given them more authority to monitor and fight practices that were against fair competition over the years by passing other laws.

The government enacted another law in 1938 that was broadly addressed to stop any deceptive or unfair practices and acts. They have continued to receive direction and discretion to govern a number of other laws that protect consumers over the subsequent years. Among these are the Pay Per Call Rule, the Telemarketing Sales Rule, and the Equal Credit Opportunity Act. Congress passed another law in 1975 that gave the Federal Trade Commission the ability to come up with rules that regulated trade throughout the industries.

The FTC has a vision for the American economy. They want to see one that has healthy competition between producers. They also desire to see consumers able to obtain correct information. Ultimately the government agency looks for all of this to create low priced and superior quality goods. They encourage innovation, efficiency in business, and choice for consumers.

This agency carries out its vision with three strategic goals. It starts with them protecting consumers by heading off trickery and deception in the business and consumer marketplace. They desire to keep competition going strong. In this role, they stop mergers and business dealings that they believe are against competition. They also work to increase their own performance with consistently improving and excellent managerial, individual, and organizational efforts.

All of these goals and efforts combine to make the FTC one of the government agencies that most impacts each American citizen's economic and personal life. They are the only government entity that possesses a mandate for both competition jurisdiction and consumer protection in large segments of the U.S. economy. They go after aggressive and effectual enforcement of the laws.

The FTC shares its knowledge with international, state, and federal groups and agencies. The group creates research tools at a variety of conferences, workshops, and hearings every year. They also develop and distribute easy to understand educational materials for business and consumer needs in the transforming technological and global market.

The FTC carries out its work through its Bureaus of Economics, Competition, and Consumer Protection. They receive assistance from the Office of General Counsel. Seven regional offices around the country help them to carry out their mandate.

Financial Analyst

A Financial Analyst refers to a salaried individual who handles analysis, financial planning, and projection for both corporations and smaller companies. These accounting field experts create future forecasts for expenditures and revenues in order to come up with projected costs and capital budgeting for company projects. Those analysts who are senior level have the opportunity to work with executives in the corporate team and Chief Financial Officers to help determine across the company investments, policies, and future strategies.

These Financial Analysts draw on strong backgrounds in compliance and accounting in order to evaluate historical financial information, to forecast results for the future, and to push policy and process improvements. Their daily responsibilities include many different elements. They must analyze past and current financial performances and information. They have to evaluate depreciation and current capital expenditures. They must also consider various opportunities for investments of the company. These professionals do a great deal of projections and report preparing using their analyses. They work to find trends in the financial performance of the firm and offer suggestions for improving them. The analysts also evaluate and establish profit plans. Finally, they deliver financial projections and models for the finance team and executives to review.

There are a number of other positions which are related to this important job in a corporation or company. Some of these include financial analysis manager, senior financial analyst, investment analyst, and financial reporting manager. It means there are always opportunities for advancement in such a career path.

In today's increasingly technologically interconnected world, it should not come as a surprise that technology plays a major part in the careers of today's financial analysts. The ones who will be most successful in this field will gain as much exposure to these systems, tools, and platforms which service the field as they possibly can. Among the most typical technological requirements of these positions nowadays is having a complete grasp of the ERP enterprise resource planning systems. Second most in importance proves to be a command of both big data systems and data analytical systems. This is increasingly the case because firms more often rely on data-driven decisions now instead of the old school intuition-driven ones.

This job has a bright outlook for the future, according to the authority in the careers and employment industry--- the United States Bureau of Labor Statistics. In fact this organization states that the career outlook is tremendously positive for this position. The field will increase by approximately 16 percent during the years from 2012 to 20122.This makes it a more rapidly growing job opportunity than the average of every other career path in the U.S. The reasoning behind it is that corporations have put the recession and global financial crisis in the perspective of the past and so are putting on more financial analysts who they feel will help them to increase both their overall corporate growth and profits for the coming years.

The bureau similarly finds that these positions remain among the most heavily demanded jobs in either finance or accounting. This is the case not only for senior level positions, but also even entry level financial analysts. The respected industry publication U.S. News and World Report recently listed these jobs as among the top 100 Best Jobs, at number 63 in the United States. For the category of Best Business Jobs, they award it the number 13 best position in the nation.

This helps to explain why in the year 2014, financial analysts who possessed even from no to two years of experience earned average salaries amounting to $49,459 with an average range of from $39,252 to $60,352. The variance and range depends heavily on the industry, size of firm, location, and other factors of the employer. Senior financial analysts who possess over four years of experience can count on earning an impressive average $74,265 salary each year.

Financial Statement

Financial statements are official records of a business' or personal financial activity. With businesses, financial statements present any and all pertinent financial activity as usable information. They do this in a clear, organized, and simple to comprehend way.

Financial statements are commonly comprised of four different types of financial accounts that come with an analysis and discussion provided by the company's management. The Balance sheet is the first of these. It is known by several other names, including statement of financial condition, or statement of financial position. The balance sheet details will outline a corporation's ownership equity, liabilities, and assets on a particular date. This will give a good picture of the general strength and position of the company.

Financial statements similarly include income statements. These can also be called Profit and Loss statements too. They outline numerous important pieces of company information, such as corporate expenses, income, and profits made in a certain time period. This statement explains all of the relevant financial details to the business' operation. Sales and all associated expenses are included under this category. This section of the financial statement proves to be the nuts and bolts of the whole document. It provides a snap shot of the company's ability to generate sales and turn profits.

A statement of cash flow is also a part of a complete financial statement. As its name implies, this section will share all of the details regarding the company's activities pertaining to cash flow. The most important ones that will be outlined include operating cash flow, financing, and investing endeavors.

The last element of a financial statement includes the statement of retained earnings. This section of the document makes good on its name to detail any changes to a corporation's actual retained earnings for the period that is being reported. These four sections of a financial statement are all combined together to make the consolidated financial statement, once they are combined with the analysis and discussion of management.

With large multinational types of corporations, such financial statements are typically large and complicated, making them challenging to read and understand. To assist with readability, they may also come with a group of notes for the financial statement that also covers management's analysis and discussion. Such notes will go through all items listed on the four parts of the financial statement in more thorough detail. For many companies, these notes for financial statements have come to be deemed a critical component of good and complete financial statements.

Financial statements are used by several different groups of people who are looking at a company. Investors use them in order to determine if the company and its stocks or bonds make a sound investment with a chance of providing good returns on investments and profits in exchange for limited risks. Banks utilize these financial statements to decide if a company is a good credit risk for their loan dollars. Institutions and other groups that may be considering a cash infusion or buyout of the company use such financial statements to decide if the company is a viable investment or acquisition target.

Financial Times Stock Exchange (FTSE)

The Financial Times Stock Exchange represents an enormous group of indices owned by the London Stock Exchange. The acronym originated in the days when it was half owned by the Financial Times newspaper and the LSE. Now this group is an entirely owned subsidiary of only the London Stock Exchange.

When individuals use the word FTSE, they are most commonly referring to the most important benchmark index of the group the FTSE 100. These 100 companies are the hundred largest British companies which the London Stock Exchange lists. As such the Blue Chip companies of the British economy represent the biggest companies by market capitalization in the U.K. Besides this FTSE 100 index, the group produces the FTSE 250, the 350, the Small Cap, and the All-Share.

The FTSE 250 companies are those next 250 largest companies after the FTSE 100. Combining the 250 and the 100 yields the 350 index. Merging the 350 and Small Cap provides the All Share Index.

London Stock Exchange launched the FTSE 100 on January 3, 1984. The companies in the index are calculated for size based on their market capitalization, or number of existing shares times the price per share. The group recalculates the indices every quarter to adjust for any of the companies in the 250 index that have moved up to the 100 index and those in the 100 group that have dropped to the 250 group.

Besides this, they have to remove companies that have been taken over or merged with others. The index must also be updated for name changes, as happened with British Gas becoming BG Group and Centrica, Midland Bank becoming HSBC, and Commercial Union Assurance becoming Aviva. Name changes, mergers, and takeovers are changed as soon as they become effective.

FTSE 100 updates its composite companies based on those which rise to a position in the top 90 largest companies on the London Stock Exchange. Those which fall to the 111th position or lower are dropped. They maintain this overlapping band so that there will not be too much change in the index in any given quarter. The group is concerned about the stability of the index and the rate of change because it forces investment companies and funds to rebalance when the benchmark 100 index changes. This is an expensive process for the large investors that the group tries to mitigate.

The 100 index and other benchmark indices are calculated up every 15 seconds throughout the trading days. The values are published in real time all day. The indices are open from 8am to 4:30pm on all weekdays that are not market holidays.

FTSE 100 is considered to be a good barometer for geopolitical and economic events throughout the world. When the major global markets soar, it does as well. When they plummet, it falls in sympathy. The largest single point drop for the 100 index happened on the day following Black Monday in the U.S. on October 20th of 1987. On this occasion, the 100 index fell 12.22% in a single trading session.

FTSE is not only a series of British stock indices. The group also produces and compiles every day more than 100,000 additional indices around the globe. Among these are the Global Equity, Italy's MIB, the China A50 and 50, the Portugal 20, and the TWSE Taiwan. In 2015 the group merged with Russell to become the FTSE Russell Group. This gave it reach into a number of American stock market indices like the Russell 2000.

Fiscal Year

The fiscal year refers to an accounting period which governments or companies choose to use for their own accounting and in developing financial statements. Fiscal years are not necessarily the same as the calendar years. The U.S. government employs a different starting and finishing point for its own fiscal year.

The IRS Internal Revenue Service permits companies to choose whether they will use calendar years or fiscal years in their tax computations. When individuals or companies discuss budgets, they often invoke fiscal years. They prove to be a useful reference point when contrasting corporate or government financial results over the medium to long term.

The IRS has its own definition of fiscal year. To them these are comprised of 12 contiguous months that conclude on the final day in any month besides December. This means that where tax reports are concerned, a fiscal year could run February 1st to January 31st. American taxpayers also have the opportunity to utilize either 52 or 53 weeks long fiscal years instead of a 12 month one. In the case of the weeks' version, the years will rotate back and forth between 52 and 53 weeks in length.

Because the IRS automatically uses a calendar year system, those who employ fiscal years will need to adjust their own deadlines for turning in specific forms and getting in different payments. The biggest difference concerns the tax filing deadline. For the majority of American households and businesses, this will be no later than April 15th after the year in question for which they file. Those taxpayers working with the fiscal year system instead must file no later than the 15th day in the fourth month that comes after the conclusion of their fiscal period. This means that a business choosing to have fiscal years that span from May 1st to April 30th will need to turn in all tax returns no later than August 15th.

The U.S. tax code makes it relatively easy for companies to use fiscal years in their income tax reporting efforts. All that they are required to do is to turn in on time their tax return which covers that particular fiscal period. The companies also have the right to opt back to using calendar years whenever it suits them. To make the change from fiscal back to calendar years, they need to obtain individual permission by asking the IRS. Otherwise, they will have to measure up to the criteria that they outline in their Form 1128 called the Application to Adopt, Change, or Retain a Tax Year.

These fiscal years have a particular way of being addressed. Individuals who are discussing them reference them either by the end date or alternatively the end year. This means that one would refer to the American federal government fiscal year that starts on October 1st and ends on September 30th by saying the government fiscal year which ends on September 30th, 2016. If instead they were referencing spending by the government that happened in November of 2015, they would have to call this expenditure one that occurred in the 2016 fiscal year.

Fixed Assets

Fixed Assets refers to tangible property which are longer term holdings by their very nature. Companies and corporations both own and utilize them in their normal everyday business operations to produce their revenues and profits. They do not typically become converted back to cash or consumed any quicker than in under minimally a year time frame. Many corporations refer to their collective fixed assets as "the plant." Classic examples of these types of assets include real estate, factories, office space and buildings, furniture, computer equipment, and other operating equipment.

There are longer term assets that do not typically qualify as fixed assets though. Among these are patents and trademarks. They are generally considered to be simply intangible assets on company balance sheets.

Such assets also go by the names of property, plant, and equipment (PP&E). Corporations purchase fixed assets to create and supply services and goods. They might also rent them out to third parties to generate a revenue stream. They could simply deploy them within the company's own internal organization as well. These often include such tangible assets as office equipment, computers, and laptops, as well as manufacturing equipment and factories. Copyrights, goodwill, patents, and trademark could fall into either the fixed or intangible assets categories, depending on the accounting method favored by the firm.

There are many different types of equipment that fall under the classification of fixed assets. Among these are office buildings and plants, software and computer equipment, land, furniture, vehicles, and machinery. It often helps to consider a real tangible example when discussing difficult concepts like this one. Think about the company Amazing Fruits and Vegetables. They sell and even deliver fresh produce. This makes their delivery vehicles a fixed asset. The firm's distribution center would also be such a fixed type of asset. Even the parking lot where customers park while they shop the fruits and vegetables stand would be considered a fixed asset.

There are several reasons why it is helpful (and often times even essential) to have reliable information on the assets of a given company. The most important is that it leads to concise and precise financial reporting, as well as a better valuation of a going concern via financial analysis. Investors rely on such reports in order to ascertain the true financial health and real value of a given company. It enables them to make well- informed choices as to whether they should trust the firm enough to loan it money or instead invest in the equity of the corporation. One thing that makes it more confusing for investors is that firms have a choice of acceptable means of recording, depreciating, and disposing of their own assets. It requires qualified analysts who are willing to read the fine print and notes on the financial statements of the company in question in order to accurately determine on what basis the numbers were compiled.

It is an inevitable fact of life that fixed assets will gradually decline in value terminally as they grow older. They do offer long term income generation, which explains why they become expensed differently than do other company items. While tangible assets become subjected to occasional depreciation, intangible assets are subjected instead to amortization. A specific portion of the costs for the asset will be expensed out yearly. The value of the asset will correspondingly diminish alongside the amount of depreciation on the balance sheet of the corporation. The firm is then allowed to match up the cost of the asset in question with the longer term value of the item.

The method that a given firm utilizes to depreciate its assets will change the book value of the firm which is based on the amount they paid for the asset. This will make the equity book value different from the current market value of the asset in question. An exception to all of this depreciation and book value discussion concerns raw real estate. Land cannot be depreciated since it does not become depleted. The exception is when it is natural resource land, as with oil land, gold or silver mining land, or timber lands. These resources are finite and become expended over time and culling.

Fixed Annuity

A Fixed Annuity refers to a particular form of annuity contract. Insurance companies make such contracts with individuals who are mostly saving for retirement or estate planning. Two main types of these annuities exist, variable and fixed annuities. The fixed one permits investors to add money to the account which is tax deferred. The investor furnishes a lump sum of money in exchange for which the life insurance provides a fully guaranteed and fixed interest rate at the same time as they also guarantee 100 percent of the principle invested. These annuities are often popular for their ability to offer the annuity holder (annuitant) a fully guaranteed income on a regular basis. This can be arranged as a specific number of years or for the remainder of the individual's life.

The motivation for a person to turn over a large sum of money to an insurance company for such a Fixed Annuity lies in the wish to obtain guaranteed returns while not having any original principal at risk. The second factor centers on the special tax advantages that these contracts with insurance companies enjoy. They receive many of the identical tax advantages from which life insurance policies benefit. Among these are earnings growth on a tax-deferred basis. This does not mean that taxes will not be paid, only that they will not be due until the contract becomes annuitized into monthly payouts or the earnings in the account become withdrawn.

There are a number of advantages to these types of Fixed Annuity investments that continue to draw investors to them year in and out. They offer guaranteed minimum rates, competitive yields which are fixed, guaranteed income payments, withdrawal ability, tax deferred growth, and principal safety.

The guaranteed minimum rates are nice but not forever it is important to note. These exist for an initial period only. The subsequent rates becomes adjusted utilizing a certain formula or alternatively employing whatever the prevailing yield is in the investment accounts of the insurers. Some fixed annuities will also offer an extended minimum rate guarantee as a protection in case interest rates decline in the future.

Competitive yields that are fixed come from the life insurance firm's investment portfolio which generates them. These investments mostly go into both high quality corporate bonds and U.S. government bonds. This yield is usually greater than a comparable yield on another investment which comes without risk. Many times this will be guaranteed by the insurance company for anywhere from at least one to as many as ten years.

To many annuity buyers, the guaranteed income payments are the greatest benefit to them. This feature becomes activated when the holder converts the fixed annuity into what is known as an immediate annuity. They can do this whenever they wish to provide a fully guaranteed monthly income payout that can last the remainder of the annuitant's life if they so desire.

Withdrawals are possible with these forms of Fixed Annuities. Holders can take an annual withdrawal every year that is as high as 10 percent of the value of the account. Any amounts greater than 10 percent will be penalized with a surrender charge if this occurs during the surrender period (usually ranging from seven to 12 years from contract start). Every year this surrender charge amount decreases until it eventually reaches zero. At that point withdrawals exceeding 10 percent of the account become penalty-free. There would still be the IRS tax penalty which amounts to ten percent (plus regular income taxes levied as well) on any withdrawals made before the owner reaches 59 and ½ years of age.

Principal safety is a rare commodity in these financially unstable times in the world. Annuities guarantee this, but the strength of the guarantee is only as good as the life insurance company that makes it. This is why investors should only invest their money with those life insurance firms which have at least an A or higher financial strength rating.

FOREX Markets

FOREX markets are the world wide foreign exchange markets. They are called FX markets as well. FOREX markets are different from all of the other major financial markets in that they are over the counter and decentralized. They exist for the purpose of trading currencies.

Unlike with other markets, the FOREX markets are also open twenty-four hours a day during the week and on Sunday, since the different financial centers around the globe serve as trading bases for a variety of buyers and sellers. This foreign exchange market is the place where supply and demand mostly decides the different currencies' values for nations around the world.

The main point and reason for the FOREX markets are to help out investment and trade internationally through permitting businesses to easily change one currency to the other one that they require. In practice, individuals or businesses actually buy one amount of foreign currency through paying for it with a given amount of a different currency.

As an example, Canadian businesses may import British goods by paying for them in British Pounds, even though their income and base currency are Canadian dollars. The foreign exchange markets allow for investors to speculate on the rising and falling values of various currencies as well. It also makes the infamous carry trade possible, where investors are able to borrow currencies with low yields or interest rates and use them to purchase higher interest rate yielding currencies. Critics have said that the FOREX markets also hurt some countries' competitiveness against other countries.

This market is extremely popular and unique for a variety of reasons. It possesses the greatest trading volume on earth, managing in the three to four trillion dollar range every single trading day. This gives it enormous liquidity. It is also geographically centered all over the world, from Wellington in New Zealand to London in Great Britain to New York in the United States. Traders love that the market runs fully twenty-four hours per day except for on the weekends, when it reopens Sunday afternoon.

Finally, an enormous degree of leverage, that can be as much as two hundred to one, allows for even people with small accounts to make potentially enormous gains. Because of all of these factors and its world wide trading base, the FOREX markets have been called the ones where perfect competition is most evident. This is the case even though central banks sometimes intervene directly in these markets to increase or decrease the value of their currency relative to a trading partners' or trading competitors' currency value.

Fortune 500

Fortune Magazine publishes a famous annual list of the biggest 500 companies throughout the United States. This list has become known as the Fortune 500. The positions in the list are based upon total revenues earned for the given year. The magazine's editors compile this list from the most current revenue figures. They consider both private and public companies. For a private company to be included, it must have revenue information that is available as part of the public domain.

Being listed as one of the Fortune 500 companies has always been deemed to be a prestigious position. Over recent years, the leaders in this important list have competed with each other for the top spots. Among the contenders for these important top rankings have been Walmart, Exxon Mobile, Apple, General Motors, Chevron, and General Electric. Energy producing companies nearly always figure prominently in the list.

The Fortune 500 list has evolved quite considerably since Fortune Editor Edgar P. Smith first conceived of it. The first year the magazine published it was 1955. At the time, only companies whose revenues came from certain sectors were considered to be included. This comprised companies in energy exploration and production, mining, and manufacturing.

Other sectors of the economy were not completely left out by Fortune Magazine. These were included in separate special lists of Fortune 50 companies. In these lists, there were companies which were ranked by assets. This included the 50 biggest commercial banks by assets, 50 largest life insurance companies, and 50 largest utilities in the United States. Other Fortune 50 companies were ranked by revenues. Among these lists were the 50 biggest transportation companies and the 50 largest retailers in America.

Fortune magazine finally expanded the definitions of what companies could be included in the benchmark Fortune 500 list in 1994. They broadened their methodology to factor in companies who were members of the services industry. This change made an enormous difference in the subsequent results immediately. The Fortune 500 list gained 291 new companies because of it. Three of the members of the coveted Top 10 spots became service companies for the first time in that ground breaking year.

Besides the Fortune 500, Fortune Magazine also publishes several other related rankings. These include such lists as the broader Fortune 1000 and the more selective Fortune 100. These lists are much less widely cited than is the gold standard Fortune 500 list. Fortune has also expanded their lists internationally in recent years. This list is known as the Global 500. Its members generally employ more people, have higher revenues, and boast higher profits than the 500 companies on the solely American based Fortune 500 list.

The all around health and performance of the U.S. economy can be measured by the results of the Fortune 500 companies. During the middle of the Great Recession back in 2008, these companies' results gave hope that there might be improvement in the overall economic picture.

In 2009 the Top 500 American corporations as a whole saw earnings increase by 335%. These more encouraging results indicated that possible economic recovery lay ahead. The subtraction from or addition to this list also speaks volumes about different sectors in the American economy. Following the collapse of the housing market in the Great Recession, home builders fell off of the list in significant numbers.

FTSE 100 Index

The FTSE 100 Index proves to be the trading world designation for the largest index managed by the FTSE Group out of London in the United Kingdom. FTSE is actually jointly owned by parent companies the Financial Times and the London Stock Exchange. This mash up of FT from Financial Times and SE from London Stock Exchange is how they arrive at the acronym FTSE. In general when analysts refer to the FTSE, they mean the FTSE 100 Index itself. This is actually a misnomer, since there are literally thousands of different FTSE indices the company owns and operates around the globe on numerous different national stock exchanges on every continent.

This FTSE 100 Index has been called the globe's most heavily referenced and most popular stock market index throughout the world. In practice, it represents around 80 percent of the entire market capitalization of the heavily multinational London Stock Exchange. The weighting system the FTSE company utilizes means that the bigger a corporation is, the larger a share of the index it occupies, thanks to it being a market capitalization-weighted index. This index is real time calculated all trading day long. The firm updates and publishes it continuously throughout the open market hours on an every 15 seconds basis.

Many analysts and investors rely on the FTSE 100 Index as some sort of prosperity indicator for British companies and the United Kingdom economy in general. This is actually a misnomer. It is all thanks to a significant constituency of the representative firms from the index being headquartered in other nations throughout the globe. It means that the index's daily movements do not truly reflect the strength of the British economy and corporations. Instead, the secondary index of the group, the FTSE 250 is more accurate a bell weather for British businesses and the economy. This is because a far smaller representation of international corporations populates the 250 index. It makes it a much better indicator for Great Britain generally speaking.

FTSE the company decides every quarter which are the 100 largest member companies on the LSE. Their tradition is to calculate this on the Wednesday after the first Friday of the month for March, June, September, and December, respectively. They utilize the business day close values from the night before to decide if any constituents should be replaced.

It is no exaggeration to call the FTSE 100 Index the Blue Chip index of the London Stock Exchange. These are the largest and most economically powerful and far-reaching corporations from Great Britain and around the world (ex the United States) in many cases.

The constituent members of the FTSE 100 as of time of publication were as follows: 3I Group, Associated British Foods, Admiral Group, Anglo American, Antofagasta, Ashtead Group, AstraZeneca, Aviva, Babcock International, BAE Systems, Barclays, Barratt Development, BHP Billiton, BP, British American Tobacco, British Land, BT Group, Bunzl, Burberry Group, Carnival, Centrica, Coca Cola HBC AG, Compass Group, Convatec, CRH, Croda International, DCC, Diageo, Direct Line, Easy Jet, Experian, Fresnillo, GKN, GlaxoSmithKline, Glencore, Hammerson, Hargreaves Lans, Hikma, HSBC Bank Holdings, Imperial Brands, Informa, Intercontinental Hotels, Intertek Group, International Consolidated Airlines, INTU Properties, ITV, Johnson Matthey, Kingfisher, Land Securities, Legal & General, Lloyds Group, London Stock Exchange, Marks & Spencer, Medi clinic, Merlin, Micro Focus, Mondi, William Morrison, National Grid, Next, Old Mutual, Paddy Power Betting, Pearson, Persimmon, Provident Financial, Prudential, Randgold Res., RDS A Shares, RDS B Shares, Reckitt Benison Group, RELX, Rentokil International, Rio Tinto, Rolls Royce Holdings, Royal Bank of Scotland, Royal Mail, RSA Insurance, Sage Group, J. Sainsbury, Schroders, Scottish Mort, Severn Trent, Shire Pharmaceuticals, Sky PLC, Smith & Nephew, Smiths Group, Smurfit Kap., SSE, St. James's Place, Standard Chartered, Standard Life, Taylor Wimpey, Tesco, TUI AG, Unilever, United Utilities, Vodafone Group, Whitbread, Wolseley, Worldpay Group, and WPP Group (the world's leading advertising company giant).

FTSE 250

FTSE 250 is a broad-based stock index maintained by the FTSE company. This company is much like Standard and Poor's in that they both concentrate their efforts on calculating indices. The FTSE is not made up of any stock exchange, though among its co-owners is the famed and historic London Stock Exchange (LSE). The other co-owner of the company is its namesake the Financial Times newspaper publishing empire.

Easily the best known of the FTSE indices is the FTSE 100. There are many thousands of indices owned, produced, and calculated by FTSE, but only one is the blue chip index of all British and international company and economy stocks based on the LSE. The second most important and widely cited index from the company is this FTSE 250. This one is made up of the 101st to 351st largest companies in the U.K. As these firms tend to be much more British and far less international than those making up the FTSE 100, they are gauged to be a superior measurement of how the British economy and U.K. based firms are actually performing.

The FTSE 250 index list is altered four times a year on a quarterly basis. This occurs reliably every March, June, September, and December month. The index itself is continuously calculated instantly in real time. The owner of the index publishes it every minute accordingly online and through financial news and media outlet feeds.

As of November 7, 2016, the 350 different constituent companies which comprise the FTSE 250 are as follows: 3i Infrastructure, AA, Aberdeen Asset Management, Aberforth Smaller Companies Trust, Acacia Mining, Aggreko, Aldermore Group, Alliance Trust, Allied Minds, Amec Foster Wheeler, AO World, Ascential, Ashmore Group, Assura, WS Atkins, Auto Trader Group, Aveva, Balfour Beatty, Bankers Investment Trust, Barr, A.G., BBA Aviation, Beazley Group, Bellway, Berendsen, Berkeley Group Holdings, Bank of Georgia Holdings, BH Macro, Big Yellow Group, B & M European Retail Value, Bodycote, Booker Group, Bovis Homes Group, Brewin Dolphin Holdings, British Empire Trust, Britvic, Brown N, BTG, Cairn Energy, Caledonia Investments, Capital & Counties Properties, Card Factory, Carillion, Centamin, Cineworld, City of London Investment Trust, Clarkson, Close Brothers Group, CLS Holdings, CMC Markets, Cobham,

Computacenter, Countryside Properties, Countrywide, Cranswick, Crest Nicholson, CYBG, Daejan Holdings, Dairy Crest, Debenhams, Dechra Pharmaceuticals, Derwent London, DFS, Dignity, Diploma, Domino's Pizza, Drax Group, Dunelm Group, Edinburgh Investment Trust, Electra Private Equity, Electrocomponents, Elementis, Entertainment One, Essentra, Esure, Euromoney Institutional Investor, Evraz, F&C Commercial Property Trust, Fidelity China Special Situations, Fidelity European Values, Fidessa Group, Finsbury Growth & Income Trust, FirstGroup, Fisher, James & Sons, Foreign & Colonial Investment Trust, G4S, Galliford Try, GCP Infrastructure Investments, Genesis Emerging Markets Fund, Genus, Go-Ahead Group, Grafton Group, Grainger, Great Portland Estates, Greencoat UK Wind, Greencore, Greene King, Greggs, GVC Holdings, Halfords Group, Halma, Hansteen Holdings, HarbourVest Global Private Equity, Hastings Group, Hays, Henderson Group, HICL Infrastructure Company, Hill & Smith, Hiscox, Hochschild Mining, Homeserve, Howden Joinery, Hunting, Ibstock, ICAP, IG Group Holdings, IMI, Inchcape, Indivior, Inmarsat, Intermediate Capital Group, International Personal Finance, International Public Partnerships, Investec, IP Group, Jardine Lloyd Thompson, JD Sports, John Laing Group, John Laing Infrastructure Fund, JPMorgan American Investment Trust, JPMorgan Emerging Markets Investment Trust, JPMorgan Indian Investment Trust, JRP Group, Jupiter Fund Management, Just Eat, KAZ Minerals, Keller, Kennedy Wilson Europe Real Estate, Kier Group, Ladbrokes Coral, Laird, Lancashire Holdings, LondonMetric Property, Man Group, Marshalls, Marston's, McCarthy & Stone, Meggitt, Mercantile Investment Trust, Metro Bank, Millennium & Copthorne Hotels, Mitchells & Butlers, Mitie, Moneysupermarket.com Group, Monks Investment Trust, Morgan Advanced Materials, Murray International Trust, National Express Group, NB Global, NCC Group, NMC Health, Ocado Group, OneSavings Bank, P2P Global Investments, PageGroup, Paragon Group of Companies, PayPoint, Paysafe, Pennon Group, Perpetual Income & Growth Investment Trust, Personal Assets Trust, Petra Diamonds, Petrofac, Pets at Home, Phoenix Group Holdings, Playtech, Polar Capital Technology Trust, Polypipe, PZ Cussons, QinetiQ, Rank Group, Rathbone Brothers, Redefine International, Redrow, Regus, Renewables Infrastructure Group, Renishaw, Rentokil Initial, Restaurant Group, Rightmove, RIT Capital Partners, Riverstone Energy, Rotork, RPC Group, Safestore, Saga, Savills, Scottish Investment Trust, Scottish Mortgage Investment Trust, Segro, Senior, Serco, Shaftesbury, Shawbrook Bank, SIG plc, Smith (DS), Smurfit Kappa Group, Softcat, Sophos,

Spectris, Spirax-Sarco Engineering, Spire Healthcare, Sports Direct, SSP Group, Stagecoach Group, St. Modwen Properties, SuperGroup, SVG Capital, Synthomer, TalkTalk Group, Tate & Lyle, Ted Baker, Telecom Plus, Temple Bar Investment Trust, Templeton Emerging Markets Investment Trust, Thomas Cook Group, Tritax Big Box REIT, TR Property Investment Trust (two listings, both ordinary & sigma shares), Tullett Prebon, Tullow Oil, UBM, UDG Healthcare, UK Commercial Property Trust, Ultra Electronics Holdings, Unite Group, Vectura Group, Vedanta Resources, Vesuvius, Victrex, Virgin Money, Weir Group, Wetherspoon (J D), W H Smith, William Hill, Witan Investment Trust, Wizz Air, Woodford Patient Capital Trust, Wood Group, Workspace Group, Worldwide Healthcare Trust, and Zoopla.

Futures

Futures prove to be financial derivatives that are also called forward contracts. Such a futures contract gives a seller the obligation to deliver an asset, such as a commodity, to the buyer at a pre set date. These contracts are heavily traded on major produced commodities like wheat, gold, oil, coffee, and sugar. They also exist for underlying financial instruments that include government bonds, stock market indexes, and foreign currencies.

The history of futures goes back to Ancient Greece where the first recorded example is detailed about an olive press arrangement that philosopher Thales entered into. Futures contracts become commonplace at trade fairs throughout Europe by the 1100's. Merchants did not feel secure traveling with significant amounts of goods, so they would only bring display samples along and then sell merchandise that they would deliver in greater quantities at future dates.

Futures contracts created an enormous bubble in the 1600's with the Dutch Tulip Mania that caused tulip bulbs to skyrocket to unthinkable levels. In this speculative bubble, the majority of money that was exchanged turned out to be for tulip futures and not the tulips themselves. The first futures exchange in the United States opened in 1868 as the Chicago Board of Trade, where copper, pork bellies, and wheat were traded in futures contracts.

In the early years of the 1970's, futures trading grew explosively in volume. Pricing models created by Myron Scholes and Fischer Black permitted the quick pricing of futures and options on them. Investors could easily speculate on commodities prices through these futures. As the demand for the futures skyrocketed, additional significant futures exchanges opened and expanded around the world, especially in Chicago, London, and New York.

Futures trading could not happen effectively without the exchanges. Futures contracts are spelled out in terms of the asset that underlies them, the date of delivery, the last day of contract trading, transaction currency, and size of ticks or minimum permissible price changes. Exchanges have developed into major and predictable markets through their standardizing of all of these various factors for many different kinds of futures contracts.

Trading futures contracts involves major leverage. This means that they carry tremendous opportunities as well as risks. Futures, with their ability to control enormous quantities of commodities and financials, have been the root causes for many collapses. Enron and Barings Bank were both brought down by financial futures. Perhaps the most famous futures meltdown involved the Long Term Capital Management group.

Even though this company had the inventors of the futures pricing models Scholes and Black working for them, the company lost money in the futures markets so quickly that the Federal Reserve Bank had to become involved and bail out the company to stop the whole financial system of the Untied States from collapsing.

Futures Contracts

Futures contracts are legally binding agreements which two parties usually enter into on a futures exchange trading floor or electronic platform. They spell out the particulars for selling or buying specific financial instruments or commodities for a pre-set price at an exact moment in the future. Such contracts have become standardized to make it easy to trade them on the various futures exchanges. They provide information on the quantity and quality of the commodity, though this depends on the nature of the underlying asset.

Futures contracts can be settled in two ways. Some of them require actual physical delivery of the commodity specified. Others simply settle between the two parties in cash. These contracts specify all important characteristics for the item which the parties are trading. This makes them different from the word "futures" that more generally refers to the markets in which these commodities and instruments trade.

There are two actual types of participants in the futures markets who utilize such futures contracts. These are speculators and hedgers. Individual traders and managers of portfolios can use them to place speculative bets on the direction of price movements for the given asset that underlies the contracts. Hedgers involve buyers or producers of the contact asset itself attempting to lock in the price for which they will later buy or sell their commodity.

There are many different commodities and assets for which futures contracts exist. The most obvious of these are hard assets such as precious metals, industrial metals, natural gas, crude oil and other energy products, grains, seeds, livestock, oils, and carbon credits. Literally dozens of the more significant stock market indices around the globe have these contracts available to trade. Some major individual stocks have their own futures contract on their shares as well. The major interest rates and most important currency pairs also have such contracts and markets to trade.

Futures contracts which require physical delivery do not often result in such physical delivery. Many investors in these contracts trade them and sell them before the date of delivery. They can roll them forward by selling the imminent to expire contract and buying a further month out to replace them.

For producers of a good, these contracts provide a unique solution to the problem of fluctuating prices. Oil producers are classic examples. They might intend to produce a million barrels of oil to deliver in precisely a year. If the price is $50 for a barrel today, and the producer does not want to risk prices falling lower, it could lock it in. Oil prices have become so volatile that they could be substantially lower or higher a year from now. By selling a futures contract, the producer gives up the opportunity to possibly sell the oil for more in a year. It also eliminates the risk of receiving a lower amount.

Mathematical models actually determine the prices of futures contracts. They consider the present day spot price, time until maturity, risk free return rates, dividends, dividend yields, convenience yields, and storage costs. This might mean with oil prices at $50 that a one year futures contract sells for $53. The producer receives a guarantee for $53 million and will have to provide the 1 million barrels of oil on the exact delivery date. It will obtain this $53 per barrel price despite the spot prices at which the markets are trading on that date.

Futures Exchange

A futures exchange refers to a central clearing marketplace that allows for futures contracts as well as options on such futures contracts to be traded. Thanks to the rapid increase in electronic trading of futures, this term also finds use regarding futures trading activities directly.

There are the two most important futures exchanges in the world today. The biggest in the United States is the Chicago Mercantile Exchange, or CME. This one became established in the last years of the 1890s. In the early days, the only futures contracts available were agricultural products' futures.

This changed rapidly in the 1970s. Currency futures appeared on the major currency pairs after the breakdown of the Breton Woods Agreement. The futures exchanges of today are massive by comparison. They allow for investors to hedge all sorts of financial products and commodities. These range from stock indices and individual stocks to energies, precious and base metals, soft commodities such as orange juice and soybeans, interest rate products, and even credit default swaps.

In today's futures exchange, it is hedging financial instruments and products which create the significant majority of activity in futures markets. Today the futures exchange markets carry an important responsibility for global financial system operations, efficient functioning, and activity. The international nature of this global futures exchange has given rise to the world's first truly international futures market, the ICE Intercontinental Exchange.

ICE is massive and important in not only futures markets. They own and operate 12 different exchanges around the world, including NYSE EuroNext, which controls the famed and venerable New York Stock Exchange and EuroNext exchange (owning the Paris and Dutch stock exchanges, among others). In Europe, this is a serious rival to the historic LSE London Stock Exchange and continental powerhouse the German Deutsche Bourse. The ICE today counts 12,000 listed futures contracts as well as securities. It trades 5.2 million futures contracts every day, as well as $1.8 billion in cash equities every day.

In energies, the Intercontinental Exchange Futures commands almost half of all the traded crude and refined oil futures contracts volume for the entire planet. It is also the location of the most highly liquid market for the European interest rates short term contracts. It controls a wide variety of global benchmarks in agriculture, energies, foreign exchange, and equity indices.

ICE only launched its international futures exchange back in 2000 with the advent of their electronic trading platform. This makes it among the newer futures exchanges in the world, and yet it is a dominant international player still. Their high tech-powered rise increased the access to and transparency of the Over the Counter traded energy markets as well as the new global futures markets exchange they opened shortly thereafter. It was 2001 when they expanded to energy futures with their acquisition of the International Petroleum Exchange.

In 2002, ICE expanded heavily into Europe by opening up their ICE Clear Europe. This represented the first new clearing house in the United Kingdom in a full century. By 2007, the Intercontinental Exchange had cemented its global position in energy trade by acquiring both the NYBOT New York Board of Trade and the Canadian-based Winnipeg Commodity Exchange.

The end result today is an entire ecosystem made up of futures and equities markets, clearing houses throughout the world, listing and data centers and services, and technology-driven solutions which together work to create a full, free, and transparent accessibility to the worldwide futures, energy, derivatives, and capital markets.

Between ICE Futures U.S.'s operations and endeavors within the United States, the futures exchange is enabling and empowering markets which allow for an effective risk management throughout the world economy. Their product offerings and solutions encompass a diverse and broad variety of futures contracts. These span internationally traded equity indexes and futures; credit derivative futures; FX futures; North American oil, power, and natural gas futures; and soft commodities and agriculture futures including sugar, cotton, coffee, and cocoa.

Government Bonds

Government bonds are debt instruments that governments issue to pay for government expenditures. Within the United States, federal government issues include savings bonds, treasury notes, treasury bonds, and TIPS Treasury inflation protected securities. Investors should carefully consider the risks that different countries' governments possess before they invest in their bonds. Among these international government risks are political risk, country risk, interest rate risk, and inflation risk. Governments generally have less credit risk, though not always.

Savings bonds are a type of United States government bonds that the Treasury department sells. They are available in an electronic form. The Treasury offers them directly from their website, or individuals can buy them from the majority of financial institutions and banks. When savings bonds reach maturity, the investors get back the bond's face value along with interest which accrued. These savings bonds may not be redeemed the first year of issue. Any investors who redeem them in their first five years of issue lose three months interest for cashing out too early.

The Treasury of the United States also issues intermediate time frame bonds known as Treasury notes or T-Notes. These notes provide interest payments semiannually at a coupon rate which is fixed. These notes typically are denominated in $1,000 face values. Those with three or two year maturity dates come in $5,000 denominations. Before 1984, T-Notes were callable and gave the Treasury the right to buy them back given specific conditions.

The U.S. government's longest term bonds are Treasury Bonds, or T-Bonds. These have maturity dates ranging from ten to 30 years time. They also provide interest payments on a semiannual basis and come in $1,000 denominated values. These T-bonds are important because they pay for federal budget shortfalls, are a form of monetary policy, and ensure the country is able to regulate its money supply. As all bond issuers, the Treasury department looks at return and risk requirements on the market when it goes to raise capital so that it can be as efficient as possible. This helps to explain the different kinds of Treasury securities and government bonds they offer.

U.S. government bonds have generally been considered to be without risk, which is why they trade so easily in extremely large and liquid markets. The downside to this is that they offer considerably lower returns than do other bonds. TIPS do provide protection against inflation so that any inflation increases will not exceed the interest rate of the bond. The prices of government bonds are based on current interest rates. This means that the fixed rate bonds will decline in value as the interest rates rise, since there is lost opportunity to obtain newer bonds at higher interest rates. Similarly, if interest rates fall, the bond's values will rise.

The federal government is able to control the money supply in part by its issue of the government bonds. If they wish to increase the money supply, they can simply buy back their own bonds. These funds then find their way to a bank and expand the money supply as banks keep small reserves and loan the rest out (in the money multiplier effect). The government is also able to lower the money supply by selling additional bonds which takes money out of circulation. If the government were to retire the funds received from the sale of these bonds, it would reduce the available money supply. More often than not, the U.S. government spends the money.

Hedge Account

A hedge account is an account established with a hedge fund. There are several reasons why a person or business would be interested in setting up a hedge account. These mostly center on the desire for investments that commonly produce higher profits or the wish to hedge, or protect, a business' operations from certain unpredictable and undesirable swings in market prices. Businesses can open up their own hedge accounts in various futures and commodities markets to protect themselves from these business impacting price movements in important related commodities.

A person who is interested in opening a hedge account will have to make application to a hedge fund. Hedge funds are typically restrictive in the types of funds that they will accept from an investor. The investor will have to prove certain income levels or asset base holdings that demonstrate that they are capable of bearing the substantial losses that could result from trades in a hedge account. They must also have liquid cash that they can tie up for long periods of time, since most hedge funds do not allow immediate on demand withdrawals.

Funds that are invested with them could be tied up for a year or longer, and minimum waiting periods apply. Because of all of these reasons, hedge funds are typically looking for people as investors who have in excess of a million dollars of liquid net worth.

Hedge accounts can also be accounts that businesses use to offset the changes in commodities' prices. A company's products may be heavily dependent on prices such as sugar and cocoa if they are a chocolate company, oil and other energy prices if they use energy intensive processes or are shipping companies, or even industrial metals such as copper if they produce wires or cables. Gold and silver mining companies, along with oil producers, routinely hedge their quantities of precious metals and energies that they expect to produce to protect against anticipated declining prices. By locking in the present price for these goods and commodities that they require or will produce later on in the year, they can insulate themselves from price swings that move against them.

This can mean the difference between having to raise prices and risk losing market share or selling goods at a much lower profit margin. Because of this, many major multinational companies around the world routinely protect themselves and their operations through the use of hedge accounts. Some of them even have individuals or departments that oversee these operations.

For a business to set up such a hedge account is not difficult. They only have to open a commodities account with one of the major commodities exchanges, such as the Chicago Mercantile Exchange, the Chicago Board of Trade, New York Mercantile Exchange, or the New York Board of Trade. These accounts can be used by companies for speculating on the price movements of underlying commodities as well, and not only for hedging their operations. In this case, care has to be taken, as the leverage provided by hedge accounts, such as commodities accounts, is enough to bring down a company overnight if they are irresponsible with the trades in the account.

Hedge Fund

A hedge fund is an investment fund which are commonly only open to a specific group of investors. These investors pay a large performance fee each year, commonly a certain percent of their funds under management, to the manager of the hedge fund. Hedge funds are very minimally regulated and are therefore are able to participate in a wide array of investments and investment strategies.

Literally every single hedge fund pursues its own strategy of investing that will establish the kinds of investments that it seeks. Hedge funds commonly go for a wide range of investments in which they may buy or sell short shares and positions. Stocks, commodities, and bonds are some of these asset classes with which they work.

As you would anticipate from the name, hedge funds typically try to offset some of the risks in their portfolios by employing a number of risk hedging strategies. These mostly revolve around the use of derivatives, or financial instruments with values that depend on anticipated price movements in the future of an asset to which they are linked, as well as short selling investments.

Most countries only allow certain types of wealthy and professional investors to open a hedge fund account. Regulators may not heavily oversee the activities of hedge funds, but they do govern who is allowed to participate. As a result, traditional investment funds' rules and regulations mostly do not apply to hedge funds.

Actual net asset values of hedge funds often tally into the many billions of dollars. The funds' gross assets held commonly prove to be massively higher as a result of their using leverage on their money invested. In particular niche markets like distressed debt, high yield ratings, and derivatives trading, hedge funds are the dominant players.

Investors get involved in hedge funds in search of higher than normal market returns. When times are good, many hedge funds yield even twenty percent annual investment returns. The nature of their hedging strategies is supposed to protect them from terrible losses, such as were seen in the financial crisis from 2007-2010.

The hedge fund industry is opaque and difficult to measure accurately. This is partially as a result of the significant expansion of the industry, as well as an inconsistent definition of what makes a hedge fund. Prior to the peak of hedge funds in the summer of 2008, it is believed that hedge funds might have overseen as much as two and a half trillion dollars. The credit crunch hit many hedge funds particularly hard, and their assets under management have declined sharply as a result of both losses, as well as requests for withdrawals by investors. In 2010, it is believed that hedge funds once again represent in excess of two trillion dollars in assets under management.

The largest hedge funds in the world are JP Morgan Chase, with over $53 billion under management; Bridgewater Associates, having more than $43 billion in assets under management; Paulson and Company, with more than $32 billion in assets; Brevan Howard that has greater than $27 billion in assets; and Soros Fund Management, which boasts around $27 billion in assets under management.

Hedging

In the world of finance, hedging is the act of putting together a hedge. Hedging involves building up a position in one market whose goal is try to counteract risk from changes in price in another market's position that is the opposite. The ultimate goal is to diminish or eliminate the business or person's possibilities of risk that they wish to avoid. A number of specific vehicles exist to help with hedging. These typically include forward contracts, swaps, insurance policies, options, derivatives, and products sold over the counter. Futures contracts prove to be the most popular version of hedging instruments.

In the 1800's, futures markets open to the public came into existence. These were set up to permit a standardized form of effective, viable, and open hedging of commodity prices in agriculture. In the intervening century, these have grown to include all manners of futures contracts that allow individuals and businesses to hedge precious metals, energy, changes in interest rates, and movements in foreign currencies.

There are countless examples of individuals who might be interested in hedging. Commercial farmers are common types of people who practice hedging. Prices for agricultural crops like wheat change all the time as the demand and supply for them fluctuates. Sometimes these price changes are significant in one direction or the other. With the present prices and crop predictions at harvest time, a commercial farmer might determine that planting wheat for the season is smart.

The problem that he encounters is that these predicted prices are simply forecasts. After the farmer plants his wheat crop, he has tied himself to it for the whole growing season. Should the real price of wheat soar in between the time that the farmer plants and harvests his crop then he might make a great amount of money that he did not count on, yet should the real price decline by the time the harvest is in then the farmer might be ruined completely.

To remove the risk from his wheat crop equation, the farmer can set up a hedge. He does this hedging by selling a certain quantity of futures contracts for wheat. These should be sold at an amount equal to the wheat crop size that he expects when he plants it. In such a way, the commercial farmer fixes his price of wheat at planting time. His hedging contract proves to be a pledge to furnish a particular quantity of wheat bushels to a certain place on a fixed date in time at a guaranteed price. Now the farmer is hedged against changes in the prices of wheat. He does not have to worry anymore about the wheat prices and whether they are falling or rising, since he has been promised a fixed price in his hedging wheat futures contract. The possibility of him being totally ruined by falling wheat prices is completely removed from the realm of possibility. At the same time, he has lost the opportunity of realizing extra money as a result of rising wheat prices when harvest time arrives. These are the upsides and the downsides to hedging; both the positives and the negatives of uncertainty are eliminated.

High Frequency Trading (HFT)

High frequency trading turns out to be a platform for program-based trades. It works with super computers that are able to run huge quantities of trading orders at incredibly rapid speeds. This HFT works with complicated algorithms. These analyze a wide range of markets and then place a number fast-paced orders depending on the conditions in the markets. The secret of the trading algorithms lies in their speed. Those traders who have the quickest trade executions usually make more money than do traders who have slower trade executions.

This high frequency trading has not always been mainstream or even possible. It grew in popularity as some of the exchanges began to provide incentives for corporations that could increase the stock market's liquidity.

As an example, the NYSE New York Stock Exchange works with a number of liquidity providers. These are known as SLPs Supplemental Liquidity Providers. The strive to provide better liquidity and more competition for the exchange and its already existing quotes.

The companies that participate in this program earn either a rebate or a fee when they increase the liquidity. This amount turned out to be $0.0019 in mid 2016 for securities that are listed on the NYSE or NYSE MKT. It may not sound like an enormous amount of money. It adds up to major profits quickly as some of these companies are engaged in millions of transactions on busy days.

The NYSE and other exchanges introduced this SLP program for a specific reason. After Lehman Brothers collapsed back in 2008, liquidity turned into an enormous concern for market participants. The SLP provided the solution to low liquidity. It also made high frequency trading a major part of the stock market in only a few years.

High frequency trading offers some significant benefits to the stock exchanges and financial markets. The most significant one centers on the significantly better liquidity that the programs provide. It has reduced bid ask spreads substantially. Larger spreads are more or less a thing of the past.

Some exchanges tested the benefits by trying to place fees on the HFT. The spreads then increased as fewer trades occurred. The Canadian government started charging fees for high frequency trading on Canadian markets. A study concluded that the end result was 9% higher bid to ask spreads.

There are many who dislike high frequency trading as well. Opponents are harsh in their criticism. Many broker dealers have been eliminated by the computer programs. The human element has been removed from many decisions on the exchanges.

When errors occur, the critics are quick to point out that human interactions could have prevented them. Part of the problem in the speed is that the programs are making decisions in literally thousandths of a second. This can lead to huge moves in the market with no apparent explanation or reason.

The best example of the mistakes that can lead to enormous and scary stock market moves happened on May 6, 2010 during the Flash Crash. The DJIA Dow Jones Industrial Average experienced its biggest drop of all time on an intraday basis. The Dow plunged over 1,000 points and dropped a full 10% in only twenty minutes. It then recovered back much of the loss in the next few hours. When the government investigated the issue, they found an enormous order which had caused the sell off to begin. The HFT computer algorithms did all the rest.

Another criticism concerns large corporate profiting at the expense of the smaller retail investors. The trade off is superior liquidity. Unfortunately, much of this turns out to be phantom liquidity. It is there for the market at one moment and then gone in another. This keeps the traders from benefiting from the liquidity.

High Yield Bonds

High Yield Bonds turn out to be bonds that possess a lower credit rating and higher yield than those corporate, municipal, and sovereign government bonds which are of investment grade. Thanks to the greater risk of them defaulting, such bonds yield a higher return than the bonds which are qualified investment grade issues. Those companies that issue high yielding debt are usually capital intensive companies and startup firms that already possess higher debt ratios. Investors often refer to such bonds as junk bonds.

The two principal corporate rating credit agencies determine the breakdown of what qualifies as a High Yield Bond and what does not. When Moody's rates a bond with lower than a "Baa" rating, or Standard and Poor's (S&P) rates then with an under "BBB" rating, then they become known as junk bonds. At the same time, all of those bonds which enjoy higher ratings than these (or the same rating at least) investors will consider to be investment grade. There are credit ratings that cover such categories as presently in default, or "D." Those kinds of bonds holding "C" ratings and below also have high probabilities for defaulting. In order to compensate the investors who take them on for the significant risks they run of not receiving either their original principal back or accrued interest payments by the maturity date, the yields must be offered at extremely high interest rates.

Despite the negative label of "junk bond," these High Yield Bonds remain popular and heavily bought by global investors. The majority of these investors choose to diversify for safety sake by utilizing either a junk bond ETF exchange traded fund or a High Yield Bonds mutual fund. The spread between the yields on the higher yielding and investment grade types of bonds constantly fluctuates on the markets. The at the time condition of the global and national economies impacts this. Industry-specific and individual corporate events also play a part in the differences between the various kinds of bonds' interest rates.

In general though, High Yield Bonds' investors can count on receiving a good 150 to 300 basis points more in yield as measured against the investment quality bonds in any particular time frame. This is why mutual funds and ETFs make imminent sense as an effective means of gaining exposure to the greater yields without taking on the unnecessary risk of a single issuer's bonds defaulting and costing the investors all or most of their original investing principal.

In the last few years, various central bankers throughout the globe have decided to inject enormous amounts of liquidity into their individual economies so that credit will remain cheaply and easily available. This includes the European Central Bank, the U.S. Federal Reserve, and the Bank of Japan. It has created the side effect of causing borrowing costs to drop and lenders to experience significantly lower returns.

By February of 2016, an incredible $9 trillion in sovereign government debt bonds provided yields of only from zero percent to one percent. Seven trillion of the sovereign bonds delivered negative real yields once adjusted for anticipated levels of inflation. It means that holding such bonds cost investors money, or provided them a real losing return.

In typical economic environments, this would drive intelligent investors to competing markets that provide better return rates. Higher yield bond markets have stayed volatile though. Distressed debts which pay minimally a yield higher than 1,000 basis points greater than a comparably maturing Treasury bond were notably affected. Energy company high yielding debt bond prices collapsed by approximately 20 percent in 2015 as a consequence of the problems in the energy sector which resulted from plummeting energy prices.

High Yield Preferred Stocks

Preferred stocks are a special type of stocks that many companies issue. These types of stocks provide investors with a different level of ownership in a given company. A preferred stock holder obtains a higher priority on the earnings and assets of a company than a common stock holder would enjoy. These preferred stocks also pay a higher dividend that has to be given out before any dividends can be paid to the common stock holders.

As such, they represent a hybrid type of security on the stock markets. They are like common stocks in that they are bought and sold as stocks and represent ownership in a company. These stocks can also trade up and down in price like a common stock. Unlike a common stock, they do not come with any rights to vote for a company board of directors or items on a company ballot at the annual meeting.

They are also like bonds in that they pay a higher dividend that must be paid out unless the company lacks the earnings to pay these holders. In this way preferred stocks have elements of bonds with their fixed rate of dividends. Every preferred stock comes with its own unique details that are set when the company issues the stock.

Preferred stocks are often higher yielding issues. They are most commonly issued by companies that are in industries such as financials, real estate investment trusts, utilities, industrials, and conglomerates. Despite this higher yield that makes them like bonds, they can be traded on the major stock exchanges. They are typically found on exchanges including the NASDAQ and the New York Stock Exchange.

As preferred stocks are a type of equity legally, they show up as equity on any company balance sheet. Both common and preferred stock holders are owners in the company. There are several advantages to preferred stocks that investors like about them.

In the past, individual retail investors were less aware of preferred stocks, but this is changing. Part of the reason they have gained in popularity surrounds market volatility. As common stocks have seen wild price swings in recent years, investors have been looking for more stable instruments in which they can invest.

Preferred stocks fit this need as they tend to be more stable in price than do common stocks. With more baby boomers looking for investments that provide higher yields, this has brought preferred stocks into the spotlight. The retirees gain the advantage of better yields and the opportunity for the price to increase in the issues as well.

Preferred stocks are not new. They have existed from the time when modern day investing began. Institutional investors have known about and invested in them for many decades. Many individual investors did not because they lacked the information they required to select and trade them.

In the past, individuals did not have any lists of preferred stocks from which to pick. The information available was difficult to come up with before the Internet made this kind of information much more readily available. Now there are tools smaller individual investors can find that provide calendar searches for ex-dividend dates.

There are also screening filters that allow individuals to narrow down their search for the best high yielding dividend preferred stocks. Preferred stocks represent another way to diversify an investor's portfolio and earn higher yields on dividends at the same time.

Index Funds

Index funds are typically exchange traded funds or mutual funds. Their goal is to reproduce the actual movements of an underlying index for a particular financial market. They do this no matter what is happening in the overall stock markets.

There are several means of tracking such an index. One way of doing this is by purchasing and holding all of the index securities to the same proportion as they are represented in the index. Another way of accomplishing this is by doing a statistical sample of the market and then acquiring securities that are representative of it. A great number of the index funds are based on a computer model that accepts little to no input from people in its decision making of the securities bought and sold. This qualifies as a type of passive management when the index fund is run this way.

These index funds do not have active management. This allows them to benefit from possessing lesser fees and taxes in their accounts that are taxable. The low fees that are charged do come off of the investment returns that are otherwise mostly matching those of the index. Besides this, exactly matching an index is not possible since the sampling and mirroring models of this index will never be one hundred percent right. Such variances between an index performance and that of the fund are referred to as the tracking error, or more conversationally as a jitter.

A wide variety of index funds exist for you to choose from these days. They are offered by a number of different investment managers as well. Among the more typically seen indices are the FTSE 100, the S&P 500, and the Nikkei 225. Other indexes have been created that are so called research indexes for creating asset pricing models. Kenneth French and Eugene Fama created one known as the Three Factor Model. This Fama-French three factor model is actually utilized by Dimensional Fund Advisers to come up with their various index funds. Other, newer indexes have been created that are known as fundamentally based indexes. These find their basis in factors like earnings, dividends, sales, and book values of companies.

The underlying concept for developing index funds comes from the EMH, or efficient market hypothesis. This hypothesis claims that because stock analysts and fund managers are always searching for stocks that will do better than the whole market, this efficient competition among them translates to current information on a company's affairs being swiftly factored into the price of the stock. Because of this, it is generally accepted that knowing which stocks will do better than the over all market in advance is exceedingly hard. Developing a market index then makes sense as the inefficiencies and risks inherent in picking out individual stocks can be simply eliminated through purchasing the index fund itself.

Initial Coin Offering (ICO)

An Initial Coin Offering refers to a non-regulated process in which the funds for new crypto-currency projects become raised. This is also popularly known by its acronym of ICO. These ICOs allow for entrepreneurs to sidestep the heavily regulated process of raising capital through more traditional means involving banks, venture capital, angel investors, or IPOs initial public offerings on stock exchanges.

With any ICO offer campaign, at least some of the crypto-currency will be sold off to those backers of the venture who become involved early. They receive this in compensation for providing traditional currency or alternative currency investment from the likes of Bitcoin. These ICOs are also known as IPCOs, or Initial Public Coin Offerings sometimes.

The process for engaging in an Initial Coin Offering is straightforward and relatively easy to do. The startup outfit begins by producing and releasing a whitepaper-based plan that reveals all of the key details on the venture. These include the needs this operation will meet when it is up and running, what percentage of the new virtual currency project pioneers will keep, what kinds of funding is allowed, the amount of cash required to make the venture a success, and what time duration the campaign will run.

In this campaign, the investors and supports of the new initiative will purchase part of the alternative coins of the new venture with real or virtual money. Such alt coins will be called tokens. They function in much the same way as do shares of stock which corporations sell their investors during an IPO initial public offering.

In cases where the funds raised are not sufficient to carry out the project requirements as set out by the firm in the white paper plan, invested sums will be given back to the investors as the ICO becomes a failure. Yet in those many cases where the funding objective are attained within the set out duration, then the money will be utilized to fund the new enterprise (or to finish it in other cases).

Naturally the upfront investors have their own motivation in purchasing such crypto-coins in the project. This is because they believe that the operation will be a success following launch. This would lead to a potentially massive gain in the value of their tokens.

One highly successful ICO proved to be the platform for the introduction of smart contracts to the world, known as Ethereum. Its coin tokens are called Ether. The Ethereum project came out in 2014. The ICO garnered $18 million worth of Bitcoins for the project's completion. This meant that the Ether tokens cost forty cents apiece. Following the live launch of Ethereum in 2015 and growing success in 2016, Ether roared higher to more than $14. In 2017, it has even topped $400 each at one point. Early investors who held to $400 realized gains of an eye-watering over 1,000 percent in less than five years.

It is true that many ICO events go off successfully. These Initial Coin Offerings are in fact highly disruptive and innovative means of fundraising. Yet they are not a serious rival to traditional stocks by a long shot. Many ICO campaigns have been deemed to be fraud. Without the imperative regulation provided by the SEC Securities Exchange Commission, their volume is likely to remain a tiny fraction of that done in IPOs on traditional exchanges for at least the foreseeable future.

ICOs have suffered from official national opposition which has hindered them as well. The People's Bank of China fully banned all ICOs in September of 2017. They declared them to be financially unstable and disruptive to an orderly economy. Banks were forbidden to provide any services having anything to do with ICOs. At the same time, these new tokens were no longer allowed to be utilized as a currency on Chinese markets. It caused the Bitcoin and Ether enthusiasts to realize that crypto-currency regulation is in the future cards. This temporarily crushed the prices of both main alternative currencies as investors realized what a serious setback it represents.

Initial Public Offering (IPO)

An IPO is the acronym for an Initial Public Offering. Such IPO's represent the first opportunity for most investors to start buying shares of stock in the firm in question. Initial Public Offerings commonly generate a great deal of excitement, not only for the company involved but also for the members of the investing community.

Private companies decide to issue stock and become publicly traded companies for a few different reasons. The main two motivating factors revolve around the need to raise more capital, as well as the desire to permit the original business owners and investors to take profits on their time and investment that they originally put into starting up the company.

It is true that private companies are limited in the amount of capital that they are able to raise, since their ownership turns out to be restricted to certain organizations and individuals. Public companies have the advantages of allowing any investor to take a stake through buying stock shares on exchanges that are publicly traded. It is far easier for them to raise money as public companies.

Initial Public Offerings that go well translate to large amounts of cash for a company. They use this for future expansion and development. Those who began the company or who were initial investors typically make enormous gains at that time in compensation for their time and effort.

Initial Public Offerings take huge amounts of preliminary work. Great amounts of paper work have to be filled in and filed with the regulatory oversight groups. A prospectus has to be created for investors to study and consider. Advertising campaigns for the first shares that will be sold must be developed. On top of these tasks, the company has to continue its normal operations. Because of this, financial firms such as Morgan Stanley or Goldman Sachs are commonly engaged to perform these tasks on the company's behalf. Such a firm is called the IPO underwriting company. With enormous sized IPO's, these tasks could even be divided up between a few different IPO underwriting companies.

Contrary to what many people think, the majority of IPO's typically do not do well initially. Besides this, a percentage of the companies will not make it, meaning that all of the investment in the IPO stock could be lost. Because of this, there is great risk and often lower rewards for sinking money into Initial Public Offerings than in traditional well established companies and stocks. Many investors buy into the enthusiasm and excitement that surrounds Initial Public Offerings. Another explanation for their euphoria may have to do with believing that there is something special in being among the first investors to acquire the next possible Apple, Coca Cola, or IBM. Whatever their reasoning proves to be, investors continue to love Initial Public Offerings and the somewhat long shot opportunities that they represent.

Insider Trading

Insider trading is a generally negative phrase, though it can also refer to a legal activity. The illegal and better known version if it involves a person purchasing or selling a security when they have information that is not publicly available on the stock. The timing involved in such a trade often determines if it is legal or illegal.

If the critical information has not yet been released to the public, then it is not legally allowed. This is because the government determined to level the playing field in investing. Trading securities when investors have special knowledge is not fair to those traders who do not have the ability to access this information.

A person who tips off other individuals is also participating in illegal insider trading. This is the case if the tipster possesses valuable and relevant information that is not available to the public. Fines and jail time can be given to those who pass along illegal insider information. The responsible body for policing this type of illegal trading is the SEC Securities and Exchange Commission. They maintain and enforce rules that protect average investors from the results of illegal insider trading.

Legal insider trading happens all the time. It is not as well known as the illegal version. A legal trade from an insider occurs when company directors buy or sell shares that they fully disclose according to the rules. This occurs every week. The transactions must be electronically turned in to the SEC in a manner that is timely. Not only must they be sent in to the SEC, the company of the person involved must disclose this transaction information on their official website.

Congress passed the Securities Exchange Act of 1934 to address this issue. This first important step pertained to company stock transactions and legal disclosure. Major owners of securities and directors of the company as well had to disclose their positions, any transactions, and any time the ownership changed hands.

Several forms allow corporate insiders to legally disclose their stock affairs. Form 3 permits them to initially file that they have a company stake.

Directors use Form 4 to make a disclosure on company stock transactions two days or less after the sale or purchase. They utilize Form 5 for earlier transactions or for transactions that become deferred until later.

It is not only company or corporate directors who are able to be tried and convicted for insider trading. Stock brokers and their clients can also be accused of this crime. Martha Stewart is a classic example of a brokerage client who the courts found guilty for placing insider trades back in 2003.

Martha Stewart received a tip from her Merrill Lynch stockbroker Peter Bacanovic concerning her shares of ImClone, a bio-pharmaceutical company. She used this information to sell her shares. Her broker had obtained this information that the Chief Executive Officer of ImClone Samuel Waksal liquidated all of his position in the corporation.

Waksal learned that the Food and Drug Administration was not going to approve his company's cancer drug Erbitux. After the two sales occurred, the FDA officially and publicly rejected the ImClone treatment drug. This caused a major selloff in the company stock of 16% in a single trading day. Stewart had saved a stock loss of $45,673 by selling out early.

The problem was that her sale had been based on the tip that CEO Waksal had sold all of his shares. This had not been publicly disclosed. Waksal became convicted and received a seven year jail sentence. Martha Steward was also convicted and forced to serve out five months in jail. She also received a number of months of house arrest and then probation.

Internal Rate of Return (IRR)

The IRR is the acronym for internal rate of return. This IRR proves to be the capital budget rate of return that is utilized in order to determine and compare and contrast various investments' profitability. It is sometimes known as the discounted cash flow rate of return alternatively, or even the ROR, or rate of return. Where banks are concerned, the IRR is also known as the effective interest rate. The word internal is used to specify that such calculation does not involve facts that are part of the external environment, such as inflation or the interest rate.

More precisely, the internal rate of return for any investment proves to be the interest rate level where the negative cash flow, or net present value of costs, from the investment is equal to the positive cash flow, or net present value of benefits, for the investment. In other words, this IRR will yield a discount rate that causes the net current values of both positive and negative cash flows of a specific investment to cancel out at zero.

These Internal Rates of Return are generally utilized to consider projects and investments and their ultimate desirability. Naturally, a project will be more appealing to engage in or purchase if it comes with a greater internal rate of return. Given a number of projects from which to choose, and assuming that all project benefits prove to be the same generally, the project that contains the greatest Internal Rate of Return will be considered the most attractive. It should be selected with the highest priority of being pursued first.

The assumed theory for companies is that they will be interested in eventually pursuing any investment or project that comes with an IRR that is greater than the expense of the money put into the project as capital. The number of projects or investments that can be run at a time are limited in the real world though. A firm may have a restricted capability of overseeing a large number of projects at once, or they may lack the necessary funds to engage in all of them at a time.

The internal rate of return is actually a number expressed as a percent. It details the yield, efficacy, and efficiency of a given investment or project. This should not be confused with the net present value that instead tells the particular investment's actual value.

In general, a given investment or project is deemed to be worthwhile assuming that its internal rate of return proves to be higher than either the expense of the capital involved, or alternatively, than a pre set minimally accepted rate of return. For companies that possess share holders, the minimum IRR is always a factor of the investment capital's cost. This is easily decided by ascertaining the cost of capital, which is risk adjusted, for alternative types of investments. In this way, share holders will approve of a project or investment, so long as its Internal Rate of Return is greater than the cost of the capital to be used and this project or investment creates economic value that is viable for the company in question.

International Monetary Fund (IMF)

The International Monetary Fund represents an international organization with membership of 189 different countries. As such it counts nearly all countries of the world among its almost global membership. This IMF seeks to achieve financial stability, helps to encourage worldwide monetary cooperation, pushes for economic growth that is sustainable and for high unemployment, helps to facilitate international trade, and attempts to lessen poverty throughout the world.

Members of the United Nations created the International Monetary Fund back in 1945 as a result of the idea initially conceived of at the important Bretton Woods UN conference held in New Jersey in the United States in July of 1944. Originally 44 nations attended this conference and looked for ways to rebuild the global economy. They wanted to create a way of fostering economic cooperation. The group collectively hoped to not repeat the mistakes of the 1930s. A currency devaluing race to the bottom had led to the Great Depression in those years.

There were a number of original goals for the IMF. The organization was to encourage stability of exchange rates and monetary cooperation on an international scale. They were to promote and aid in the growth of a balanced international trade. IMF also had to help build up a system for balance of payments that was multilateral in scope. They also were designed to provide emergency resources to member states that suffered from problems with their balance of payments. Safeguards on the resources loaned out would b required.

With the early 1970's dissolution of the fixed exchange rates based on the gold standard set up at the Bretton Woods conference, their role changed some. They were no longer responsible for stable exchange rates and a balance of payments system based on pegged exchange rates. They became more of an organization that helps out member states in emergency economic need.

Today the IMF counts among its largest emergency borrowers Greece, Portugal, Ukraine, and Ireland. It also issues precautionary loans to members who may need to borrow based on particular conditions within their countries. The countries with the largest precautionary loan amounts agreed on include Poland, Mexico, Colombia, and Morocco. Between the two groups, the IMF has committed itself to $163 billion. Of this amount $137 billion has not yet been drawn.

The International Monetary Fund still works to safeguard the global monetary system. They watch over the system of international payments and free floating exchange rates so that nations and their populations can engage in transactions with each other. In 2012, the fund received an expanded mandate in part as a result of the chaos in the Great Recession. This bigger mandate includes all issues pertaining to the financial sectors and all macroeconomic issues that have to do with global stability.

The International Monetary Fund has its headquarters in Washington, D.C. Their governance is by an executive board. The board is made up of 24 directors. Each of these directors represents either a group of nations or a single nation. The IMF maintains a global staff of 2,600 individuals who hail from 147 different countries.

The majority of the IMF's money comes from its quota system. Every member is given a quota that they must contribute. This amount is based on the nation's economic size in the global economy. The member state's maximum contributions are limited to this quota. When countries join, they pay as much as one-quarter of their quota in a widely traded foreign currency like the pound, euro, dollar, or yen or as SDR Special Drawing Rights made up of a basket of these currencies. The other three-quarters they pay from their own currency.

Intraday

Intraday refers to trades that occur during the normal course of the day. These price movements are especially important for traders who practice short term trading. They attempt to earn profits trading repeatedly throughout the one day trading session. Sometimes the term is utilized to refer to securities which engage in normal trading on the stock exchanges throughout the regular hours' session. This would include ETFs exchange traded funds and company stocks.

On the other hand, investors must purchase mutual funds from dealers directly. Their transactions typically occur after the stock market exchanges close for the day. This happens because the mutual funds must calculate their closing NAV Net Asset Value before they can lock in the buying and selling prices for their fund shares each market day.

Intraday also can be employed to explain a new low or high for a given security. It is always illuminating to consider a real example of such concepts. When dealers or analysts refer to a new Intraday low, they signify that the security touched a new low as compared to its other price points throughout the day in a single trading session. There are many cases where such an intraday low or high is the same as the final closing price for the given security.

Short term traders are always interested in these single day price movements. They watch them carefully with computer power-generated real time charts. This helps them to ascertain the right points to trade in and out in an effort to make money on the short term volatility and movements in the underlying issue stock prices. These shorter term time frame traders generally deploy 60, 30, 15, five, and one minute charts as they are trading in a single session and day. They might employ the five and one minute charts for scalping, while they would utilize the 60 and 30 minute charts for holding periods of a longer several hours.

There are a range of advantages and disadvantages to such Intraday trading. The greatest benefit to it lies in the fact that any unforeseen after market news can not impact the prices of the securities themselves. As an example, consider a surprise earnings report or important economic data release. There are also broker downgrades and upgrades which might happen after the market has closed or before it even opens. By only trading stocks on a throughout the day basis, short term and scalping traders avoid these pitfalls which can cause dramatic price swings and shocks. Intraday trading also permits tighter stop loss orders, greater opportunities for learning, and higher leverage limitations.

Disadvantages in such trading are that there is not always enough time for various stock prices to gain sufficiently in profit. Commission costs are also significantly higher as the traders on a short term basis are often in and out of positions repeatedly throughout he day, raising the costs of trading.

Short term traders are not without their effective strategies that help them to realize profits on an intraday basis. Some of them are range trading in which they work off of resistance and support levels in order to decide sell and buy entry and exit points. There are also scalping trades that seek to earn a large number of profits on minute changes in the price of the securities in question. News-based trading seeks to gain advantage on the increased volatility levels surrounding announced news which may make for interesting and exciting trading opportunities on an intraday basis. Finally, there are high frequency trading strategies. These employ expensive and complicated computer algorithms to take advantage of tiny inefficiencies in the single day trading markets.

Junk Bonds

Junk bonds are almost the same as regular bonds with an important difference. They are lower rated for credit worthiness. This is why in order to understand junk bonds, individuals first must comprehend the basics of traditional bonds.

Like traditional bonds, junk bonds are promises from organizations or companies to pay back the holder the amount of money which they borrow. This amount is known as the principal. Terms of such bonds involve several elements. The maturity date is the time when the borrower will repay the bond holder. There will also be an interest rate that the bond holder receives, or a coupon. Junk bonds are unlike those traditional ones because the credit quality of the issuing organization is lower.

Every kind of bond is rated according to its credit quality. Bonds can all be categorized in one of two types. Investment grade bonds possess medium to low risk. Their credit ratings are commonly in the range of from AAA to BBB. The downside to these bonds is that they do not provide much in the way of interest returns. Their advantage is that they have significantly lower chances of the borrower being unable to make interest payments.

Junk bonds on the other hand offer higher interest yields to their bond holders. Issuers do this because they do not have any other way to finance their needs. With a lower credit rating, they can not borrow capital at a more favorable price. The ratings on such junk bonds are often BB or less from Standard & Poor's or Ba or less by Moody's rating agency. Bond ratings such as these can be considered like a report card for the credit rating of the company in question. Riskier firms receive lower ratings while safe blue-chip companies earn higher ratings.

Junk bonds typically pay an average yield that is from 4% to 6% higher than U.S. Treasury yields. These types of bonds are placed into one of two categories. These are fallen angels and rising stars. Fallen angels bonds used to be considered at an investment grade. They were cut to junk bond level as the company that issued them saw its credit quality decline.

Rising stars are the opposites of fallen angels. This means the rating of the bond has risen. As the underlying issuer's credit quality improves, so does the rating of the bond. Rising stars are often still considered to be junk bonds. They are on track to rise to investment quality.

Junk bonds are risky for more reasons than the chances of not receiving one or more interest payments. There is the possibility of not receiving the original principal back. This type of investing also needs a great amount of skills in analyzing data like special credit. Because of these risk factors and specialized skills that are needed, institutional investors massively dominate the market.

A better way for individuals to become involved with junk bonds is through high yield bond funds. Professionals research and manage the holdings of these funds. The risks associated with a single bond defaulting are greatly reduced. They do this by diversifying into a variety of companies and types of bonds. High yield bond funds often require investors to stay invested for minimally a year or two.

When the yield of junk bonds declines below the typical 4% to 6% spread above Treasuries, investors should be careful. The risk does not become less in these cases. It is that the returns no longer justify the dangers in the junk bonds. Investors also should carefully consider the junk bond default rates. These can be tracked for free on Moody's website.

Key Performance Indicator (KPI)

Key Performance Indicators are measurements that aid companies and other organizations in assessing the progress they are making towards their key goals. It is important for any organization to start out by deciding on its mission and determining its goals. Once they have done this effectively, they can decide on the best means of measuring their incremental progress to reaching the goals.

A characteristic of Key Performance Indicators is that they are measurements that are quantifiable. They must also be relevant to the organization's particular benchmarks of success. These will be different for various organizations. A business and a community service organization will not have the same KPIs.

Businesses could have KPIs that relate to their total profits or amount of income that they derive from repeat customers. Customer service departments could use KPIs that measure the number of calls they answer in under a minute. Schools' Key Performance Indicators could center on the percentages of students who graduate. Community service organizations might look at a KPI that revolves around the number of individuals they are able to assist in a given year.

There is no one right or wrong Key Performance Indicator. KPIs only need to be measurable, relevant to the goals of the organization, and a core part of the group's success. As an outfit's goals evolve or are met, the KPI goals may shift as well.

Key Performance Indicators have to be definable and measurable to be useful. It is no good setting a KPI that is subjective or a matter of opinion. Their definitions also should be consistent year in and year out. This is the only way that the targets set for each KPI will be meaningful.

If a company sets a goal to be the best employer, then they might use their company Turnover Rate each year as a Key Performance Indicator. This will work so long as they are using the same turnover rate definition and measurement each year. Reducing turnover by a certain percent annually is an understandable goal that different departments can act on and address.

Another important attribute of these Key Performance Indicators is that they have to be relevant to the organization and its goals. A business whose goal is to become the most profitable company in the sector will need to use KPIs that address profits and relevant finances. They might choose profits before taxes. Schools that are not interested in turning profits would not utilize such KPIs.

For Key Performance Indicators to be helpful they also need to be a core part of an organization's success. KPIs are only practical so long as they relate to the elements that the organization needs to work on so that they can attain the goals. Another important facet of these KPIs is that there should not be too many of them.

The idea is for the members of the organization to be able to focus on the identical Key Performance Indicators. It is possible for the organization as a whole to have three to five KPIs while departments have several others that help to support the overall goals. So long as these goals can be neatly categorized under the company's larger ones, this is acceptable.

Key Performance Indicators make a good tool for performance management. When everyone in the organization is aware of the goals, then they can take appropriate steps to help reach them. KPIs can be posted on company websites, in employee break rooms, and in company conference rooms. All of the activities of the members of the organization should be focused towards meeting or even surpassing those KPI goals.

Loan Discount Rate

The Loan Discount Rate refers to an interest rate which commercial banks and various other financial institutions pay on loans they take from the discount window of their regional branch of the Federal Reserve Bank. It can also pertain to the discounted cash flow or DCF analysis interest rate. This rate would set the current value of all future cash flows.

Where the DCF analysis is concerned, the discount rate considers more than simply the time value of money. It also factors in the insecure future cash flows. The higher a future uncertainty risk may be for the uncertain cash flows, the higher the discount rate will prove to be. There is also a third meaning to the discount rate term. This is the rate which insurance companies and pension plans utilize to discount their liabilities. In general, the first definition above is the primary one for this phrase, and the one we will mostly consider in greater detail throughout this article.

The Federal Reserve is the government institution tasked with setting and administering the primary interest rates which the Federal Reserve banks set. It is not the market that sets these rates. The Fed offers these loans via its discount window as a lender of last resort to its member financial institutions when they are in trouble. This window became extremely popular back in the end of 2007 and 2008 when the national economic and financial situation in the U.S. declined dramatically almost overnight.

The Federal Reserve then engaged in necessary emergency steps in order to deliver significant liquidity to the struggling financial system. That year, the borrowing from the discount window made a new all-time record high of $111 during this crisis peak of the Global Financial Crisis and Great Recession of October in 2008. The Board of Governors of the Federal Reserve System then slashed the loan discount rate to a low of .5 percent not seen since the end of the Second World War on the date of December 16th of 2008.

It is always instructive to consider a real world concrete example of a challenging concept such as this one. If an individual anticipates that he will receive a thousand dollars in a certain year, he may need to ascertain how much the present value of said thousand dollars is right now. To determine this, he would have to choose a given interest rate at which to discount the present value. If the individual employed a ten percent rate, then the money a year from now would be worth $909.09 today. This is $1,000 divided by 110%. If the anticipated receipt date of the thousand dollars was for two years in the future, then the present value of the money would today be $826.45.

Companies often need to figure out an appropriate discount rate to deploy on a given project. A great number of firms utilize the WACC Weighted Average Cost of Capital when the risk profile of the project proves to be similar to the company profile as a whole. In scenarios where the risk profile of the project is significantly different from the company's operations in general, they will instead utilize the CAPH Capital Asset Pricing Model. This delivers a project-specific discount rate which might more appropriately reflect the risk of the given project.

The loan discount rate should never be confused with discount points. These are a kind of prepaid fees in lieu of interest which mortgage borrowers are able to buy at their closing. They reduce the amount of the interest dollars which the borrowers will have to pay out in later re-payments. Such points typically cost a percent of the entire loan amount. Every point reduces the interest on the loan by from an eighth to a quarter of a percentage point.

Loan Modification

A loan modification proves to be a set of changes on the original terms and conditions of a mortgage loan agreement. These must be agreed to by both the borrower and the lender. The housing crisis of 2007 caused many American homeowners to be on the verge of foreclosure. The numbers of imminent and in process foreclosures increased dramatically.

Loan modifications were amended to be a means for home owners to stay out of foreclosure and keep their houses. The process is not simple or quick, and it can be time consuming. Consumers also have to watch out for scams that prey on the vulnerable owners of homes.

Before the financial crisis erupted, a loan modification turned out to be a means for borrowers to ask for better interest rates on their mortgages without having to undergo an entire refinancing ordeal. Every mortgage company did not offer them. The ones that featured these would provide them for a cost to borrowers on the condition that their mortgage had not been resold to another firm. Now they are far more commonplace since lenders needed unorthodox solutions to help homeowners who were struggling to keep up with their payments and avoid foreclosure.

For the process of a loan modification to begin, the borrower must first request such a change to the loan terms. These changes once only affected the interest rate and made them lower. The more recent packages offered since the Great Recession are even able to change adjustable rate mortgages into standard fixed rate types. It is possible that a lender could suggest such a change to its borrowers as a possibility. Usually the borrowers initiate the process by determining they can not keep up with their loan payments and asking for help and a modification.

The next step is for the lender to consider the borrower's request. They are not required to agree to these petitions. A great number of lenders have very strict guidelines on which borrowers they will approve for modifications and which they will not. This is the case even when the homeowner has foreclosure looming. It is partly because such modification programs were not created to save home owners from rising adjustable interest rates or payments they could not handle. They were made to create a cheaper way of refinancing down to better interest rates. Each lender makes its own rules for which modifications they will accept and which they will reject.

Finally the lender will decide whether to approve or reject the modification request. They will then notify the borrower in writing. Many borrowers are rejected because they have been late with their mortgage payments frequently or too recently. Other lenders might not be in possession of the original loan any more. Whatever the reason is, the lender will state this in the letter.

If the request for modification gains approval, the request goes through to the department that handles loan servicing. There the loan will be modified to the new terms and conditions. Usually this will only reduce the interest rate and not change the loan's amortization. It may require several payment periods before these changes take effect. This is why borrowers should always keep making the payments in the amount and time for which they are scheduled.

Loan Servicing

The term loan servicing refers to the procedure of either a mortgage bank or servicing firm gathering up the regular principal and interest payments from the mortgage and loan borrowers. The amount of such service depends on the kind of loan in question and the particular terms that have been arranged between investors looking for such services and the servicing firm.

In the roaring days of the housing expansion, mortgage servicing got to be substantially more profitable than it had been in the past. Loan servicers sought out borrowers who were likely to have trouble making their payments on time. They did this with the hope of bringing in a greater number of lucrative late fees. After the financial collapse and in the Great Recession, this strategy came back to haunt them, as greater and greater numbers of homeowners defaulted on their mortgages and other types of loans.

Loan servicing outfits commonly make their money in the form of a percentage of the remaining balance on any loans that they are servicing. While the actual fees vary, they typically range from twenty five basis points down to a single basis point. This has much to do with the loan's size, amount of service necessary, and whether the loan is backed up by residential properties or commercial properties.

Loan servicers carry a certain value on their balance sheets from these loans. The current net value of the payment flow obtained in servicing the loans minus the anticipated costs for servicing them generates the asset that goes on the balance sheet. Such asset values commonly prove to be highly volatile when refinancing becomes more common. This is because the loans are commonly paid off in advance, leading to an end to the servicing fees that are collected.

A number of companies have traditionally been major players in the loan servicing field. These include Bank of America, JP Morgan Chase, Wells Fargo, and Citigroup as the biggest participants. GMAC is another major servicer. Between them they handle in excess of sixty percent of all American residential mortgage debt.

For special borrower cases that are near default or already behind, another industry of loan servicing has grown up. This is dominated by two companies. Ocwen Financial and Litton Loan Servicing, which Goldman Sachs owns, overshadow the industry. While it is the case that the big servicing companies are capable of handling borrowers who are unable or unwilling to pay, they do it inefficiently. As many as twenty-four different employees of the major loan servicing companies become involved from the first call of a collection agent down to the final foreclosure.

Loan Syndication

Loan Syndication refers to the procedure of getting a few different lenders involved in delivering a few different components of a loan. This activity typically happens in those situations where borrowers need to borrow a huge amount of capital. In these cases, the money required might be more than any one lender will feel comfortable providing or could be higher than certain lenders' levels of allowed risk exposure. This is why many lenders choose to work hand in glove on such projects in order to deliver the financing a borrower requires.

Corporate borrowing typically involves this type of loan syndication such firms look for loans to cover a wide range of needs. It is most often needed as companies are attempting to perform an acquisition, a merger, or a share buyback, or for other kinds of capital intensive projects. With a capital project of this nature, significant loans will be involved. This is why these loan syndications are utilized for these types of projects or merger and acquisition activity.

This kind of Loan Syndication permits any single lender to be involved with more than only a single huge loan. It also allows it to keep a more manageable and sensible level of credit exposure since it is not the one creditor involved with the deal in question. In these types of multi bank underwritten deals, the various lenders' terms will commonly be identical to the borrower, although there are incidents where this is not the case and they instead vary. The various lenders will often require different amounts of collateral. These requirements can vary significantly. It is common however for there to almost always be a single loan agreement which governs the whole of the syndicate group.

With the majority of Loan Syndication, one financial institution plays the role of lead bank. They will then arrange all terms and particulars of the deal itself. This lead financial institution is commonly referred to as the deal's syndicate agent. Such an agent is commonly responsible to handle all particulars of the deal. This means they will arrange the upfront transaction, compliance reports, fees, loan monitoring, reporting, and repayment arrangements in the life of the loan. They do this on behalf of every lender who is a party to the deal.

There can be specialists brought in to help with some aspects of the deal in question. These are typically third parties which are not a part of the loan syndicate. They often handle such important administrative functions as monitoring and report making. With loan syndications, there are many times higher fees to cover the huge reporting requirements as well as to finalize, package up, and handle the loan servicing and processing. This means that fees can run up to 10 percent of the principal of the loan amount.

For the year 2015, the company with the greatest amount of loan funded syndications on its books was Charter Communications. They boasted of $13.8 billion in syndicate amounts thanks to the merger transaction with Time Warner Cable. The lead financial institution on the syndication was Credit Suisse. For the loan market of the United States, the banks which represent the foremost lead institutions with loan syndications prove to be Bank of America Merrill Lynch, Wells Fargo, JPMorgan, and Citi.

There is an umbrella organization which covers the corporate loan market. This is the LSTA Loan Syndications and Trading Association. There goals are to offer resources for those firms interested in participating in loan syndications as well as those companies that require the services of loans in this capacity. It brings together all of the various important players in the market, delivers market research on relevant topics, and even lobbies industry regulators to impact procedures for compliance in Washington, London, and other important loan syndication cities around the world.

Loan to Cost Ratio

Loan to Cost Ratio, or LTC, proves to be a measurement utilized by finance companies in extending loans for commercial real estate projects. It is employed ultimately to make comparisons of the offered financing for a given building project versus the expenses of completing said project. With the LTC ratio, lenders of commercial real estate loans are able to decide on the risks involved in backing a particular construction project via loans. The LTC ratio is similar to the LTV loan to value ratio. They both compare the amount of the construction loan to the value in fair market terms of the project in question.

Lenders work with the Loan to Cost Ratio in order to decide what loan percentage or dollar amount the financier is agreeable to finance. They do this with a basis on the firm costs stated in the construction project budget. After construction completes, these projects then possess a new and often times significantly higher value. Future values can often be double what the construction costs prove to be. This means that on a loan for $200,000 in construction, the future value of the project is likely to be $400,000 once it is fully concluded.

Consider how LTC will look in this example. With $200,000 in construction costs, and an 80% LTC ratio, the lender would be willing to loan out $160,000 on the total project. Using a similar 80% LTV ratio metric instead would significantly change the amount of money the lender is wiling to extend to $400,000 x 80% for $320,000.

Lenders never completely finance 100% of construction costs. This is because they feel that the builders also need to have significant exposure to the project in order to guarantee they will give their all to see them succeed. This is what is meant by the colloquial expression "skin in the game." It prevents a builder from simply getting up and walking away from a project gone bad. It is why the majority of lenders will require a builder to kick in minimally 10% to 20% of the construction costs to secure a financing deal.

Loan to value ratios are not the same as the Loan to Cost Ratio, though they have much in common up to a point. LTV evaluates the loan issued versus the project value once it will be fully completed. Since most banks assume that construction projects will double in value once they are finished, this is why an identical LTV percentage to the LTC ratio will yield twice the loan amount.

Lenders hold firmly to the LTC ratio. It helps them to clearly express the levels of risk in a given financing project for commercial construction. In the end, using a greater Loan to Cost Ratio will entail a significantly riskier project from the lender's perspective. This is why the overwhelming majority of reputable mainstream lenders will not surpass a pre-determined percentage when they consider any given project. They usually limit this amount strictly to a maximum of 80% of the project's LTV or LTC. When lenders are willing to become involved at a higher percentage and ratio, they will most always insist on a substantially greater project and loan interest rate to compensate them for the additional level of risk to which they are consenting.

Lenders will also have to consider other information and circumstances beyond simply Loan to Cost Ratio and Loan to value ratios when extending such financing. They take into consideration the value of the property and its location for where the project will be constructed. They also contemplate how much creditworthiness and experience the commercial builders in the application possess. Finally, they consult both the borrowers' loan payment histories on other loans and their credit record as demonstrated in their company credit report.

Margin Call

Margin Call refers to a demand from a broker that the account holding investor (who is utilizing margin) deposit additional funds or securities in order to restore the margin account to a minimum preset maintenance margin level. This could occur with a stock, futures, or commodities margin account. Such margin calls happen as the account value falls to a ratio which that specific brokerage deems unacceptable. Many brokerage houses use their own unique formulas to determine the amount at which they will issue such a call for more funds or securities.

Investors get into this unpleasant position when one or many of their securities they have purchased (utilizing money they borrowed from the brokerage) drops to a specified value point. That is when the call goes out from the broker for more money to restore the account to an acceptable minimum value. Investors will have two choices. They could comply with the request for additional funds and make an urgent deposit. Otherwise, they could sell off some or all of the positions in the account to reduce the need for minimum margin maintenance or raise the account equity position. The third choice of completely disregarding or ignoring the margin call would result in the broker force-selling positions to reduce this maintenance amount required.

Margin calls would not be necessary at all if investors did not buy securities, futures, or commodities with a combination of their own cash plus money they borrow off of the broker. This is why many experts recommend not utilizing such margin accounts unless an investor is a both seasoned and experienced trader.

Investors have equity in these margin-purchased investments. This amount equals the securities market value less the funds they originally borrowed to complete the purchase in the first place. If and when this equity of the account holder drops to lower than the brokerage-set percentage requirement of maintenance margin, then such a margin call becomes issued. Such maintenance margins do vary somewhat significantly from one broker to the next.

The constant is the Federal minimum maintenance margin requirements.

These are set at a lowest common requirement of 25 percent, regardless of who the responsible broker is. The brokers can choose to utilize a higher margin maintenance level than this amount, but they can not ever reduce their own limit to less than the 25 percent set by the Feds. Brokers can decide to change their maintenance level higher or lower than their present set one with little to no advance warning or notice, so long as they do not drop it below the government-mandated minimum amount. Raising their margin maintenance requirements may also result in creating a margin call.

Looking at a tangible example helps to clarify the concept and make it more understandable. Investors might purchase $50,000 worth of stocks via a combination of $25,000 of their own funds and through borrowing the balance $25,000 off of the brokerage firm. Assume that this particular broker chooses to utilize the government-set minimum of 25 percent maintenance margin. The investor has no choice but to honor this.

When the investors open the trade, at that point the equity positions of the investments prove to be $25,000 (or $50,000 minus the $25,000 borrowed). This makes the investor equity percentage an even 50 percent (using the $25,000 equity divided by the $50,000 original securities market value). This is twice the required minimum 25 percent margin maintenance.

Yet a week later, our investors suffer a drastic decline in the value of their securities, which precipitously drop to $30,000. The investors' equity is now down to a mere $5,000 (or $30,000 minus the $25,000 borrowed). Yet the brokerage (and government regulations which are the same in this scenario) requires that they keep a minimally $7,500 worth of equity for the account to remain margin-eligible (which is 25 percent of the borrowed amount of $30,000).

It means that there is presently a $2,500 deficit ($7,500 requirement minus the $5,000 actual market value). The broker will then issue a margin call for $2,500 in additional cash to be deposited immediately. Should the investors refuse or take their time, then the broker is legally bound and permitted to sell off some of the securities to reach the minimum $7,500 in account equity value.

Margin Trading

Margin trading is the practice of buying investments on margin. This is accomplished through borrowing money from your broker in order to buy stocks. Another way of understanding margin trading is taking out a loan from your broker to buy greater amounts of stock shares.

Margin trading generally requires a margin account. Margin accounts differ from cash accounts that only allow you to trade with the money that your account contains. Brokers have to get a signature from you in order to open up a new margin account. This could be as an extension of your existing account and account opening forms or as a separate and new agreement. Minimum investments of $2,000 are necessary to open such a margin account. Some brokers insist on larger amounts. Whatever the final margin requirement deposit is, it is called the minimum margin.

After the margin account is up and running, you are able to purchase as much as fifty percent of a stock with margin trading money. The money that you use to buy your part of the stock is called initial margin. Margining up to the full fifty percent is entirely optional. You might borrow only fifteen or twenty percent instead.

Margin trading loans can be held for as long a period as you wish, assuming that you continue to meet the margin obligations. A stock maintenance margin has to be maintained while the loan is outstanding too. This maintenance margin is the lowest account balance that can be held by the account in advance of the broker making you deposit additional funds. If you do not meet this minimum or resulting margin call for extra funds, then the broker has the right to sell your stocks in order to reduce your outstanding loan.

Borrowing money from your broker is not done for the sake of charity. Interest has to be paid on the loan. Also, the marginable securities in the account become tied up as collateral. Unless you pay down the loan, interest charges will be applied to the loan balance. These interest amounts can significantly increase the debt level in the account with time. Higher debt levels in your account lead to still higher interest charges. Because of this, buying stocks on margin is typically utilized only for shorter time frame investments. This is true since the greater amount of time that you hold the margin loan in the investment, the higher a return you will require in order to break even on the margin trade. When you maintain such a margin based investment over a long time frame, it becomes difficult to turn a profit after the expenses are cleared.

It is also important to remember that not every stock qualifies for purchase using margin. The rules pertaining to which stocks can be purchased with margin are set by the Federal Reserve Board. In general though, Initial Public Offerings, penny stocks, or over the counter traded stocks are not allowed to be purchased utilizing margin as a result of the daily volatility and trading risks associated with such kinds of stocks. Besides this, each brokerage can restrict whichever other stocks that they wish.

Merger

A Merger refers to a financial transaction which combines two preexisting companies into a single larger resulting firm. A few different kinds of mergers exist today. There are a variety of reasons for why companies engage in such mergers. These mergers and acquisitions often go through with an eye to extending a firm's customer base and product reach, increasing its market share, or moving into new markets and industry segments. In the end, the ultimate motivation is to make shareholders happy by adding shareholder value.

These combinations occur as two firms join forces into a new larger single company. They are nearly identical to takeovers and acquisitions. The main difference lies in the stock shareholders of each firm holding on to an interest in the share of the new corporation. With acquisitions though, a single company buys out all of or a controlling interest in the stock of the target company. This leads to an unbalanced ownership within the newly formed corporation. Practically the whole process of such mergers is generally kept under wraps so that the members of the investing public are completely unaware of it until after they are announced.

Most personnel at both companies are kept in the dark as well. In fact, the lion share of such merger efforts fail. With the majority of them completely secret, it is hard to say with any accuracy the number of possible mergers that become discussed and considered any year in question. The number ought to be extremely high as the quantities of successful ones prove how desirable such mergers are for a great number of corporations.

There are so many different explanations for why two firms wish to combine. Some of these are ideal for shareholders while others are actually not. A profitable company could be combined with a loss-making firm. This would allow the profitable company to employ the losses of the losing target as a tax write off against its own considerable profits. It would simultaneously grow the entire new corporation.

A good reason for these types of combinations is to boost the market share of a given firm. This is especially helpful with bigger corporations which cannot easily grow their market share organically any longer because of their sheer scope and size. When major competitors combine, the new company might be able to overwhelmingly dominate the industry, providing it with a wide range of choices in setting prices and buyer incentives. In these cases, the Sherman Clayton Anti-Trust laws often come into play to stop the merger and prevent the formation of a new monopoly.

There is another popular motivation to combining two existing companies. When they make products which are distinctively different yet still complementary, it presents an opportunity for cost savings. It could be that the acquiring firm wants to obtain the assets of a target firm which is a part of its product supply chain. As an example, there could be significant manufacturers who wish to obtain control over the warehousing chain. This would enable the buyer to save considerable costs on warehousing and to earn profits from the business it buys out at the same time.

A real world tangible example of this type of merger occurred when PayPal merged with eBay a few years ago. eBay became capable of sidestepping the considerable fees it had to pay PayPal previously. The complementary product line was actually a good match also.

It is usually investment bankers who handle the particulars details of and arrangements in a merger. They help with the transfer of ownership of the company itself via stock sales and strategic issuance. This does give incentive to investment banks to encourage mergers between existing clients. It could happen even when a merger would not be in the best interests of the two companies' underlying shareholders.

Money Laundering

Money laundering refers to the methods for taking income from corruption and crime and turning them into legal assets. Many countries and jurisdictions have re-defined the term to focus on financial or business crime, often used to support drug dealing empires or terrorism financing. The phrase can also refer to improperly utilizing the financial system for a variety of reasons. In these cases, it might involve digital currencies, traditional currency, credit cards, and even securities.

In recent years money laundering has become associated with international sanction avoidance and financing of terrorist acts. The pursuit of this focuses on the source of money while that of terrorism financing is worried about the destination of this money.

Throughout history, countries, kingdoms, and rules created regulations designed to seize wealth from their citizens. This eventually caused the formation of tax evasion and offshore banking. Though these are not crimes in all countries, the ones that do penalize and pursue it consider it to be a form of money laundering.

In the early years of the 1900s, wealth began to be seized as a means of stopping crime. This began in earnest during the American Prohibition of the 1930s. Law enforcement agencies and the government became concerned with tracking down and seizing money involved in illegal alcohol sales. Organized crime had obtained an enormous boost because of the major new source of funds illegal alcohol vending provided.

The emphasis for fighting money laundering shifted in the 1980s to drug dealers and empires in the American led war on drugs. Governments and law enforcement became concerned with seizing the financial rewards from drug related crime as they pursued the drug empire founders, managers, and dealers. These laws required individuals to demonstrate that their seized funds were from legitimate sources in order to get them back.

The most recent focus of this illegal activities pursuit centered around terrorism empires that began with the 9/11 attacks in 2001. The Patriot Act in America and comparable legislation passed around the developed world gave a new motivation for such rules which would help fight terrorism and its financing.

The G7 Group of Seven wealthy nations created its Financial Action Task Force on Money Laundering to pressure other governments around the globe. They wanted greater observation and monitoring for financial transactions with information sharing between nations. This resulted in improved monitoring systems for financial transactions and stronger anti-laundering laws from 2002.

These regulations have created a far heavier burden for international banks. Enforcement of perceived money laundering breaches has led to severe investigations and steep fines against major international financial institutions. British banking giant HSBC received a hefty $1.9 billion fine from the U.S. in December of 2012. French bank BNP Paribas reeled from a steep $8.9 billion fine from the U.S. government in July of 2014.

A number of nations have also instituted stricter rules on the amount of currency which is allowed to be physically carried across borders. Governments have set up central transaction reporting systems to make all of the financial institutions report every electronic financial transaction. The American Department of the Treasury established its Office of Terrorism and Financial Intelligence to seek out and exploit weaknesses in the networks of money laundering operations through national and international financial systems.

Money Market Account (MMA)

Money Market Account refers to a type of savings account which commonly includes advantages such as a debit card and check writing privileges. Besides this, it usually has interest rates which are higher than those which normal savings accounts provide. Such money markets generally have a higher minimum account balance than the average savings accounts do. These accounts are sometimes referred to by their acronym of MMA.

For those individuals who are contemplating a safe depository vehicle for bigger sums of cash and who wish to earn some interest while keeping the funds entirely liquid, these money market accounts can be an optimal solution. Among their pros are that the balance funds are available without advance notice, that they earn a relatively higher interest rate, that they provide the capability of writing as many as six checks each month, and that the debit card attached to them can be utilized as many as six times every month.

For any person who is going to place at least a few thousand dollars into a bank account and desires the clear cut safety provided by the FDIC Federal Deposit Insurance Corporation guarantee of funds, these can be a solid choice. Both credit unions and banks offer them as a reliable place to keep customers' emergency day purpose funds. The money is kept segregated from an account holder's daily utilization checking account funds this way. It can grow quicker than money kept in a comparable savings account thanks to the higher interest rate commonly attached to these MMAs. They provide the added convenience of check writing, which allows for easily covering any unexpected or emergency expenses.

Yet these accounts should not be confused with either checking or savings accounts. In fact they have stark differences from either of the two competing types. For starters, MMAs are not at all checking accounts. They may include the debit card maximum use feature or limited check writing privileges. Yet as with a savings account, they are Federal Reserve-regulation limited to maximum of six monthly withdrawals or transfers in a given month. This includes transactions made by check, debit card, or online/in person transfer. For those individuals who will need more than these half a dozen uses, interest bearing checking accounts make more practical sense than do money market accounts.

Besides this MMAs are similarly not strictly savings accounts either because of their debit cards and check writing capabilities. For those people who do not feel the need of having checks or even the debit card convenience with the account, there are sometimes better interest rates on balances available through what are known as high yield online savings accounts.

One of these types is the CD or certificate of deposit. Cd's may require that the owners agree to tie up their funds for as little as from months to as long as for years. MMAs will certainly permit more convenient and immediate time framed withdrawals than this. Yet CDs will pay better rates for those who can afford to lock it down for some time.

Finally, such money market accounts should not be confused with money market funds. The latter are instead investments whose principal value will decline if the market plunges. All MMAs carry the full FDIC backing when they are operated by banks, and by the NCUA National Credit Union Administration when they are held at credit unions. This amount of protection is equal to $250,000 per depositor or account.

For those individuals who decide that money market accounts are well suited for them, the best policy is to pursue those that come without any associated monthly fees and that pay the highest possible interest rates. It is also critical to ensure that they do not require too high a minimum account balance. This is critical to pay attention to since some financial institutions mandate that depositors open the account with and maintain a $10,000 account balance for these MMAs.

Moody's

Moody's is a company that creates credit ratings, analysis, research, and tools which help to make markets easier to understand and more transparent for investors and clients around the world. Moody's Corporation acts as parent company to the two divisions of Moody's Investors Service and Moody's Analytics.

The Investors Service offers research and credit ratings on securities and debt instruments for a large range of companies, cities, municipalities, nations, and supra national organizations. The Analytics division provides customers with cutting edged advisory services, software, and research for economic and credit analysis and managing financial risk. In 2015 the company itself boasted a staff of nearly 11,000 individuals with offices in 36 countries that generated $3.5 billion in revenues.

The company is best known for its famous system for rating securities that they originated over 100 years ago. John Moody created this method for securities ratings back in 1909. The idea behind such ratings is to offer investors an easy to understand grading system that they can use to gauge securities' creditworthiness in the future.

Moody's Investors Services grades credit using ratings symbols. Every symbol was deigned to categorize a group where all of the elements of the credit worthiness are generally similar to one another. The company limits the system to nine different symbols. The ones with lowest credit risk start with A and gradually decrease to C to show the securities with the highest credit risk. These ratings grades are Aaa (highest possible), Aa, A, Baa, Ba, B, Caa, Ca, and C (lowest possible). Besides these the Investor's Service also adds the numbers 1, 2, or 3 to all of the classifications of ratings from Aa through Caa.

Sometimes there are no ratings given out to a company. Other times the company has ratings that have since been withdrawn. This does not mean that the issue has problems with its credit worthiness. It could be that the company placed the issue privately. There may not be enough important information available on the issuing company or their actual issue. Other times the issuing company or its particular issues are part of a group that the company simply does not rate. Finally, applications for ratings may not have been turned in to the Investor's Service or may not have been approved for one reason or another.

Ratings can also be withdrawn. It might be that the Investor's Service can no longer perform adequate analysis to update a rating. The data could be out of date so that proper judgments may not be formulated. When bonds are redeemed or called in, ratings are also withdrawn.

Moody's Investor's Service also changes the ratings it issues on securities, companies, and governments. This is because for the majority of issuers the quality of their credit improves or deteriorates naturally over time. This is why the service is interested in updating the ratings to properly reflect any changes in the strength of the issuing entities and their various obligations.

With individual issues, these ratings changes can happen at any time. When Moody's discerns that there has been a significant change in the quality of credit or that the earlier rating did not accurately reflect the actual quality of the issue, then they may intervene with a new rating. Bonds with lower ratings tend to receive more frequent changes than would bonds that possess superior ratings. Holders of any quality of bonds are encouraged to check the ratings consistently to make sure that their credit rating has not changed.

Moody's also rates sovereign countries, cities, counties, municipalities, and supranational organizations for their debt. Very few countries anymore qualify for the coveted Aaa rating since the financial crisis of 2008 and Great Recession destabilized the finances and debt positions of even some of the most dependable developed country economies in the world.

Mortgage Backed Obligations (MBO)

Mortgage Backed Obligations are also called mortgage backed securities, or MBS. These are real estate-based financial instruments. They represent an ownership stake in a pool of mortgages. They can also be called a financial security or obligation for which mortgages underlie the instrument.

Such a security offers one of three different means for the investor getting paid. It might be that the loan becomes paid back utilizing principal and interest payments that come in on the pool of mortgages which back the instrument. This would make them pass through securities. A second option is that the security issuer could provide payments to the investing party independently of the incoming cash flow off of the borrowers. This would then be a non-pass through security. The third type of security is sometimes referred to as a modified-pass through security. These securities provide the security owners with a guaranteed interest payment each month. This happens whether or not the underlying incoming principal and interest payments prove to be sufficient to cover them or not.

Pass-through securities are not like non-pass through securities in key ways. The pass through ones do not stay on the issuer of the securities' or originators' balance sheets. Non-pass through securities do stay on the relevant balance sheet. With these non pass through variants, the securities are most frequently bonds. These became mortgage backed bonds. Investors in the non-pass through types often receive extra collateral as a letter of credit, guarantees, or more equity capital. This type of credit enhancement is delivered by the insurer of the mortgage backed obligation. The holder of the MBO will be able to count on the security which underlies the instruments in the event that the repayments the pools of mortgages make are not enough to cover the payments (or fail altogether) for the bond holder investors.

These offerings of Mortgage Backed Obligations, Mortgage Backed Bonds, or Mortgage Backed Securities are all ultimately backed up by mortgage pools. Analysts and investors usually call these securitized mortgage offerings. When such types of investments are instead backed up by different kinds of assets and collateral then they have another name. An example of this is the Asset Backed Securities or Asset Backed Bonds.

They are backed up with such collateral as car loans, credit card receivables, or even mobile home loans. Sometimes they are referred to as Asset Backed Commercial Paper when the loans that underlie them are short term loan pools.

With these Mortgage Backed Obligations, they are often grouped together by both risk level and maturity dates. Issuers, investors, and analysts refer to this grouping as tranches, which are the risk profile-organized groups of mortgages. These complicated financial instrument tranches come with various interest rates, mortgage principle balances, dates of maturity, and possibilities of defaulting on their repayments. They are also highly sensitive to any changes in the market interest rates. Other economic scenarios can dramatically impact them as well. This is particularly true of refinance rates, rates of foreclosure, and the home selling rates.

It helps to look at a real world example to understand the complexity of Mortgage Backed Obligations and Collateralized Mortgage Obligations like these. If John buys an MBO or CMO that is comprised of literally thousands of different mortgages, then he has real potential for profit. This comes down to whether or not the various mortgage holders pay back their mortgages. If just a couple of the mortgage-paying homeowners do not pay their mortgages while the rest cover their payments as expected, then John will recover not only his principal but also interest. On the other hand, if hundreds or even thousands of mortgage holders default on their payments and then fall into foreclosure, the MBO will sustain heavy losses and will be unable to pay out the promised returns of interest and even the original principal to John.

Mortgage Backed Securities (MBS)

Mortgage backed securities turn out to be a special kind of asset which have underlying collections of mortgages or individual mortgages that back them. To be qualified as an MBS, the security also has to be qualified as rated in one of two top tier ratings. Credit ratings agencies determine these ratings levels.

These securities generally pay out set payments from time to time which are much like coupon payments. Another requirement of MBS is that the mortgages underlying them have to come from an authorized and regulated bank or financial institution.

Sometimes mortgage backed securities are called by other names. These include mortgage pass through or mortgage related securities. Interested investors buy or sell them via brokers. The investments have fairly steep minimums. These are generally $10,000. There is some variation in minimum amounts depending on which entity issues them.

Issuers are either a GSE Government Sponsored Enterprise, an agency company of the federal government, or an independent financial company. Some people believe that government sponsored enterprise MBS come with less risk. The truth is that default and credit risks are always prevalent. The government has no obligation to bail out the GSEs when they are in danger of default.

Investors who put their money into these mortgage backed securities lend their money to a business or home buyer. Using an MBS, regional banks which are smaller may confidently lend money to their clients without being concerned whether the customers can cover the loan itself. Thanks to the mortgage backed securities, banks are only serving as middlemen between investment markets and actual home buyers.

These MBS securities are a way for shareholders to obtain principal and interest payments out of mortgage pools. The payments themselves can be distinguished as different securities classes. This all depends on how risky the various underlying mortgages are rated within the MBS.

The two most frequent kinds of mortgage backed securities turn out to be collateralized mortgage obligations (CMOs) and pass throughs. Collateralized mortgage obligations are comprised of many different pools of securities. These are referred to as tranches, or pieces. Tranches receive credit ratings. It is these credit ratings which decide what rates the investors will receive. The securities within a senior secured tranche will generally feature lesser interest rates than others which comprise the non secured tranche. This is because there is little actual risk involved with senior secured tranches.

Pass throughs on the other hand are set up like a trust. These trust structures collect and then pass on the mortgage payments to the investors. The maturities with these kinds of pass throughs commonly are 30, 15, or five years. Both fixed rate mortgages and adjustable rate ones can be pooled together to make a pass through MBS.

The pass throughs average life spans may end up being less than the maturity which they state. This all depends on the amount of principal payments which the underlying mortgage holders in the pool make. If they pay larger payments than required on their monthly mortgages, then these pass through mortgages could mature faster.

National Association of Securities Dealers (NASDAQ)

The NASDAQ is the acronym for the National Association of Securities Dealers Automated Quotation Systems, though the organization has dropped the Automated Quotation Systems part of the name as obsolete. This NASDAQ is the country's second largest stock exchange. It represents the principal rival to the NYSE, or New York Stock Exchange, which is the largest stock exchange in the country and only one larger than it.

The NASDAQ is also the largest equity securities trading market in the U.S. that is based on an electronic screen. When market capitalization, or the value of its stock per share multiplied by the number of outstanding shares, is considered, it is the fourth largest trading exchange in the world. The NASDAQ actually records a higher trading volume than does any competing electronic stock exchange on earth with its actively traded 2919 ticker symbols.

NASDAQ became established in 1971 by the NASD, or National Association of Securities Dealers. The system originally represented the successor to the OTC, or Over the Counter traded market. It later developed into an actual stock exchange of sorts. By 2000 and 2001, the NASD sold off the NASDAQ into the NASDAQ OMX Group, who presently own and operate it. Its stock is listed under the symbol of NDAQ since July 2 of 2002. The FINRA, or Financial Industry Regulatory Authority, oversees and regulates the NASDAQ stock market exchange.

The NASDAQ made major contributions to the world of electronic stock exchange trading as the first one of its kind on earth. When it began, it started out as a computer bulletin board system that did not literally put buyers and sellers in touch. Among its great achievements, the NASDAQ proved to be responsible for decreasing the spread, or the bid and the asking prices' difference for stocks. Many dealers disliked the NASDAQ in the early days, as they made enormous profits on these higher spreads.

In subsequent years, the NASDAQ evolved into a typical stock exchange through adding volume reporting and trade reporting to its new automated trading systems. This exchange became the first such stock market in America to advertise to the public. They would highlight companies that traded on the NASDAQ, many of which were technology companies. Their commercials closed out with the motto the stock exchange for the nineties and beyond, that they eventually changed to NASDAQ, the stock market for the next one hundred years.

The NASDAQ is set to become a trans Atlantic stock exchange titan with its purchase of the Norway based OMX stock exchange. This will only enhance its European holdings that presently include eight other stock exchanges throughout Europe. Besides its NASDAQ stock exchange in New York City, the group possesses a one third stake in the Dubai Stock Exchange in the United Arab Emirates. With its double listing arrangement in place with the OMX exchange, the NASDAQ OMX is set to become the major competitor for NYSE Euronext in bringing in new listings.

Net Asset Value

The Net Asset Value refers to a mutual fund and its per share value. It is also known by its acronym NAV. Exchange traded funds, or ETFs, can also be referenced by the NAV. These values which the companies themselves compute for investors only provide a snap shot of the NAV at a particular time and date. In either security type, the fund's per share dollar value arises from the aggregate value of every security within its portfolio minus any liabilities the fund may owe. Finally this is expressed over the total number of outstanding shares in order to arrive at the shares' ultimate NAV.

Where mutual funds are concerned, the Net Asset Value is derived one time every trading day. They utilize the closing market prices for every security within the fund's holdings in order to determine this. Once this is done, the fund is able to settle all sell and buy orders which are outstanding on the shares. These prices will be set by the NAV of the mutual fund in question for the value per the trade date. Investors will always be required to wait to the next day in order to obtain their actual trade-in or trade-out price.

Because mutual funds do pay out nearly all their capital gains and income, such NAV changes are never the optimal gauge for the performance of the given fund. Instead these are better determined by looking at the yearly aggregate return, or total return.

With ETFs, these are actually closed end types of funds. This means that they actually trade more like stocks do. The shares of these Exchange Traded Funds therefore constantly trade at the market value. It might be a literal value which is higher than the NAV. This would be trading at a premium to the Net Asset Value. It could similarly trade under the NAV. This would mean the prices were trading at a discount to the NAV.

With these ETFs, the Net Asset Value becomes computed once at the markets' close so that the fund can correctly report the ETF values. During the day however, these are figured differently than the mutual fund computations. This is because the ETFs will compile the during-the-day NAV in real time at numerous points in every minute of the trading day.

It is helpful to consider an example of how the mutual funds compute their Net Asset Value calculations. The formula is actually very straightforward. It is simply that the NAV is equal to the mutual fund's assets less its liabilities with the difference divided by the total number of shares outstanding. The assets in the case of mutual funds include cash equivalents and cash, accrued income, and receivables. The main portion of their assets commonly are their investments, which will be priced per the end of the day closing values. Liabilities equate to the complete longer-term and shorter-term money owed, along with each accrued expense. Among these expenses will be utilities, salaries of the staff of the fund, and various operational costs for running such a fund.

Consider that the fictitious Diamond Stocks Mutual Fund counted $200 million in investments, figured utilizing the end of day closing prices of all their assets. Besides this, it has $14 million in cash equivalents and cash and another $8 million in receivables in total. The daily accrued income amounts to $150,000. Besides this, Diamond Stocks owes $26 million in its shorter-term liabilities and has $4 million of longer-term liabilities. The daily accrued expenses amount to $20,000. With 10 million outstanding shares, the net asset value would equate to $19.21 in the case of the Diamond Stocks Mutual Fund.

Net Operating Income

Net Operating Income can refer to two different concepts. It may be used in regards to companies and corporations, or to properties and their annual incomes. Where companies are concerned, Net Operating Income, also known by its acronym NOI, is the income after deducting the company's operating expenses. It is figured up in advance of taking off interest and income tax deductions.

When this number proves to be a positive number, it is called net operating income. If the number turns out to be a negative value, then it is referred to as a Net Operating Loss, also known by the acronym of NOL. Many analysts like to look at the Net Operating Income as a realistic picture of how a company is performing. They feel that this number is more difficult for management to manipulate than are other numbers in the income statements of a company.

Pertaining to properties, Net Operating Income equals the annual gross income minus the expenses for operating. In this respect, the gross income is comprised of real income from rentals as well as other incomes like laundry receipts, vending receipts, parking charges, and every type of income that is related to properties. Operating expenses prove to be the expenses that are encountered in the typical maintenance and operating of the property in question. Among these expenses are insurance, maintenance, repairs, utilities, management fees, property taxes, and supplies. Some costs are not deemed to be operating expenses, such as capital expenditures, interest and principal payments, income taxes, depreciation, or amortization of the points on a loan. So, calculating the Net Operating Income on a property involves first taking the various forms of annual gross income and adding them all up. Then the operating expenses should be taken and added up. Finally, the operating expense total is subtracted from the operating income total to achieve the Net Operating Income figure.

In real estate, Net Operating Income is utilized within two critical real estate ratios. The Capitalization Rate, also know as the Cap Rate, is employed to come up with an estimate of the actual value of properties that produce income. For example, maybe a property being considered for purchase possesses a market capitalization value of ten. Coming up with the market cap rate is achieved by considering the financial information from the sales of properties that produce income and are similar in a particular market.

The other important real estate ratio that relies on Net Operating Income is the Debt Coverage Ratio, also know as the DCR. The Net Operating Income proves to be a critical component of this DCR ratio. Investors and lenders alike utilize the debt coverage ratio to determine if a property has the capability of covering both its mortgage payments and operating expenses together. A result of one is deemed to be the break even point. The majority of lenders want at least a 1.1 to 1.3 ratio in order to contemplate making a commercial loan to a given property. The higher this debt coverage ratio works out to be in a banks' opinion, the safer the loan will ultimately be.

Net Profit

Net Profit refers to the remaining sales dollars which are left over after a firm pays for all of its operating costs, interest on debt, preferred stock dividends, and taxes. Common stock dividends are not included in the amounts deducted from the firm's aggregate sales revenue. Sometimes analysts call this type of profit the net income, the bottom line, and/or the net earnings.

A simplistic (but useful) way of thinking about this form of profit is that it is all of the money which remains after all of the expenses of the going concern are paid in full. Calculating the net income is done when aggregate expenses are subtracted from total revenue. Because these net earnings traditionally occur on the final line in an income statement, companies often refer to it as their "bottom line."

It remains true that this Net Profit is still among the most closely watched business indicators in the world of finance. Because of this, it has a substantial part in the computations of financial statement analysis and ratio analysis. Stake holders in the corporations also scrutinize this bottom line carefully since it ultimately proves to be the way they become compensated as shareholders in the firm. When corporations are unable to realize enough profits to pay their shareholders, stock prices plunge. On the other hand, when corporations are growing and in solid financial health, the more available profits become reflected in greater stock prices.

A common mistake that many individuals make is in their understanding of what net profits actually represent. Net profit is never the metric for the total cash earnings a firm realized in a certain period. The reason for this confusing fact is that income statements also showcase a range of expenses that are not cash-based. Some of these are amortization and depreciation. In order to understand the true amount of cash which corporations actually generate, investors and analysts must carefully review the cash flow statement.

In fact any changes to net profit will be constantly and thoroughly reviewed, examined, and discussed. When firms' net profits are negative or even lower than anticipated, there are a host of issues that could be causing it. It might be that the customers' experience is negative. Sales could be decreasing for one or more reasons. Expenses at the company could be out of control or simply poorly managed and monitored. New management teams may not be performing at the anticipated or promised levels.

In the end, the Net Profit will range wildly from one firm to the next and according to which industry they represent. One industry's profits will likely be substantially different from another industry's. It is not a useful comparison to make between one corporation and another since these profits are quantified in dollars (Euros, pounds, Swiss francs, or yen). It is also a fact that no two corporations will be exactly the same size by either revenues or assets.

This is why many analysts prefer to make comparisons between corporations and industries by utilizing what they call profit margin. This is the net profit of a company as a percentage amount of its total sales. Sometimes analysts and investors will also look at the P/E Price to Earnings Ratio alternatively. This widely cherished ratio reveals to considering investors what the price is (in the form of stock price) for every dollar of net profit the corporation actually generates.

Analysts still like the metric of net profit despite these limitations. A survey conducted querying around 200 marketing managers who were senior level revealed that an incredible 91 percent agreed that they believe this measurement to be very useful.

New York Mercantile Exchange (NYMEX)

The New York Mercantile Exchange proves to be the biggest physical commodity exchange for futures buying, selling, and trading in the world. Since they merged, it is comprised of both the NYMEX Division and the COMEX Division. At NYMEX, traders are able to trade platinum, palladium, and energy markets.

COMEX is where they trade FTSE 100 index options as well as silver, gold, and copper futures. NYMEX still keeps a place for the open outcry system where traders shout and make hand gestures to indicate their purchases. This operates only during the day time. After normal business hours, the electronic trading system takes over for the night.

The NYMEX origins go back to an association of Manhattan dairy merchants. In 1872, a group of them came together and formed the Butter and Cheese Exchange of New York. Once eggs joined the various dairy businesses handled on the exchange, they changed the name to Butter, Cheese, and Egg Exchange. By 1882 they had added canned goods, dried fruits, and poultry to the offerings. The name received its final change to reflect the broader product offerings as the New York Mercantile Exchange at this time.

Though COMEX Commodities Exchange and NYMEX used to be separately owned and run exchanges, they merged together to become two divisions of the NYMEX Holdings, Inc. back in 1994. They listed on the New York Stock Exchange on November 17, 2006 trading under the NMX ticker symbol.

In March of 2008, the CME Group of Chicago committed to a conclusive agreement to buy NYMEX holdings for $11.2 billion combination in cash and stock offerings. In August of 2008 the deal finished and NYMEX and COMEX began to function as DCM Designated Contract Markets for the CME Group. They joined sister exchanges the Chicago Board of Trade and Chicago Mercantile Exchange as part of the four DCMs.

In 2006, the New York Mercantile Exchange became almost entirely electronically traded. NYMEX keeps a smaller venue operating for those traders who prefer to engage in the open outcry historic and sentimental form of trading. There they utilize complicated hand signals and shouting while standing on a physical trading floor to buy and sell. The hand signal system is being preserved by a project published on the subject.

NYMEX's headquarters is found in the Battery Park City area of Manhattan in Brookfield Place. They also maintain offices around the world in such cities as Washington D.C., Boston, San Francisco, Atlanta, London, Dubai, and Tokyo. The options and futures traded here on precious metals and energy commodities have developed into important tools for companies that are seeking to mitigate their risk through hedging their own positions. Because these various instruments are traded so easily and liquidly, companies are able to discern future prices and to hedge their future needs. This is why NYMEX has grown to become such a critical part of global activities in hedging and trading environments.

Today the NYMEX manages literally billions of dollars in metals, energy carrier, and other commodities that companies and traders sell and buy every day for delivery in the future. This is handled on either the physical trading floor or the electronic trading system by computers.

These prices on the exchange and its numerous transactions become the basis of pricing for individuals and companies who purchase commodities around the globe. The Commodity Futures Trading Commissions agency of the U.S. government actually regulates the NYMEX floor. Trading on the exchange is performed by independent brokers sent by specific companies.

New York Stock Exchange (NYSE)

The NYSE is the acronym for the world's largest stock exchange, the New York Stock Exchange. With a market capitalization of companies listed on it totaling at $11.92 trillion dollars in August 2010, it also possessed an average day trading value of around $153 billion in 2008. By market capitalization, the NYSE has no rivals for size.

The New York Stock Exchange is owned and operated by the NYSE Euronext company. This outfit came into being in 2007 when the NYSE merged with the completely electronic Euronext stock exchange. Four rooms make up the trading floor of the NYSE that is found at 11 Wall Street. Its main building is found at 18 Broad Street on the corners of Wall Street and Exchange Place. This building became a National Historic Landmark back in 1978, along with its sister 11 Wall Street Building.

Occasionally known as "the Big Board," the New York Stock Exchange allows for sellers and buyers of stocks to exchange shares in all of the companies that are listed for public trading. Its trading hours prove to be 9:30 AM to 4:00 PM on Monday to Friday. Holidays are spelled out in advance by the exchange itself.

The NYSE has always operated as an in person trading floor since its inception in 1792. Today, this works in an auction format that is ongoing. Floor traders here are able to make stock transactions for investors. They simply gather together surrounding the particular company post where there is a specialist broker working as auctioneer in open outcry format to get buyers and sellers together and to oversee the auction itself. This specialist works directly for the company that is an NYSE member and not the exchange itself. These specialists will commit their own money to assist the trades about ten percent of the time. Naturally, they also give out information that serves to bring together sellers and buyers.

In 1995, NYSE began making the automation transition for the auctions. This started with hand held computers that were wireless. Like this, traders were capable of executing and getting orders electronically. This ended a 203 year tradition of paper based trades.

From January 24 of 2007, most every stock on the NYSE is able to be traded on the electronic Hybrid Market. With this ability to send in customer orders for electronic confirmation immediately, orders can also be sent to the floor for auction market trade. More than eighty-two percent of the NYSE order volume came to the floor electronically in only the first three months of that first year.

Only those who own one of 1,366 actual seats on the exchange are permitted to trade shares directly on the exchange. Such seats are sold for enormous sums. The highest price paid for one amounted to $4 million in the tail end of the 1990's. The highest price ever paid adjusted for inflation proved to be $625,000 in 1929, which would amount to more than six million dollars in terms of 2010 dollars. Since the exchange became a public company, the seats have been instead sold in one year licenses.

Nikkei 225

The Nikkei is an abbreviation for Japan's foremost, best known, and most respected stock index of Japanese companies. Its full name is the Nikkei 225 Stock Average. This index is price weighted and made up of the top 225 industry leading companies which investors trade on the Tokyo Stock Exchange. The United States equivalent of this Nikkei is the Dow Jones Industrial Average.

This stock index originally came into existence as the Nikkei Dow Jones Stock Average. Investors knew it by this name during the years 1975 to 1985. Today's Nikkei 225 carries the name of the Japan Economic Newspaper "Nihon Keizai Shimbun" which is generally referred to as Nikkei. This newspaper is the sponsor for the index and its calculation. There has been a calculation of this index going back to September of 1950. There are many well known firms that make up this index. Some of the most recognized are Toyota Motor Corporation, Sony Corporation, and Canon Inc.

The Nikkei 225 proves to be Asia's oldest stock index in existence. The country founded it in its industrialization and reconstruction efforts that followed the end of World War II. Stocks which make it up are not ranked by market capitalization like in the majority of such indices around the world. Instead they are ranked and listed based on their share prices. The denominations of every stock's value are in Japanese yen. Each September the Nikkei's make up undergoes review so that necessary changes can be made effective for October.

The actual Tokyo Stock Exchange began operating in 1878. This exchange received a major boost in the heat of World War II when the Japanese government decided to merge Tokyo's Stock Exchange with five other exchanges to make a single, unified national Japanese Stock Exchange. This pan-Japanese exchange had to be shut down in August of 1945 towards the conclusion of the war. It finally opened again on May 16 in 1949 as part of the new legislation the Securities Exchange Act.

An enormous asset bubble engulfed Japan during the late 1980s. The government bore responsibility for this as they employed both monetary and fiscal stimulus programs to attempt to offset the nation's currency led recession. The yen had risen 50% in the beginning of the decade. From 1985 to 1989, both land and stock prices tripled in value. When the bubble reached its peak, Tokyo's Stock Exchange comprised an astonishing 60 percent of all capitalization for global stock exchanges.

This bubble exploded in 1990. That year alone the Nikkei 225 Index dropped by a third. This economic and stock market stagnation continued for decades so that in the midst of the Great Recession in October 2008, the Nikkei's value had dropped below 7,000. This represented an astonishing plunge of over 80 percent from the high set back in December of 1989. The government worked to re-inflate the index powerfully from June 2012 to June 2015 as it rose 150 percent. The government's economic stimulus programs coupled with efforts of the Bank of Japan assisted in this asset appreciation. Even at these loftier levels, this still proved to be almost 50 percent under the high set in 1989.

Investors who wish to invest in the index may not buy it directly. A few different ETF Exchange Traded Funds track its performance. These include the Japan iShares Nikkei 225 by Blackrock and the Nikkei 225 Exchange Traded Fund by Nomura Asset Management. Investors can trade the index via ETFs in dollars on the New York Stock Exchange by purchasing or selling shares of the Nikkei 225 Index ETF by Maxis.

Offshore Account

Offshore accounts are accounts that you have in a bank that is located in another country. The term originally came from banks and accounts that were found in the Channel Islands, which were literally off shore from Great Britain. Interestingly enough, the majority of offshore banks and offshore accounts are still found on islands to this day.

Individuals and businesses might use offshore accounts for a variety of purposes. The popular conception of offshore accounts is that spies and criminals utilize them as places to store their cash. In fact, most offshore accounts are completely legitimate. People and even businesses have them as places to deposit their money, make investments, or use as trading accounts. When they are used as trading accounts, the person utilizes them to place online trades in stock markets.

Offshore accounts can also be employed to hide assets from governments and taxes, even though this is not the case for most such offshore accounts. A number of offshore banking accounts exist, such as HSBC Offshore Banking in Gibralter, Barclays Offshore Banking in the island of Jersey, and Griffon Bank in the island of Dominica in the Caribbean. These accounts provide all types of services for the banking needs of people and businesses, one of which is Internet banking.

Among the advantages of offshore accounts is privacy. Offshore banking institutions keep offshore account information secret. Such banks are forbidden to declare this information concerning the status of the account or any of its particulars to any individual or entity who is not the account holder. The only exception to this is when offshore banks believe the holder of an offshore account may be using the account for illegal purposes like drug trafficking, support of terrorism, or criminal money laundering.

Another good reason for putting your money into an offshore bank account is because they typically offer better interest on money. It is a well known fact that offshore banks provide better interest rates for their customers. Such rates depend on the location and the offshore bank in question. Reasons for higher interest rates have to do with the lower operating costs in these islands or other locations, as well as the higher interest rates in the prosperous countries where they are based.

Tax advantages prove to be another motivating factor for offshore banking and having offshore accounts. A number of countries will provide tax benefits to investors who are foreigners in order to attract their money. While this is different for every location too, many offshore banks and their hosting countries will not levy taxes on investment returns and interest earned in such offshore accounts.

Offshore Banking

Offshore Banking is a means of banking by keeping your funds in a bank that is outside of the country in which you primarily reside, or literally "offshore." These days it has acquired a negative connotation consistent with money laundering, criminal activities, or tax evasion. Yet none of these mental pictures are accurate any longer. All an offshore bank account truly means is that it is overseas or international. When individuals choose to keep part of their bank deposits internationally, this is a sensible, legitimate, and legal practice.

The old model of the Swiss Offshore Banking account has expanded to numerous other countries. Today places as far flung as Singapore, Hong Kong, Panama, Malta, Liechtenstein, Bermuda, Jersey, the Isle of Man, Gibraltar, and the Cayman Islands all participate in the concept. Some of the highest-rated and most financially stable Offshore Banking centers are Singapore, Hong Kong, and Liechtenstein.

There are a number of good reasons why ordinary people (as well as wealthy clients) opt to move their checking and savings accounts overseas to an Offshore Banking center. For starters, this protects assets from legal or government malfeasance. It is not an exaggeration to claim that any individuals who choose to maintain all of their assets and funds within the exact same country in which they work and live are taking on substantial legal (and hence financial) risk. The United States proves to be by far the most litigious society and nation which has ever arisen in all of world history. It is the shocking truth that any government agency or court can freeze any individual's private bank accounts with only one phone call and with no due process.

A second good reason for using Offshore Banking concerns the fact that the banks in other countries outside of most Western nations are far safer and sounder financially. Many banks in the so-called first world or developed world are in perilous financial condition. This became painfully obvious back in 2008 during the Western-based Financial Crisis and Great Recession. Some of the largest American, British, and European banks failed or went to the brink of bankruptcy. Examples of this are Wachovia Bank, Washington Mutual Bank, Bear Stearns, Lehman Brothers, and

Merrill Lynch.

Many others would have gone under but for desperate and generous government support of the likes of Citibank, Royal Bank of Scotland, and Lloyds TSB. While many of them have recovered somewhat, others like Credit Suisse, UniCredito, and Deutsche Bank remain in dangerous financial condition. In fact in Europe there are even entire banking systems as in Italy, Greece, Spain, Ireland, and Cyprus that had to receive sometimes multiple bailouts in order to survive at all. The jury is still out on the large and too big to fail Italian banking system.

American banks also keep dangerously low levels in their liquidity. This means that they do not have nearly enough cash and cash equivalent assets to pay their depositors back in the event of a customer "run on the bank." Yet in Offshore Banking centers like Malta, Singapore, Hong Kong, and Liechtenstein, the banks are conservative to a fault. They practice extreme caution with their depositing customers' money and keep huge and conservative liquidity and capital ratios. Many of these same jurisdictions are governments with little to no debt and highly solvent and very well-capitalized banking insurance funds.

Finally, Offshore Banking centers often pay significantly higher interest rates for U.S. dollar deposits. While major Western central banks in the United States, Great Britain, Europe, and Japan have absolutely slashed their interest rates to historic low rates or even negative interest rates, others are still paying decent returns overseas. In some of these, investors can receive even in excess of four percent on U.S. dollar-denominated deposits in low to no risk banks and regulatory regimes and jurisdictions.

Offshore Bonds

Offshore Bonds are sometimes called offshore investment bonds. These investment vehicles allow individuals to gain control over what point they pay tax, to whom they will pay such tax, and how much they will ultimately pay in the end. These types of bonds are offered internationally from some of the mega global multinational life insurance firms like Britain's Old Mutual International and Friends Provident International, Genarali Worldwide, RL360, and Zurich International.

Such Offshore Bonds would not ever be domiciled in the United Kingdom or the United States. Rather they would be based in such offshore tax havens as Luxembourg, Guernsey in the Channel Islands, or the Isle of Man. More and more these days, international expatriates choose Dublin, Ireland for a domicile for these investments. This is because of the perception that Ireland offers tax efficiency and effective regulatory protection.

When money like this is not brought back into most countries (beside the United States) where the citizen is from in the form of either capital appreciation or income, then it will not be subject to those jurisdictions' taxes. This is why investors have to consider the tax jurisdiction where they are residents when they cash out their Offshore Bond. It means that selecting the best location and provider of the bond is extremely critical, since this will determine which access and taxation rules apply in the event of a cash out scenario.

A great number of the Offshore Bonds prove to be inexpensive, completely transparent, and tax efficient planning investment vehicles. Investors still have to be careful that they are not abusing this type of tax and investment vehicle. Reality is that whether a bond is offshore or onshore, it truly is an investment masquerading as an insurance contract. This delivers to the investors an array of some helpful tax benefits.

There are a number of good reasons for why investors (and especially those who are not U.S. citizens who can not escape from their own taxing regime the IRS no matter where they live unless they give up their citizenship) utilize such investment vehicles as Offshore Bonds. For starters, an offshore bond will not be considered an income generating asset. Because of this truth, trustees and individuals do not have to fill in any tax returns which require self assessment.

Income which is reinvested in the Offshore Bonds will not produce income tax events. These bonds have advantages over pensions and retirement accounts as well, since investors can assign them to another individual or legal entity at will. Money kept inside of the bond may be switched around and still will not require any Capital Gains Tax payment or even tax reporting situations.

There are similarly income tax-free events with these Offshore Bonds. It is possible to draw out as much as five percent of the premium originally deposited or paid without creating any taxing liability. This can be done over a span of 20 consecutive years. When owners make their five percent withdrawals, this is not an income-generating event, but instead simply a return of original capital to the bond holder. These bonds may also be put inside of a trust and then removed from it without creating an income taxing event.

Without a doubt, these Offshore Bonds have proven to be enormously popular with expatriates living abroad. They provide tremendous possible tax advantages for anyone who will reside outside of their native country (besides for citizens of the U.S.). The reason for this is that investors are able to claim tax relief for those gains which they make when residing offshore. This significant benefit is known as time apportionment relief.

For British residents as an example, they are able to lower the tax which must be paid commiserate with the amount of time they resided outside of the United Kingdom. So if they were bondholding residents of Spain for half the life of holding the bond, then this would lower the amount of taxes they had to pay for any income or gains in Britain by half.

The danger of course is that some commission-based financial advisors will try to take advantage of the investors in this type of program. When they are not correctly established with extreme transparency, the unscrupulous financial advisor may draw out a significant amount of the savings percentage wise. This transfer of wealth is not illegal, as it is merely a case of high fees and commissions. These Offshore Bonds can be dangerously opaque if investors are not careful.

Operating Cash Flow (OCF)

Operating Cash Flow is also known by its abbreviated acronym OCF. It refers to a metric for the quantity of cash which a corporation or company's typical daily business operations produce. As such, it provides a good insight into a firm's ability to generate enough cash flow in order to either grow or at the very least maintain its existing operations. It might also prove that a going concern requires outside financing in order to fund its expansion plans.

Publically traded firms must calculate their Operating Cash Flows through employing an indirect method of calculation. This GAAP Generally Accepted Accounting Principles mandate means that they have to adjust their net income into a cash basis. They do this by making alterations to their accounts that are not cash. This includes accounts receivable, depreciation categories, and inventory changes.

In fact the Operating Cash Flow is a true representation of the cash portion of the firm's net income. This will also take into account other non-cash items thanks to the requirements which the GAAP sets out for net incomes to be done as accrual-based reporting. This means that amortization, compensation which is based upon stock shares, and incurred but as of yet not paid for expenses would be included in the calculations.

Besides this the actual net income has to be adjusted to reflect changes to working capital kinds of accounts in the balance sheet of the corporation. Especially important is the fact that any accounts receivable increases actually equate to booked revenues for which no collections have been completed. Because of this, these increases have to be taken off of the net income figure. This is partially offset at least by any reported accounts payable increases that are due but as of yet not paid, since this remains in the net income number.

Analysts have opined that such Operating Cash Flow represents the most accurate and basic form of outflows and inflows of cash as a company engages in its normal operations of the daily business. Where the health of a firm is concerned, this represents among the most crucial of metrics. Yet it most appropriately and usefully works for those corporations that are not overly complex.

The Operating Cash Flows focus on the both outflows and inflows which a corporation's principal business activities involve. This includes buying and selling inventory, paying employee salaries, and delivering services. It is important to remember that all financing and investing activities will not be included in the Operating Cash Flow. These become reportable separately. A part of these excluded activities would be purchasing equipment and factories, borrowing money, and engaging in share holder dividend payouts. Finding this cash flow number is easy by looking at the corporation's cash flows statement. This statement will break out the numbers into several categories including cash flows from operations, from financing, and from investing.

Operating Cash Flow is a very important number on a company balance sheet. Many financial analysts and investors would rather consider such cash flow measures since they reduce the impacts of confusing and opaque accounting tricks. It also delivers a better, sharper big picture for the business operations' health and reality.

Consider the following examples. When a firm concludes a big sale, this delivers a major increase to its revenues. This is irrelevant though if the firm can not collect on the money owed. It does not represent a real gain for the corporation. At the same time, firms could be producing elevated operating cash flow numbers. Despite this, they might have an abysmally low net income number if they employ an accelerated depreciation calculation or possess many fixed assets.

OTC Bulletin Board (OTCBB)

The OTC Bulletin Board (OTCBB) proves to be a service for electronic trading that the NASD National Association of Securities Dealers maintains and provides to investors and dealers. It delivers live quotes on volume and pricing data to both investors and traders on stocks which trade OTC over the counter.

Every company which is listed on this backwater exchange has to be current in its filings of financial statements with regulatory oversight group the SEC Securities and Exchange Commission or some other applicable regulatory body. Other than this, there are no minimum listing requirements on the OTC Bulletin Board exchange; unlike with sister monster exchanges the NYSE New York Stock Exchange or the NASDAQ.

The OTCBB turns out to be a fairly young stock quoting system. It began in 1990 following the passage of the Penny Stock Reform Act of 1990. This legislation mandated that the SEC had to come up with some form of system for electronic quotes for those firms which were not able to qualify for listing on one of the rival major stock exchanges such as NYSE or NASDAQ. Those securities which trade on the over the counter basis does so between individuals who are utilizing either phones or computers to place trades. Every stock which trades on the OTCBB contains an ".OB" in its suffix.

It is important for potential investors in OTC Bulletin Board stocks to remember that this is not an extension of any major stock exchange. Instead, it is because these stocks are not well known, heavily traded, or largely capitalized that they are trading on the over the counter electronic quoting system basis in the first place.

These stocks are well known for their substantial risk and rampant instability and volatility. This is why the very few of the OTCBB stocks which enjoy great success eventually migrate over to the NASDAQ or even NYSE once they are able to meet the strict listing requirements of the relevant larger exchanges. The bid-ask spreads on OTCBB are commonly much higher since the volume is so much less.

OTC Bulletin Board serves a critically important role and fills a much-needed vacuum with its existence and services. In truth there are many individual tiny companies which will never qualify for the stronger listing requirements so that their issues are allowed to trade on the major national stock exchanges.

The OTCBB gives them another avenue to float stock shares to a national investor audience so that they can obtain significant capital for their expansion needs. As long as investors recall that this is not a true exchange in any practical sense of the word, but merely an electronic quotation system, then investors will go into a potentially severely loss-making investment scenario with their eyes wide open. These securities which trade through the OTC Bulletin Board are actually a bunch of shares that exist in a tangled web of market makers who are trading them using the various quotes the system provides on a secure network computer which is only accessible by pay to play subscribers.

Another form of exchange network trading is via the so-called Pink Sheets. There are some parallels between the two systems. They are not at all related in fact though. Pink Sheets is an individually and privately held company which offers its own proprietary system of quotations. Companies whose securities trade as part of the Pink Sheets are not required to file any financials with the SEC. They also do not have to make any certain minimum docs available to members of the public or investing community at large. This is why some smaller firms prefer the simplicity and anonymity provided by the Pink Sheets operations and service.

Paper Assets

Paper assets have three different meanings depending on whether you are discussing business, investments, or fiat currencies. Where business is concerned, paper assets are assets that you can not easily use or change in to cash. These paper assets possess extremely low liquidity, meaning that they are difficult to sell too. The term in this case literally arises from assets that are valuable on paper, or that have a paper only value.

In investments, paper assets mean something entirely different. They refer to assets that are representations of something. Paper assets in investments literally are pieces of paper that define ownership of an asset. Classic examples of investing paper assets prove to be stocks, currencies, bonds, money market accounts, and similar types of investments. For paper assets to have a tangible value, there must be a working financial system in order to back them up and exchange them. In the cases where a financial system collapses, paper assets commonly sharply decline along with it. The majority of Americans have placed an overwhelming percentage of their money in paper assets, and as the Financial Crisis of 2007-2010 showed, this makes them extremely vulnerable to economic calamities.

Paper assets stand apart in contrast to hard assets. Hard assets contain actual value in the nature of the item itself. There are many forms of hard assets, but among the most popular are gold, silver, diamonds, oil, platinum, land, and other such physical holdings. While financial collapses can cause a set back for the value of hard assets, these types of assets almost always hold up far better than do paper assets.

Many people are shocked by the fact that the U.S. dollar is also a paper asset, as are all Fiat currencies in the world except for the Swiss Franc. These paper currencies are no longer backed up by the long running gold standard. Instead, they only have value because their respective issuing governments, as well as the underlying currency users, say that they do. The Swiss Franc is a lonely exception. The Swiss constitution requires that for every four paper or electronic currency Swiss Francs in existence, there must be one Swiss Franc worth of gold in the Swiss National Bank vaults. Since the Swiss only value their gold holdings at around $250 per ounce, and gold has been trading between $1,300 and $1,400 per ounce for some time now, the Swiss actually have a greater gold backing to their currency than one hundred percent.

Penny Stocks

Penny stocks are those securities that usually trade for comparatively lower prices, off of the big stock exchanges, and with smaller market capitalizations. Many analysts and investors look at these securities as higher in risk and extremely speculative. This is because they feature significant bid and ask spreads, less liquidity, smaller followings, and lesser capitalization and disclosure requirements. Many of these smaller stocks trade on the pink sheets or OTC Bulletin Board in what is known as the "over the counter market."

Penny stocks used to be those which traded for under a dollar, but thanks to the SEC this is no longer the case. The SEC altered the definition so that all stock shares which trade for less than $5 are now considered to be a penny stock. These companies have fewer listing requirements, regulations, and filings which govern them.

It is important to remember that penny stocks best suit investors who can stand more risk. They come with greater amounts of volatility which can lead to steep losses or possibly greater returns. The lower volumes and greater amounts of risk are why the moves in these stocks can be staggering. These companies struggle with fewer resources and less cash, but sometimes achieve breakthroughs that can catapult their share prices higher. It is safer to trade or invest in penny stocks which are listed on the NASDAQ or the AMEX American Stock Exchange because these exchanges more vigorously regulate their constituent companies.

Four factors make these micro cap stocks so much riskier than traditional blue chip stocks. The information which the public has access to is usually lacking. It is harder to make well informed decisions on companies that do not provide sufficient information. Other information that is offered on such micro cap stocks can come from less than reputable sources.

Another feature that makes penny stocks so risky is that they do not have a common set of minimum standards. Neither the pink sheets nor the OTCBB require these companies to live up to minimum requirements to stay listed. They will have to file certain documents in a timely manner with the OTCBB, but not with the pink sheets. These standards traditionally offer a safety cushion that helps to protect investors. They are a benchmark for other smaller companies to achieve.

A third difficulty with these micro cap stocks is they lack history. A great number of such companies could be nearing bankruptcy or recently founded. This means that their track records are either non existent or poor at best. A lack of historical data compounds the difficulty of assessing a company's future and their stock's near and long term possibilities.

A final danger with penny stocks is their lack of liquidity. This creates two problems. An investor may not be able to sell out of the stock at an acceptable price. With low liquidity, there may be no buyer available at any price. Lower liquidity also leads to the possibility for traders to manipulate the prices of the stocks themselves. They can purchase enormous quantities of the issue, promote it themselves, and then sell it at higher prices to other investors who become stuck with it. This is called a pump and dump strategy.

Ponzi Scheme

Ponzi Schemes prove to be frauds surrounding investments that are related to the pay out of returns to investors in the scheme that are covered using contributions from new investors. The individuals who run Ponzi schemes are able to attract newer investors through boasting of tremendous opportunities that will guarantee terrific investment returns, typically with little to no risk.

With a great number of these Ponzi Schemes, the managers of the scheme concentrate their efforts on constantly bringing in new sums of money in order to be capable of giving out the payments that they promised investors from earlier time periods. Besides this, they utilize the new money for their own personal expenses. Rarely does any energy actually go into real investment opportunities and strategies.

Ponzi schemes always fail at some point in time. This eventually happens since there are no real earnings to distribute. Because of this problem, Ponzi schemes need constant money flowing into them from newer investors in order to survive. As attracting newer investors becomes more challenging, or if a great number of currently involved investors request their money back, then the Ponzi Scheme will likely fall apart.

Ponzi Schemes actually earned their name from a famed early con artist Charles Ponzi. He became famous after he tricked literally thousands of well to do New Englanders into pouring their money into his speculation in postage stamps in the 1920's. The allure of his scheme proved to be hard to resist, since bank accounts were paying only five percent annual returns while he offered investors incredible returns of fifty percent in only ninety days. In the early days, Charles Ponzi really did purchase a small quantity of international mail coupons to support his investment scheme. Before long, he decided to employ the money that came in to cash out earlier investors.

The most successful Ponzi Scheme of all time proved to be the one run by Bernie Madoff. Madoff ran an over thirty year, over thirty billion dollar investment scheme that tricked thousands of investors out of their money. Madoff proved to have a different angle on his Ponzi scheme in that he did not offer his investors who were short term amazing returns. Rather than this, he sent out fake account statements that constantly demonstrated moderate but always positive gains, no matter how turbulent the market proved to be.

Bernie Madoff is presently undergoing a one hundred and fifty year sentence in federal prison for his activities. His investment advisory company began back in 1960 and did not come down until the end of 2008. All during the years that his scheme ran, he served as Vice Chairman of the National Association of Securities Dealers, and even as a member of the board of governors and chairman for the NASDAQ stock market.

The Securities Exchange Commission is ultimately responsible for discovering and prosecuting Ponzi Schemes. They typically utilize emergency actions to freeze assets while they break up the schemes. In 2009 as an example, the SEC actually pursued sixty different Ponzi schemes, the highest profile one of which turned out to be Robert Allen Stanford's $8 billion Ponzi scheme.

Private Equity Fund

A Private Equity Fund refers to a fund that is not carried by a public stock exchange and which does not have to be regulated by the SEC Securities Exchange Commission. Private equity itself is made up of the range of investors and funds who choose to invest directly in privately held companies. They might also pursue mergers and acquisitions to cause public companies to be delisted by taking private the companies which were public.

The capital for such private equity comes from retail and institutional investors. Such funding is useful for many types of purposes. It might bolster working capital, make possible research into a new technology, provide for acquisitions of public or other privately held companies, or simply improve a given company's balance sheet.

Such private equity funds derived most of their resources from accredited investors and institutional investors. These deep pocketed entities are able to allocate enormous amounts of money into an investment (that might possibly fail) for longer term time frames. Generally these longer investment holding time frames become necessary for such private equity investments. This is because working with distressed companies or waiting on liquidity events like IPO initial public offerings or selling the private company to a public one needs time.

This private equity fund market has grown rapidly from the 1970s to date. Nowadays, funding pools can be started by private equity firms so that they can take enormous public companies private. A substantial quantity of these private equity operations engage in what analysts call LBO leveraged buyouts. With an LBO, large purchases can be affected in the markets thanks to the pooling of enormous resources. Once the transaction is completed, the private equity firms will do their very best to better the profits, prospects, and all around financial condition of the newly privatized company. Their greatest hope and plan is to resell the company back via an initial public offering or alternatively through selling the company to another larger firm.

It is worth noting that the fee arrangements of these private equity funds are different from one fund to the next. They generally start with a management fee and add a performance-based fee to the costs as well. Some firms will assess an approximately two percent management fee each year based on the value of the assets under management. They usually also get 20 percent of all profits realized when selling any companies.

When investors hand over their money to one of these private equity funds, they are throwing their lot in with an adviser that is actually a private equity firm. These funds are something like a hedge fund or mutual fund in many respects. All three of them are comprised of pooled resources that an advisor combines to utilize for investment purchases for the common good of the fund. There are differences between these types of pooled funds though.

Private equity firms will usually concentrate their efforts on longer term time framed investment possibilities. They will often look for those assets that require significant amounts of time in order to sell investments. This given investment horizon will require many times at least 10 years and sometimes significantly longer than this.

A common strategy of investing with these private equity funds proves to be engaging in minority stake investments in startups or companies which are rapidly expanding in a promising industry. Others focus solely on the previously mentioned leveraged buyouts. In either case, transparency of these funds is an issue that has been growing since 2015. The high incomes for these funds have raised questions about what they are doing with the enormous sums of money they receive.

From 2016, some states began to pursue regulations and bills that provided more clarity on what the inner workings of such private equity firms is really like. The congress has so far resisted these investigations and tried to limit the ability of the SEC Securities and Exchange Commission to access the funds' privately held proprietary information.

Proprietary Trading

Proprietary Trading refers to a type of trading in which the bank or other financial institution invests its own funds for its own benefit. They do this instead of investing the money of and for their clients and gaining a commission fee for trading for their customers. Such trading happens as a firm makes the choice to engage in market profiteering instead of existing on the tiny commissions which they realize for taking and processing others' trades.

Those banks and companies which pursue such proprietary trading feel certain they enjoy some from of competitive advantage. It is this which provides them with the confidence in their own abilities to make outsized returns versus other traditional investors.

Proprietary trading is actually a dangerous and risky type of trading. Rather than safely carrying out the orders of their clients and collecting their fair commissions, the bank traders take on real positions using the capital of the company. In other words, they will enjoy the entire profit or suffer from the brunt of the full loss of such a position. These firms will do this entirely electronically to boost their speed of execution. They will employ the firms' own leverage in order to multiply the size of their positions as well as the hoped for returns or actually realized losses which they incur.

This actually occurs because the company's own trading desk at these huge financial institutions decides they can do it for themselves. These companies are typically investment banks or brokerage firms. They will then utilize their own corporate balance sheet and capital of the company in order to make transactions in the financial or stock markets. Such trades are commonly speculative. The products in which they trade are commonly complicated and dangerous investment vehicles such as derivatives and credit default swaps.

Naturally these financial companies receive benefits from proprietary trading on their own behalf. The biggest one is that they often do enjoy higher profits, at least until a financial crisis hits like with the one in 2007-2009 that nearly overthrew most of the American, British, and continental European banking system financial institutions. With these proprietary trades, the brokerage firm or investment bank gets to keep all of the investment gains which they realize from their investments.

A second benefit which these large financial firms enjoy is that they will be capable of inventorying an impressive array of securities. It allows them to offer their speculative inventory directly to their clients who could not have obtained it any other way. It also helps the institutions to be well-supplied with securities in the event of illiquid or declining markets when it is more difficult to buy such securities on the free markets.

The last benefit pertains to the second one. With such proprietary trading, financial firms can evolve into an important market maker. They gain the ability to offer liquidity for a particular security or even range of securities through dealing in such investments. They can realize profitable spreads and fees when acting in this capacity.

The ugly truth is that this proprietary trading has led to enormous losses for the investment banks in particular. Thanks to the likes of such one time investment banking firms as Merrill Lynch, Bear Stearns, Lehman Brothers, and others engaging in such dangerously over-leveraged proprietary trading schemes before the outbreak of the financial crisis, they nearly brought down the entire financial system.

The Lehman Brothers moment refers to the point where the company failed completely. All other investment banks began to crater at this point. Bear Stearns ceased to be a going concern. Merrill Lynch the one-time largest investment bank and brokerage had to be bought out by Bank of America in order to survive. Both Morgan Stanley and Goldman Sachs, the only remaining two of the big five, were forced to change into traditional banks, backstopped by the FDIC, This helped them to stave off total collapse at the height of the Global Financial Crisis of 2008/2009.

Because of these unmitigated disasters, the Dodd-Frank Legislation and Volcker Rules were passed. These made it increasingly more difficult to engage in such trading for a financial firms' own benefits and with their leveraged balance sheets and company capital.

Return on Assets (ROA)

Return on Assets is also known by its acronym ROA. It is also sometimes called return on investment. This proves to be an indicator of a company's profitability compared to its aggregate asset base. With ROA, investors and analysts can learn about the big picture of the efficiency of an organization's management compared to the deployment of their company assets which produces earnings.

This is figured up relatively easily. To calculate the ROA, simply take the corporation's annual earnings (or income) and divide these by the firm's total assets. The final answer is the percentage amount of ROA. Other investors will do a slight variation on the formula by adding back in the corporate interest costs to the net income. This allows them to employ operating returns before the net cost of debt.

Thanks to Return on Assets, analysts and investors can learn the amount of earnings that the invested capital or assets produced. Such a figure ranges dramatically from one publically traded company to the next. Every industry's ROA varies substantially. For this reason, analysts prefer to compare and contrast the ROA primarily against the company's own prior figures or alternatively versus another company which is both similar and in the same industry.

Company assets are made up of equity and debt together. The two kinds of financing will jointly fund most corporations' various operations and projects. Because of this Return on Assets number, investors are able to discern the efficiency with which the firm converts its investable money into actual net income. Higher ROA numbers are always considered to be superior. They mean that the corporations can bring in larger revenues and earnings on a smaller amount of investment.

Consider a real world example for clarification. If Imperial Legends Strategy Games produces a net income of $2 million on aggregate underlying assets of $6 million, then it has a Return on Assets of 33.3 percent. Another company Joy Beverages may enjoy the same earnings but against a full asset base of $12 million. Joy Beverages would have an ROA of only 16.7 percent in this scenario. This means that ILSG does twice the job of converting its all around investments into profits as does Joy Beverages. This matters because it speaks volumes of the quality of management. There are not too many managers who are able to turn over significant profits utilizing small investments.

The Return on Assets provides observers with a snapshot and analysis of a business that is distinctive from the usual return on equity formula. Consider that certain industries need to pay more careful attention to the ROA figure than other ones do. In banking, some firms managed to avoid the various banking crises of the last few decades. The ones that sidestepped the problems better than others had something in common. It was that they were more conservative based on the ROA they deployed. The more successful banks did not allow their return on assets numbers to become too unnaturally high. They did this by contemplating the underlying fine details in the loan book. Too many loans that yielded too high a return indicated that management was taking excessive risks. Yet in the business of software development firms, these enterprises are not leveraged, so this ROA comparison is less important.

An important difference separates asset turnover from Return on Assets. Asset turnover specifies that companies have sales which amount to a certain amount per asset dollar on the corporate balance sheet. Conversely, the ROA explains to investors the amount of post tax profit that a firm creates for every $1 of assets it has. This is to say that the ROA compares all of the company earnings relating to the entire resource base the company claims, including both long-term debt and the capital from shareholders. This makes the relevant ROA a strict test of shareholder returns. When companies possess no debt, then their two figures of ROA and ROE Return On Equity will be identical.

Return on Equity (ROE)

Return on equity proves to be a useful measurement for investors considering a given company. This is because it takes into account three important elements of a company's management. This includes profitability, financial leverage, and asset management. Looking at the effectiveness of the management team in handling the three factors gives you as an investor a good picture of the kind of return on equity that you can expect from an investment in such a company.

Return on equity is very easy to calculate. You can figure it up by collecting two pieces of information. You will need the company earnings for a year and the value of the average share holder equity for the same year. Getting the earnings' figure is as simple as looking up the firm's Consolidated Statement of Earnings that they filed with the Securities and Exchange Commission. Alternatively, you might look up the earnings of each of the last four quarters and add them up.

Determining share holder equity is easiest by looking at the company's balance sheet. Share holder equity, which proves to be the difference of total liabilities and total assets, will be listed for you there. Share holder equity is a useful accounting construct that reveals the business assets that they have created. This share holder equity is most commonly listed under book value, or the quantity of the share holders' equities for each share. This is also an accounting book value of a corporation that is more than simply its market value.

To come up with the return on equity, you simply divide the full year's earnings by the average equity for that year. This gives you the return on equity. Companies that produce significant amounts of share holder equity turn out to be solid investments, since initial investors are paid off using the money that the business operations generate. Companies that create substantial returns as compared to the share holder equity reward their stake holders generously by building up significant amounts of assets for each dollar that is invested into the firm. Such enterprises commonly prove to be able to fund their own operations internally, which means that they do not have to issue more diluting shares of stock or take on extra debt to continue operating.

The return on equity can also be utilized to determine if a corporation is a cash generating machine or a cash consuming entity. The return on equity will simply show you this when you compare their actual earnings to the share holder equity. You can learn at almost a glance how much money the company's present assets are producing. As an example, with a twenty percent return on equity, every original dollar put into the company is creating twenty cents of real assets. This is also useful in comparing subsequent cash investments in the company, since the return on equity percentage will demonstrate to you if these extra invested dollars match up to the earlier investments for effectiveness and efficiency.

Return on Investment (ROI)

ROI is the acronym for return on investment. This return on investment is among the most often utilized methods of determining the financial results that will arise from business decisions, investments, and actions. ROI analysis is used to compare and contrast both the timing and amount of investment gains directly with the timing and amount of investment costs. Higher returns on investment signify that the results from investments are positive when you compare them against the costs of such investments.

Over the past couple of decades, this return on investment number has evolved into one of the main measurements in the decision making process of what types of assets and equipment to buy. This includes everything from factory equipment, to service vehicles, to computers. ROI is similarly utilized to determine which budget items, programs, and projects should be both approved and allocated funds. These cover every type of activity from recruiting, to training, to marketing. Finally, return on investment is often employed in choosing which financial investments are performing up to expectations, as with venture capital investments and stock investment portfolios.

Return on investment analysis is actually used for ranking investment returns against their costs. This is done by setting up a percentage or ratio number. With the vast majority of return on investment calculation methods, ROI's that are higher than zero signify that the returns on the investment are higher than the associated expenses with it. As a greater number of investments and business decisions compete for funding anymore, hard choices are increasingly made using the comparison of higher returns on investment. Many companies believe that this yields the better business decision in the end.

There is a downside to relying too heavily on the return on investment as the only consideration for making such business and investment decisions. Return on investment does not tell you anything regarding the anticipated costs and returns and if they will actually work out as forecast. Used alone, return on investment also does not explain the potential elements of risk for a given investment. All that it does is demonstrate how the investment or project returns will compare against the costs, assuming that the investment or project delivers the results that are anticipated or expected. This limitation is not unique to return on investment, but similarly plagues other financial measurements. Because this is the case, intelligent investment and business analysis also relies on the likely results of other return on investment eventualities. Other measurements should also be used along side the return on investment to help measure the risks that accompany the project or investment.

Wise decision makers will demand more from return on investment figures than simply a number. They will require effective suggestions from the person making the return on investment analysis. Among these inputs that they will desire are the means of increasing an ROI's gains, or alternatively the means for improving the ROI through decreasing costs.

Risk Arbitrage

Risk arbitrage is also known as statistical arbitrage. It is different from pure arbitrage as it involves risk or speculation. It is also far more accessible to retail traders than real arbitrage. Because of the reasonably high probability that risk arbitrage offers traders, experts generally consider it to be playing the odds. Despite the risk involved, this form of arbitrage has grown to be among the most practiced type by retail traders. Three main types of this arbitrage exist, liquidation, merger and acquisition, and pairs trading arbitrage.

Liquidation arbitrage is a kind that involves determining the liquidation value of a business' assets. If a company possesses a book value of $100 per share and trades at $70 per share, it falls under this type. If the company determines it will liquidate, there would be an opportunity to make $30 per share on the dissolution of the company. When bigger companies practice this they buy companies whose parts are worth more than the whole of the company. They then sell off the various parts or assets to make money.

Merger and acquisition arbitrage remain the most practiced form of the strategy. The goal is to find a company that is undervalued at its current share price. If it is selected by another company as a takeover target, then it presents opportunity. The offer for this target will raise the company share price to near this level. The earlier investors get in on such a prospect, the more they are likely to profit from it.

If the merger does not go on as planned, the share prices will probably drop. Speed is the necessary factor to make this type of arbitrage work. Traders who practice this type usually receive streaming market news and trade on Level II trading. When a merger deal is announced, these traders attempt to buy in before everyone else does.

An example of this type of a deal would be a company trading at $40 which received a takeover bid for $50. The share price will rapidly rise towards $50 but not reach it until the merger actually closes. It might move to $48 per share. Those who get in on it immediately have a chance to make as much as $10 per share, or a 25% return. Others who buy in at $48 only have a $2 per share arbitrage opportunity for 4%. So long as the takeover happens as planned, both parties will make their returns. If it fails in the end for some reason, they will both likely take losses. The amount they lose depends on the price they paid and how far the stock falls back down on the failed acquisition.

Pairs trading arbitrage may be less common than the other two but it is especially useful in sideways trading markets. The idea is that investors find stock pairs which trade at a high correlation. They could be unrelated or related so long as their historical trading chart demonstrates that they trade in near tandem. Usually pairs with the greatest likelihood of success turn out to be larger stocks competing in the same industry.

The goal is to wait until one of these pairs has a price divergence in the 5% to 7% range. The variance also needs to last for some significant amount of time like two or three trading days. Investors then buy the cheaper stock long and sell the more expensive one short.

The last step is to wait for the prices to approach each other again. Once the prices are back in line, this type of arbitrage closes the trade and pockets the percentages they were apart initially. If the investor both bought the one long and sold the other short, then the gains can be twice the percentage the pair was apart.

Russell 2000 Index

The Russell 2000 Index represents a British-based American stock market index which measures the actual price performance of around 2,000 small cap companies located in the United States. It is actually a portion of the far larger capitalized Russell 3000 Index, comprised of the 3,000 largest American stocks. The Russell 2000 still equates to the major benchmark for the United States' based small cap stocks today.

The way these two indices work is that the complete index is the Russell 3000. The lower capitalized 2,000 stocks in this 3000 Index are the ones comprising the Russell 2000 Index itself. FTSE Russell is the subsidiary company of the world renowned London Stock Exchange Group, based in the United Kingdom, which created and maintains the popular benchmarking index.

Without a doubt or real rival, the Russell 2000 Index proves to be the most frequently relied upon benchmark for the various families of mutual funds that present themselves in their prospectuses as small cap funds. Conversely, with large cap stock-based mutual funds, they rely on the S&P 500 index. It means that this Russell 2000 is easily the most frequently and universally referenced measurement for the aggregate performance in the mid cap to small cap company space and their corporate stock prices. Though it is the bottom 2,000 issues in the Russell 3000 Index, the market capitalization weighting of the 2,000 bottom stocks only turns out to be a mere eight percent of the overall market cap within the all around Russell 3000 Index.

The ticker symbol for the Russell 2000 is ^RUT on most platforms and trading systems. Per March 31st of 2017, the market capitalization weighted average for companies in the Russell 2000 remains about $2.3 billion, while the median market cap proves to be approximately $809 million. The biggest company in this popular market index has a market cap amounting to nearly $13.3 billion. The index first traded higher than the 1,000 point mark between May 21st and May 22nd in 2013.

A similar but not serious rival to this small cap behemoth index is the S&P 600, produced by Standard & Poor's. It is far less frequently sourced and cited, as are other competitors maintained by various rival financial providers.

One unique breakdown of the Russell 3000 and Russell 2000 indices is for a special sub index called the Russell 3000 Growth Index. Included in this special index are companies which demonstrate greater than average levels of growth. This is why this growth index is utilized as a best measurement gauge of the American growth segment stocks. In order to be included in the Russell 3000 Growth Index, they must demonstrate higher forecast earnings and greater price to book values.

The company Russell Investments has a precise procedure for determining these various indices component stocks. They screen the biggest 3,000 common stocks in the United States to form the Russell 3000 Index. The biggest 1,000 companies screened are named composite members of the Russell 1000 Index, while the subsequent 2,000 companies become members of the Russell 2000 Index. Russell Investments has strict rules on those issues which can not be included in their indices. They may not be either foreign stocks or ADR American Depository Receipts. They also can not be components of the BB bulletin board stocks or OTC pink sheet stocks.

It is interesting to note that investors who like this Russell 2000 Index have a number of options in both exchange traded funds as well as mutual funds that do their best to replicate its real performance. None of them match it perfectly though. This is because there are trading costs and expenses involved in acquiring the various 2,000 component companies, stock selection market cap imbalances, and changes to the index's constituent companies which are difficult to replicate with precision. Investors can not directly invest in the index itself, or any stock market index for that matter.

S&P 500 Index

The S&P 500 Index refers to a world famous American stock market index. It is comprised of 500 stocks today which analysts and investors view to be the leading indicator for American stocks and equities. They call this the mirror of the large cap world performance. Economists are the ones who select the components of the S&P 500.

The S&P 500 Index itself proves to be weighted based on market value. It is among the three most significant benchmarks of the American stock markets along with the Dow Jones Industrial Average and the NASDAQ Composite. There are also various other lesser known S&P indices which focus on either mid cap firms or small cap companies which boast lower market capitalizations of from $300 million to $2 billion. A wide range of investment products exist that trade on the S&P 500. Among these are both ETF exchange traded funds and index funds in which investors can speculate or invest.

Most investors consider the S&P 500 Index to be the most crucially accurate measurement of the large cap American equities performance. It is true that this index only concentrates on the bigger capitalized portion of the stock markets. Yet it is deemed to be representative of the overall market simply because it covers a substantial part of the entire U.S. stock market value.

It is the S&P Index Committee that picks out the 500 constituents of this index. This committee is comprised of a team made up of economists and analysts who work for Standard & Poor's. The professionals in this group contemplate a number of different characteristics when they decide on the 500 constituent companies that make up the index. Some of the most important considerations are liquidity, market size, and grouping of their industry.

In recent years, the S&P 500 Index has become so widely followed and popular that it has surpassed the DJIA Dow Jones Industrial Average as the preferred benchmark metric of United States' stocks. Part of the reason for its inevitable success is that the S&P 500 includes an impressive and more representative 500 different American firms versus the only 30 companies in the Dow Jones Industrials.

Besides this, another major difference exists between the two popular indices. While the S&P 500 employs a market capitalization methodology that delivers greater weight to bigger companies, DJIA utilizes a different price weighting procedure that provides greater weight to stocks which are more costly by price. Many economists and investors consider the market cap weighting method to be more true to life of the way the market itself functions.

It is difficult for individual investors to personally duplicate the S&P 500 alone. This is because the portfolio would require for them to purchase stocks from fully 500 individual companies in set quantities in order to replicate the methodology for the index. This is why it is so much easier for investors to simply buy into one of the good S&P 500 products. Some of these are the SPDR S&P 500 ETF, the Vanguard S&P 500 ETF, and the iShares S&P 500 Index ETF.

There are other S&P indices in the S&P 500 Index family. The 500 index is also a member of the S&P Global 1200 family. Besides this, there are the popular indices including the S&P Small Cap 600 Index with its smaller capitalization firms, the S&P Mid Cap 400 Index with its mid cap corporations, and the composite of the three S&P 500, 600, and 400 indices--- the S&P Composite 1500 Index.

The original name of the S&P 500 Index was the Composite Index. This arose in 1923 to track a small group of American stocks. Standard & Poor's expanded the index in 1926 to 90 stocks and finally to the present 500 in 1957.

SDR Denominated Bonds

SDR denominated bonds are a fairly recent phenomenon. These are bonds issued in special drawing rights currency units. SDR units are a basket of the world's most important currencies including the U.S. dollar, Euro zone euro, Japanese Yen, British pound sterling, and the Chinese Yuan. The International Monetary Fund's executive board approved a framework to issue such bonds to member nations and central banks back on July 1, 2009.

The principle of these SDR denominated bonds was intended to be allocated in SDRs. The market for such bonds was established initially as the official sector of IMF members. This meant it was to include primarily the member nations, relevant central banks, and another 15 holders of SDRs.

Included in these 15 prescribed holders are four central banks which were regional, eight developmental organizations, and three monetary agencies which were intergovernmental. Others allowed to trade in them were the fiscal agencies of the members. This means that a number of sovereign wealth funds were allowed to participate as there are not always distinguishing lines between national monetary authorities and their sovereign wealth funds. This is the case with Hong Kong and Saudi Arabia.

The IMF issued SDR denominated bonds were to start with three month maturities that could be extended to as long as five years. Interest payments on these instruments were quarterly. China signed an agreement to buy upwards of $50 billion of them, while Russia, India, and Brazil intended to buy as much as $10 billion each.

SDR denominated bonds again gained the international spotlight in August of 2016 when the World Bank's IBRD International Bank for Reconstruction and Development priced the first such bond in the Interbank Bond Market of China. This bond raised 500 million SDR units, which were equal to about $700 million US dollars. These bonds came with a three year maturity date. Their coupon interest payment rate was .49% per year. What made them most notable was that the payments are issued in Chinese Yuan.

This group of bonds is only the first batch. The full size of the issue approved by the World Bank SDR Denominated Issuance Program in August 12, 2016 is for 2 billion SDR's, making them equal to roughly $2.8 billion US dollars.

Even in China, placing so many SDR denominated bonds is a challenge. This is why the joint lead managers for the Interbank Market were several important banks with great depth in China. These included HSBC Bank of China Company Limited, the Commercial Bank of China Limited, China Development Bank Corporation, and China Construction Bank Corporation.

The issue was a great success. The significant interest in them led to a 2.5 times oversubscribing. Orders amounted to roughly 50. Fifty-three percent of them came from bank treasuries, 29 percent from central banks and official institutions, 12 percent from asset managers and securities firms, and six percent from insurance companies. These bonds will mature on September 2, 2019 with all payments coming from the World Bank's IBDR to be made to bond holders in Chinese Yuan.

Securities and Exchange Commission (SEC)

The SEC is the acronym for the Securities and Exchange Commission. This Federal government agency actually governs the buying and selling of stock securities and other types of related investments. The SEC also works to safe guard investors against impropriety and fraud. They encourage the development of the market with the end goal of keeping America in the first place as the world's leading economic giant.

The Securities and Exchange Commission came into existence in 1934. The stock market crash in 1929 prompted a tremendous regulatory response where the national government observed that it had to oversee and monitor investments within the U.S. The SEC is headquartered today in Washington D.C. Its staff is comprised of five commissioners who are appointed, as well as the personnel working in eleven different regional offices throughout the country. They work together to create, amend, and enforce the laws that regulate investments in the country.

The SEC has various critical missions. Among the most significant one is their role in ensuring that the markets are transparent. To do this, they significantly regulate securities trading within the U.S. Companies are required to turn in a variety of legal financial documents during the year so that investors may obtain a true picture of the total financial health of the firm in question.

The documents are kept on file in a database that is available to the public. Anyone who is interested is allowed to inspect them by logging on to the SEC's website and working through their system of electronic documentation. The SEC has great powers that it exercises in enforcing the rules. It is able to mandate company audits if it has suspicions of illegal behavior. Those it finds in violation of its rules may be brought by the SEC to court.

In keeping with the SEC's mandate to help safe guard investors, they monitor the trading of stocks and the individuals responsible for selling them. This means that exchanges, their dealers, and all stock brokers are required to work through the Securities and Exchange Commission. They can be subjected to inspection from time to time to be certain that they are properly taking care of their customers. Consumers have the right to report practices that are unfair to the SEC directly. If you are an investor, you ought to avail yourself of the SEC's wide range of documents on the various publicly traded corporations that they keep in their database on their website.

The SEC additionally governs companies that are interested in undergoing Initial Public Offerings in order to become public companies. Such interested firms have to file a significant quantity of documents with them first. To help them accomplish this, the SEC engages a big staff. Their document database includes regulations and directions for filing such documents. Consultation help is available if companies run into difficulties.

The SEC also promotes education. If you are an investor who wants to learn more about safe investing, then simply go to their website. They have workshops and publications on the site to help all investors. This is in addition to all of the companies' documents kept on file there.

Selling Short

Selling short, or short selling, is a strategy used in trading stocks. In the selling short process, you borrow the shares of the stock in question from your stock broker. You then turn around and sell the stock shares borrowed for a certain price that the market offers. Your hope is that the price of the stock will drop, so that you can buy back the stock shares for a lesser amount. This creates a profit for your transaction. The practice is buying low and selling high done in the reverse order.

If the price of the stock drops, then this process of short selling makes you money. The down side to it is that when the price of the stock instead rises, then you lose money. Detractors of selling short claim that you can subject yourself to an unlimited amount of risk, since stock prices could rise without stopping. This means that you could potentially lose more than the amount of money that you invest if a given stock that you sold short took off and ran away without you closing out the transaction. Profits are limited by the distance of the stock price to zero, since a share's price can never decline below zero.

Such selling short trades are closed out by repurchasing the shares that you sold short earlier. When it is time to close out the transaction by buying back the shares, this is called covering. The other names for this process are buy to cover or simply cover.

There are risks involved in selling short stocks. The biggest risk is that the stock could go up indefinitely. For example, you might sell short ten shares of IBM's stock at $100 per share. This means that you have put a thousand dollars into the trade. If the stock later declined to ninety, then you would realize a gain of one hundred dollars. If instead it rose to $130 before you covered it, then you would lose three hundred dollars. While the lowest that the IBM shares might decline is to zero, potentially making you as much as one thousand dollars in profits, they could also rise to three hundred dollars, losing you two thousand dollars.

Short sellers can also fall victim to a short squeeze. As the stock price that you have shorted rises, some investors who shorted it will choose to limit their losses by buying the stock back. Still other investors may have no choice but to buy back the shares in order to satisfy any margin calls on their declining valued position. All of this buying back to cover creates a bigger increase in the price of the stock. The final outcome is a large move up in the price of the stock that creates significant losses for those who continue to be short the stock.

Share Repurchase

Share Repurchase refers to a company program where the corporation purchases back some of its own shares off of the stock markets or from its own individual investors. There are various reasons why a company would choose to spend its excess profits or cash reserves on such an activity. Generally management believes the price of the stock is unfairly undervalued. This repurchase activity allows them to decrease the total number of shares which are outstanding while making a vote of confidence in the company's prospects.

The company can go about this in one or more of several ways. They might purchase shares directly from the stock market. They could also provide their existing shareholders with the opportunity of selling their shares back to the firm at a set and agreed upon price.

Companies would be interested in decreasing the quantity of shares which are outstanding on the markets as this directly boosts the earnings per share when they retire the shares which they have repurchased. Shares that they buy back they either cancel out or keep as treasury stock. In either case, they are no longer held by investors or traded publically.

This kind of share repurchase does a number of beneficial things for the financial balance sheets of the firms which engage in them. Since it decreases the aggregate assets of the business in question, this means that the firm's return on equity, return on assets, and various other measurements of corporate health all improve. The earnings per share (EPS), cash flow, and total revenues also increase faster with fewer outstanding shares. When the business decides to still pay out the identical sum of cash in dividends to its shareholders each year, and the full number of existing shares decreases, then each shareholder will receive a bigger yearly dividend amount.

When the corporation in question increases both its earnings per share and accompanying all around dividends declaration, then reducing the outstanding numbers of shares will boost the dividend growth rate as well. Stock holders are demanding by nature and will expect their company to continue to pay out consistent and growing dividends year in and year out.

These share repurchase actions reduce the amount of reserve capital which the business must keep on hand to match the par value of outstanding shares so that they could return a greater amount of capital back to shareholders when they decrease the outstanding amounts of shares.

It is easier to visualize this with a tangible real world example. A company may wish to give out 75 percent of the total earnings to the stake holders and still maintain a consistent dividend payout ratio of 50 percent. The other 25 percent of earnings they could distribute by engaging in a share repurchase program via buying back shares as a complement to the dividend.

Companies buy back their shares because they are convinced that their stock price is significantly undervalued. They believe that this is an efficient means of sinking company money into a vehicle which is also putting the money back into the pockets of shareholders. Each share gains a larger percentage ownership of the company as a result of this endeavor, increasing the value and percentage of each stakeholder's position in the corporation. Such a share repurchase program will also convince potentially skeptical investors that the business maintains more than sufficient minimum capital reserves for difficult economic cycles and corporate emergencies.

A possible downside to such share repurchase plans lies in the impression that they can convey to analysts and investors alike. It might give out the possibly erroneous idea that the firm has no better prospects in which to sink its excess funds. This could mean that they recognize no good potential opportunities to grow the business. For those investors seeking both revenue and turnover increases, this is the wrong message to send. It is also true that spending the company rainy day fund to buy back shares will prove to be a terrible idea if there is a dramatic downturn in the economy afterwards.

Share Consolidation

Share Consolidation refers to a reverse split. In this corporate operation, a number of shares of stock become merged together into only one single share. These share consolidations can take place either in the forms of reverse stock splits or as stock share funded buyouts.

With reverse stock splits, the corporation simply decreases the quantity of shares of its own stock available in order to increase the price per share. When a stock buyout takes place, the acquiring corporation creates more shares of its corporate stock with which to buy out the chosen target company. The target firm's shareholders then receive this newly created stock from the acquiring company in lieu of receiving cash payments for the target company shares they own.

There are a number of advantages to Share Consolidation buyouts done through stock funded purchases. The acquiring firm is able to buy the target corporation without having to deploy its own cash reserves or without getting a loan. This does not mean the transaction is free or completely without cost.

In creating the new shares, this diminishes the stock price of the buyer's shares. This can happen as investors decide that the target firm is worth less than the total number of shares which the acquirer is willing to pay. The present shareholders then own a lesser percentage of the firm and its future earnings. This is the case whether or not the value of their shares decreases or instead remains constant. It explains why many companies will instead utilize combination efforts of both cash and stock buyouts in order to successfully pay for an acquisition.

When a target firm becomes a part of the acquiring company, then its own corporate shares do not trade individually on the stock exchange any longer. One hundred percent of the target corporation's shares will be traded in exchange for the shares of the buying corporation as the transaction concludes. At this point, shares of the target firm will be delisted from all market indices they may trade in, as well as from the exchanges on which they were listed themselves. This also changes the aggregate value for the index the target company used to comprise. Managers of indices often choose to substitute in another corporation in place of the target corporation to maintain the same number of companies within the index in question.

The number of outstanding shares following the buyout will vary based on the relative values of the stock issues of both the selling and buying firms. When the shares of the seller prove to be higher priced than those of the acquirer, a greater number of shares will exist following the merger. As corporations merge their own shares in a reverse stock split, fewer remaining shares will exist following the operation or alternatively the combination.

When corporations choose to consolidate their shares utilizing reverse stock splits, this typically gives a warning that the corporation has run into trouble. The firm will quite possibly no longer be able to build up its share value via increasing its sales. This would be why they are trying to boost the share price to make it seem more valuable and expensive for the investors.

Once stock prices decline below the minimum allowed price set by the hosting stock exchange, they will be involuntarily delisted off of the exchange. This is why firms which are nearing bankruptcy may attempt to consolidate the price of their share to keep them over the threshold of this minimum price. For example, the NYSE New York Stock Exchange removes any corporation when the average price for its corporate stock drops under a dollar for any rolling 30 day long period.

Short Sale

Short sales are real estate sales where the money received from the sale is not sufficient to cover the balance that is owed on the property loan. This commonly happens as a result of borrowers being unable to keep up with the mortgage payments for their home loan. In this case, the bank or other lending institution will likely determine that it is in their best interest to take a reasonable loss on the sale of the property instead of pressuring the borrower to make the payments that he or she can not afford.

Both parties come together and agree on the short sale process, since it permits them both to stay out of foreclosure. Foreclosure is a negative outcome for the two parties, as it lowers credit scores of borrowers and costs banks in expensive fees. Borrowers must be careful, since a short sale agreement does not always absolve the borrower from having to cover the additional balance left on the loan. This remaining balance is called the deficiency.

The process of a short sale starts with the two parties concurring on a short sale being the best option to resolve a mortgage that the borrower is unable to keep up with as a result of financial or economic difficulties. The home owner actually sells the house in question for an amount that he or she is able to realize, even though it is less than the remaining loan balance. They give the money to the bank or lender. This is really the most economical answer for the problem in this scenario, since short sales are less costly and quicker than foreclosures that damage both lender and borrower.

Banks commonly employ loss mitigation departments. Their job is to contemplate the short sales that are possible or likely. Most of them work with criteria that they have set up in advance. In the difficult days following the financial crisis of 2007-2010, they have become more flexible and willing to entertain offers from borrowers. The banks will usually decide on how much equity is in the house by ascertaining the likely selling price that they will be able to receive either through a Broker Price Opinion, appraisal, or Broker Opinion of Value.

Even when Notice of Defaults have been sent out to borrowers beginning a foreclosure process, many banks will still consent to short sale requests and offers. They have become more understanding and accepting of short sales in the wake of the financial crisis than they ever were before. This means that for the countless borrowers who own houses on which they owe more than they are worth and who can not sell them, there is a better option open to them than foreclosure.

Too Big To Fail

Too Big To Fail refers to the disturbing but proven concept that some businesses have become so enormous and systemically important that the jurisdictional government has no choice but to save them from failing with whatever means necessary. The governments feel they must deliver material assistance to the firms in order to prevent a catastrophic rogue wave effect from reverberating across the entire economy.

The simple explanation for how a company can be so important to an entire economy is this. When such an enormous firm fails, all of the companies that count on it for parts of their revenue can also be compromised and fail, as well as its debt holders and ancillary services providing companies that work with the failing massive firm. Jobs then become eliminated en masse. For this reason, the expenses involved with a simple bailout or government backed guarantees of the mega corporation are significantly less than the cost of overall widespread economic failures. It explains why governments will often opt for the bailout as the less expensive answer to the moral problem.

Too Big To Fail especially pertains to commercial banks and financial services firms. These financial companies are so critical for the United States' and other Western economies that it would create havoc and spread financial ruin if they declared bankruptcy. Because of this, the American and British governments especially opted in the Global Financial Crisis of 2008-2009 to spare the banks and other financial service firms.

They saved the bank creditors and holders of counter party risk. As an unwished for side effect, they allowed the managers and company board members to keep their enormous salaries and incredible bonuses. Throughout the last years of the 2000's, the United States' Federal Government doled out approximately $700 billion in order to shore up such critical failing corporations as Bear Stearns, AIG, and the major banks which stood on the edge of financial ruin.

It was investors' total evaporation in confidence of the major financial institutions that led to their near-downfall back in the years 2008 and 2009. Especially the investment banks ran into trouble as they had become unbelievably leveraged (to the tune of from forty to one and eighty to one) when suddenly their mortgage loan-based assets and derivatives plunged in value as the subprime mortgage crisis spiraled out of control. Both stake holders and creditors quickly began to have doubts in their financial solvency as their balance sheets crumbled.

The defining moment in the Too Big To Fail crisis erupted when the government did not step in to prevent Lehman Brothers investment bank from failing. This has become widely known as the "Lehman moment." As widespread chaos erupted in the financial markets, regulators suddenly became painfully aware that these largest companies were so intricately connected that it would take enormous financial bailouts in order to stop literally half of the U.S. financial sector from collapsing.

Once the bailouts had intervened to save the major Too Big To Fail investment banks, only two remained standing. Even the survivors Morgan Stanley and Goldman Sachs were both forced to convert to traditional commercial banks so that they could be backstopped by the FDIC. Bear Stearns was effectively wound down, Lehman's skeleton was bought out by Barclays of Great Britain, and once-mighty Merrill Lynch became a subsidiary of Bank of America. The shadow banking industry had all but disappeared overnight.

The government then attempted to address the issues of Too Big To Fail financial firms. The U.S. Congress passed the Dodd-Frank Wall Street Reform and Consumer Protection Act of 2010. The idea was to create restrictions which would make it far more difficult for such conditions to flourish again. They hoped to sidestep having to extend other bailouts in the future.

The Act made the financial institutions create forms of "living wills" so that their plans are in place in order to rapidly liquidate assets if they have to file for bankruptcy. An internationally based consortium of financial regulators came up with a new set of rules in November of 2015 to force the major global banks to raise their capital by $1.2 trillion more in additional debt funding which they are able to convert into equity or write off if they suffer catastrophic losses again.

Trader

Trader describes any person who participates in selling and buying financial assets on any of the global financial markets. These individuals might do this on their own behalf or instead on that of an institution or another individual. Some people have the tendency to confuse the titles trader and investor. The primary difference between the two pertains to the amount of time that each type of individual holds on to the asset in question. Traders generally keep assets for much shorter time frames in an effort to take advantage of rapidly developing trends. Investors on the other hand usually possess a longer time frame horizon for investing.

Such a trader might work on behalf of a financial institution. When this is the case, he or she will trade utilizing the firm's credit and money. The person is then typically a salaried employee who has the opportunity to earn bonuses which are based on performance and returns garnered for the employing firm. Many other traders are self-employed. In these scenarios, they use their own money and credit to trade and also get to keep any and all of the profits personally.

There are definite disadvantages to trading shorter term. Among these are the spread between bids and ask that must be paid each time both in and out of the instrument and also the commission fees. This is how traders are able to run up substantial commission costs, as they often pursue such short term trading strategies in and out of financial instruments in an effort to realize profits. Thanks to the growing quantities of extremely competitive discount brokerage firms (like TD Ameritrade, E*TRADE, and Interactive Brokers), commission fees have become less of a disadvantage. With the advent of the all-electronic trading platforms offered (such as Meta Trader 4), foreign exchange market spreads have tightened considerably.

Still, the tax situation in the United States disadvantages traders and short term speculators on purpose. The Internal Revenue Service in America assesses steeply higher capital gains taxes on what they consider to be short term capital gains. Traders pay taxes on this money as if the gains were ordinary income, while longer term capital gains assess at a flat 20 percent rate.

With the institutions, they often fit out and maintain dedicated trading rooms to provide a work space for their proprietary traders to purchase and sell huge varieties of financial products for their companies. In these interesting scenarios, every trader receives a specified and pre-determined limit for how big their positions can be, how great a loss they are allowed to accrue before the positions will be force closed out, and the maximum amount of maturity time on the given positions. Because these institutional trading firms run all of the associated trading risk, they have the privilege of keeping the majority of any and all of the profits. The traders are engaging in this activity as employees who work for a salary and potential bonuses for a job well done.

The vast majority of individuals instead trading for their own personal accounts do this either from a small office or from the convenience of their own home. They will choose to work with electronic trading platforms (whenever possible) provided through a competitive discount broker in order to keep trading costs as low and reasonable as possible.

The advantage to the discount brokers is that they assess far lower commission fees per transaction. The disadvantage which is the flip side of this coin is that they do not offer financial advice, or they instead provide a bare minimum amount of it. A great number of the discount brokers do provide margin trading accounts to their members. This helps the traders to quickly and effectively borrow money off of the broker (without having to provide advance notice of a trade) in order to engage in a larger purchase. While this boosts the position sizes they can afford, it also multiplies the potential for losses at the same time.

Treasury Bills

Treasury Bills prove to be among the largest category of United States issued Treasuries. They are also called T-Bills for short. Treasury Bills have maturities of a year or less. They never pay investors interest before they mature, making them somewhat like zero coupon bonds. The government instead sells Treasury Bills at a face value discount, which causes there to be a positive yield to maturity. Numerous economists and ratings agency consider Treasury bills to be the lowest risk investments that American and foreign investors can purchase.

T-bills come issued with varying maturity dates. These typical forms of weekly Treasuries can have four week maturity dates, thirteen week maturity dates, twenty-six week maturity dates, and fifty-two week maturity dates. Every week, the government runs single price auctions for its Treasury bills. The quantity of thirteen week and twenty-six week Treasury bills available for purchase at auction are actually announced every Thursday. They are then offered on Monday and issued on the next Thursday.

Four week T-bill quantities get announced Mondays for next day auctions. The bills become issued on Thursday. Fifty-two week bills become announced only on the fourth Thursday, to be auctioned the following Tuesday and issued that Thursday. Associated purchase orders have to be received before 11 AM on Monday auctions at Treasury Direct. Minimum purchases for these T-bills are a reasonable $100, marked down from the former $1,000 minimum. The Treasury redeems T-bills that mature every Thursday. The biggest buyers of T-bills prove to be financial institutions such as banks, and primary dealers in particular. These Treasuries in their individual issue all get one of a kind CUSIP numbers.

Sometimes the Treasury cash balances are lower than usual. At these times, the Treasury often opts to sell CMB's, or cash management bills. They sell these in much the same way as T-bills, at auction with a discount. Their main difference lies in their irregular amounts and shorter terms of fewer than twenty-one days. They also possess different week days for auction, issue, and maturity. As these CMB's mature on the identical week day as typical T-bills, commonly Thursdays, they are termed on cycle.

When they instead reach maturity on another day, they are known as off cycle.

Treasury bills are regularly sold on the secondary market too. Here, they are both quoted and sold via annual discount percentages, known as a basis. The secondary market trades these T-bills heavily.

The Treasury has modernized its means of offering T-bills to investors recently. Treasury Direct is their means of selling T-bills over the Internet, so that funds can be taken out and then deposited straight to the individuals' bank accounts. This permits investors to make better rates of interest on their savings than with simple bank account interest.

Treasury Bonds

Treasury Bonds are also called T-Bonds. These financial instruments prove to be government debt issued by the United States federal government at a fixed rate of interest. Such debt securities come with maturity dates of longer than 10 years. The T-bonds offer interest payments twice per year. Because they are federal debt instruments, their earned income may only be taxed by the federal level authorities of the Internal Revenue Service. Though nothing is really risk free in the investing world, investors generally consider these bonds to be virtually without risk, since they are issued by the United States federal government. Investors perceive them to have a minimal amount of default risk.

Such Treasury Bonds turn out to be among the four kinds of Department of Treasury issued debt. They employ all of these to finance the runaway spending activities of the Federal Government. In these four debt types are the T-bills, Treasury notes, T-bonds, and TIPS Treasury Inflation Protected Securities. Each of these different debt securities is different according to both their coupon payments and their varying maturities.

Despite this, every one of them are the benchmarks for their particular fixed income categories. This is because they are American government backed, almost free of risk, and guaranteed by the revenues and tax base of the United States Treasury. In theory the Treasury can always levy higher taxes to make sure the interest and principles are repaid on these financial instruments. As they are all the lowest returns in their investment category, they are also deemed to be benchmarks for the various fixed income types of investments.

Such Treasury Bonds come standard issued with maturities which vary from 10 years to as long as 30 years. Their denominations start at $1,000 minimums. Each coupon interest payment pays out on a semi-annual basis. The bonds themselves sell via an auction system. The most of them that investors can purchase is $5 million when the bid proves to be non-competitive or as much as a full 35 percent of the entire issues when the bids turn out to be competitive.

It is important to understand what a competitive bid actually is. These types of bids declare that the bidder will accept a certain minimum interest rate bid. These become accepted according to the comparison versus the bond's set rate. With noncompetitive bids, bidders are guaranteed to receive the bonds so long as they will take them at the pre-set interest rate. Once the bonds have been auctioned off, the buyers may sell them off via the secondary market.

Investors call the active market for Treasury bonds re-sales the secondary market. Thanks to this enormous market, T-bonds and T-bills are extremely liquid. It means they can be easily resold on a constant continuous basis. It is this secondary market that causes the T-bonds' prices to gyrate considerably in the markets. This is why both yield rates and current auction rates for the T-bonds determine their prices via the secondary market.

As with all other kinds of standard bonds, these Treasury bonds will experience declining prices as the rates at auction increase. Conversely, the bonds will experience rising prices when the auction rates decrease. The reason for this inverse relationship is that the future cash flows of such bonds becomes discounted according to the higher rate.

T-bonds are also important because they are part of the yield curve for the fixed income markets. As one of the four principal investments which the American federal government offers, they make up this yield curve. The curve is critical because it pictorially displays the range of maturity yields. It is typically sloping upward since lower maturities provide lower rates than do the farther out maturity varieties. There are cases though when the farther out maturities experience peak demand. This causes the yield curve to become inverted. In such a scenario, the farther out maturities will have lower rates than the closer dated maturities.

Trust Fund

A trust fund proves to be a specific kind of legal entity. It contains property or cash which it holds to benefit another group, individual, or organization. Numerous different kinds of trusts exist. They are governed by almost as many provisions that determine how they work. Every trust fund involves three critical parties. These are the grantor, the beneficiary, and the trustee.

A grantor is the individual responsible for creating the trust fund. Grantors can do this with a variety of assets. They might give stocks, bonds, cash, mutual funds, real estate, private businesses, art, or other items of value to the fund. They also determine the terms by which the trustee will manage the fund.

Beneficiaries are the individuals who receive the benefit of the fund. The grantor sets it up on their behalf. The assets the grantor places inside of the trust fund are not the property of the beneficiary. The trustee oversees them so that the financial gain benefits this individual according to the rules laid out by the grantor at the time he or she establishes it.

Trustees are the managers of these funds. They could be an institution like a the trust department of a bank, an individual, or a number of trusted advisors. Their job is to make sure that the fund fulfills its duties spelled out by the governing law in the trust documents. Trustees typically receive small management fees. The trustee could manage the assets directly if the trust specifies this. In other cases, trustees have to pick out investment advisors who are qualified to manage money.

Trust funds come to life under the rules of the state legislature where the trust originates. Different states offer advantages to certain types of trusts. This depends on what the grantor wants to do by establishing the fund. This is why attorneys help to draft the trust documents to make sure they are correct and most advantageous. As an example, there are states which allow perpetual trusts that can continue forever. Other states make these illegal because they do now want to enfranchise a class of future generations who receive substantial wealth for which they did not work.

Special clauses may be inserted into these trusts. Among the most heavily used is the spendthrift provision. This keeps the beneficiary from accessing the fund assets to pay debts. It also allows parents to ensure that any irresponsible children they have do not find themselves destitute or homeless despite poor decisions they may make.

Trust funds provide a large number of benefits. They receive special protection from creditors. They ensure that family members follow wills after the grantor passes away. These trusts also help estates to avoid as many estate taxes as possible so that wealth can reach a greater number of generations.

Trusts can be an ideal way to ensure the continuity of a business. Sometimes business owners wish to protect a company and their employees after they die. They might still wish for the profits to benefit their heirs. In this case, the trustee would oversee the management of the business while the heirs reaped the financial rewards but could not break up or ruin the company through mismanagement.

Trusts can also be used with life insurance to transfer significant amounts of money which will benefit the heirs. A small trust could purchase a grantor life insurance. When the grantor dies, the insurance money funds the trust. The trustee will then buy investments and give the rents, interest, and dividends to the beneficiaries.

Trust Account

A trust account refers to a type of account which a trustee holds on the behalf of the beneficiary. The trustee does not have the ability to utilize the funds in any personal capacity, but merely to safe keep, disburse, and invest them for the advantage of the beneficiary.

An example of this type of arrangement is when an attorney holds funds for the benefit of the client. The attorney will not be able to draw upon the funds until after a certain protocol takes place. As the attorney earns the lawyer fees, the client will have to first review and then actually approve the bill from the attorney before he or she can transfer the client funds from this trust account over to the general account of the attorney for settlement of bills.

There are a number of reasons and situations in which individuals may opt to establish a trust account. In some scenarios, people wish to disperse a pre-determined sum of money to their family or other loved ones over a number of years or throughout the remainder of their natural lives.

As a real world example, consider the following. Parents may wish to establish some trust accounts which will provide money to their dependents and/or children every month if and when they die. In such a scenario, it would normally be banking brokers who would manage such accounts. In fact these broker trustees would draw down the account values by the appropriate amount every month or year as they disbursed the either monthly or yearly funds to the beneficiaries for the individuals who originally formed the trust.

There are other common kinds of trusts as well. One of these is a property tax trust account. Such accounts will be established by entrepreneurs of real estate who own a variety of properties. Rather than have to be concerned about the property tax funds and disbursements to the appropriate taxing authorities themselves, they elect to form a trust account which will pay the taxes. This prevents the entrepreneurs from forfeiting their valuable properties because they forgot to pay the property taxes. There are a number of monetary benefits to having such an account. One of these is that estate taxes will not apply to properties contained in such a trust when the owner dies.

There are two different main types of trust accounts. These are revocable and irrevocable trusts. With revocable trusts, these represent deposit accounts whose owners chose to name one or several beneficiaries. These beneficiaries would then obtain the deposits in the account once the holder of the account died. As the name implies, such revocable trusts may be terminated, revoked, or altered on demand whenever the holder of said account wishes. In this particular case, the owner is the trustor, settlor, or grantor of the revocable trust in question. These types of trusts will be established as either informal or formal. While trustees are powerful and have a broad scope of authority over the assets of the beneficiary, they are not omnipotent, but must be bound by the laws and regulations of the jurisdiction which pertain to trust accounts.

Irrevocable trusts on the other hand are similarly deposit accounts but they are not titled in the name of the owner. Instead these become titled as an irrevocable trust for the name. The owner, trustor, settlor, or grantor also makes deposits of money or other valuable assets to the trust account. The principal difference is that the owners forfeit all ability to alter or cancel the trust once they have established it. These types of trusts also become created once an owner of a revocable type of trust dies. They can be set up through a judicial order as well, or even by a statute as appropriate.

U.S. Treasury Bonds

U.S. Treasury bonds are bonds that the United States government issues so that it is capable of paying for Federal government projects. When a person or business purchases a Treasury bond, they are actually loaning the Federal government money. Like with all loans, the principal is paid back along with a set rate of interest.

Treasury bonds carry the full faith and credit guarantee of the United States government. This translates to them having very low risk, as the government is always able to print extra money to repay the loan. Another benefit to U.S. Treasury bonds lies in their being tax exempt from local and state taxes. You would still have to pay Federal taxes on all money that you make in interest.

The primary market is where the government markets its Treasury bonds through auctions. You might also buy them on the secondary market using a broker. While the government does not charge fees for partaking in their auctions, brokers likely will expect to receive fees for selling you a U.S. Treasury bond. The Treasury bonds are marketable securities since you are able to sell or buy them once you have obtained them initially. They are considered to be extremely liquid too, since the secondary market for them is very active. The prices for Treasury bonds both at auction and via the secondary market are set by their interest rates. Today's Treasury bonds can not be called back by the government before maturity, which means that you continue to receive interest until they mature.

Treasury bonds are not without their downsides. Should interest rates rise while you have a Treasury bond, then your money will be making lower interest than it might in another investment. If the interest rates were to increase, then the bond's resale price would also go down. Inflation that goes up also cuts into the Treasury bonds' interest that they pay. With practically no risk of the U.S. government defaulting on these bonds, Treasury bonds pay a low return on investment, so higher inflation rates will wipe out all or most of the interest profits as they lower the real worth of the principal and interest repayments.

If you are interested in becoming involved in government auctions to buy the Treasury bonds straight from the Federal Reserve Bank, then you can do so. Simply open a Treasury Direct Account. The government does not charge fees for such an account until it has in excess of $100,000. For these larger accounts, they collect tiny maintenance fees.

Besides Treasury bonds, the government also sells two other kinds of securities. These are Treasury bills and Treasury notes. Treasury bonds are distinguished from these other two types by their length of time till maturity. Treasury bonds do not mature until from twenty years to thirty years elapse. They do make coupon payments of principal and interest in every six month period, like with Treasury notes. Thirty years maturities prove to be more common than do the twenty year maturities with these Treasury bonds.

Value Investing

Value investing is the strategy that Benjamin Graham developed for investing in stocks. Warren Buffet later made it famous after he left Graham's company and went on to found Berkshire Hathaway. Buying stocks this way involved a level of discipline practiced by insurance underwriters. The method focuses on several key ideas. Investors have to consider risks involved carefully, avoid stocks which show a high amount of uncertainty, and allow a margin of safety.

Graham developed his different investing techniques while managing money as President of his Graham-Newman Corporation. He focused on net working capital investments, arbitrage, diversification, and tangible assets. Investors continue to use all of these but the first one over seventy years later.

Net working capital originally functioned as a cornerstone of value investing until changes in transparency rules and market technology made it obsolete. Net working capital investments were those where the stock's shares traded at a large 30% or higher discount to their amount of working capital.

The idea was that a value investor could buy dollar investments for effectively 70 cents or less. Some of these companies failed. This was mitigated by diversifying into many different stocks. On a combined basis, these companies brought Graham and his investors good returns. Warren Buffet utilized this category of investments heavily in his early years running the Buffet Partnership that eventually became Berkshire Hathaway.

Arbitrage proved to be the value investors' secret weapon. Graham passionately believed arbitrage would routinely provide 20% annual returns. This boosted the total return on the overall value investing portfolio. Arbitrage seeks to make money on discrepancies in price with little or even no risk.

If a company makes an offer for a rival at $60 per share, but the shares trade at $57, there is a $3 price discrepancy between that point and when the deal closes. This amounts to possibly 5% that investors can acquire in a matter of a few months. Assuming the deal closes, there is no risk in this trade. Value investors simply use arbitrage as a way to profit from a security and the money time value that is literally undervalued.

Diversification remains a critical component of Graham's investing strategy. He believed in diversifying into as many individual investments as made sense. He also practiced diversification into different kinds of asset classes. Value investing puts a certain percentage into common stocks, preferred stocks, mutual funds (which did not yet exist when Graham created the strategy), and bonds. This went along with the main premise that first investors must avoid losing their money. Receiving a good return on investment money is secondary to this idea.

Tangible assets is another value investing principle that still holds today. Graham was interested in the actual physical assets that lay behind his common or preferred stocks and bonds. This might include factories, office buildings, equipment, real estate, or rail cars. He would only buy into companies whose assets were great enough to fully back up the principle and dividend or interest payments. They would have to liquidate these assets to get back their investment money. Graham told those who valued invested to constantly look at the bonds they held and be prepared to change to other bonds if they had stronger assets.

Benjamin Graham and value investing also proved to be among the earliest groups to practice tactical asset allocation. If investors studied and determined stocks were overvalued, they should sell stocks and move money into bonds. When stocks were undervalued, he counseled investors to sell bonds and go heavier into stocks. This is still a cornerstone idea of investing today.

Venture Capital

Venture capital refers to the process of investors purchasing a portion of a start up company. Firms or individuals that engage in this are called venture capitalists. They pour money into a firm that offers a high rate of growth but that also contains high risk. The typical venture capital investment time frame generally proves to be from five years up to seven years. Such investors anticipate getting a profit back on their investment through one of two ways. Either they hope to sell their stake in an Initial Public Offering to the public, or they hope to sell the company outright.

Investors who involve themselves in venture capital investments often wish to obtain a certain percentage of the company's ownership. They might also request being given one of the director's seats. This makes it easier for the investors to ask to be given their funds back either through insisting that the company be sold or reworking the deal that they made in the first place.

Venture capitalist investments are comprised of three different kinds. One of them is early stage financing that might be broken down into seed financing, first stage financing, or start up financing. Seed financing means that a tiny dollar amount of venture capital is paid to an inventor or other entrepreneur who wants to open a business. This might be employed to come up with a business plan, do market research, or bring on a good management team.

First stage financing is the type needed as companies look to boost their capital so that they can begin full scale operations. Start up financing instead is venture capital distributed to a business that exists for under a year. In this stage, a product will not be on the market already, or will only just have been put on the market for sale.

A second type of venture capital investments is known as expansion financing. Expansion financing is comprised of both bridge financing as well as second and third stage financing. Bridge financing refers to investments that only receive interest and are short term. They are mostly employed for company restructurings. They might also be utilized to cash out early investors.

Second stage financing proves to be investment money for the purpose of growing a company already up and running. While such a company may not yet demonstrate actual profits, it is producing and selling merchandise. It also possesses inventories and accounts that are expanding.

Third stage financing is investments that venture capitalists make in companies that have at least broken even on costs or are even starting to demonstrate profits. In this case, venture capital is employed to grow the business further. For example, third stage financing could be utilized to develop more or better products, or to purchase needed real estate.

Still a different popular version of venture capital investing is known as acquisition financing. In this type of venture capital, the investment goes into gaining a stake in or the entire ownership of a different company. Management could also choose to use this venture capital to buy out yet another business or product line, whatever its development stage proves to be. They might acquire either a public or a private company in this way.

Wall Street Journal

The *Wall Street Journal* refers to the United States-based and -focused business publication in English. This daily newspaper with an impressive history stretching back well over a century has been based in New York City, the American publishing hub. Fully six days each week, the *Journal* is published alongside its European and Asian editions. Dow Jones & Company the division of News Corp, publishes the newspaper according to a broadsheet format and also online.

According to circulation the Wall Street Journal represents the closest thing to a national newspaper, boasting the biggest circulation in the United States. The Alliance for Audited Media claims that while USA Today enjoys 1.7 million daily subscribers, the *Journal* counts approximately 2.4 million daily customers, when its 900,000 online subscriptions are counted (as of March 2013).

The newspaper is also among the most award-winning daily publications in the United States. To date in 2017, they have garnered an impressive 40 Pulitzer Prizes. The daily gets its name from its base of operations in the heart of Lower Manhattan's national Financial District. The Journal can claim to have been published without interruption every day since it began appearing on July 8th of 1889 when Charles Dow, Edward Jones, and Charles Bergstresser began publishing the venerable newspaper. Nowadays, the publication has also expanded into a lifestyle and luxury news format under the name of WSJ.

Interestingly enough, the *Wall Street Journal* did not represent the very first products which Dow Jones & Company published. Originally they started with brief news bulletins. They called these flimsies. Their personnel delivered them all through the trading day to stock exchange participants back in the early years of the 1880s. Next, they began compiling these together in a daily printed summary they called the Customers' *Afternoon Letter*. They finally converted this to the Wall Street Journal full scale edition when Charles Dow, Edward Jones, and Charles Bergstresser changed the format on the 8th of July in 1889. At this time they also started their celebrated Dow Jones News Service over the telegraph, hence the name Dow Jones Newswire.

They next utilized the base of the nationally known newspaper to launch the Dow Jones Industrial Average indicator in 1896. This represented the original of a number of different stock- and bond-based compilations on the New York Stock Exchange. The publication's original column was the "Review & Outlook" column. More than a hundred and twenty years later, it is still a regular feature of the daily newspaper. Legendary reporter Charles Dow originally penned it for the publication.

By 1902, the journalist Clarence Barron bought controlling interest in the firm for a then hefty sum of $130,000. At the time, the newspaper's considerable circulation tallied to 7,000 per day. Yet by the end of the roaring 1920s, it had exponentially grown to 50,000. Barron and his associates created an environment for independent and fearless financial reporting. This was a truly novel approach in the first days of financial journalism. Barron's went on to found his premier financial weekly with the same name in 1921. Barron himself passed away in 1928 and did not live to see the terrifying events of Black Tuesday and the ensuing Great Depression. The Bancroft Family was the descendants of Barron. They maintained the company as a successful family enterprise for nearly a century until 2007.

It was in the 1940s that the Wall Street Journal attained its current national prominence and layout during this era of booming industrial expansion within the U.S. The managing editor of the financial publication became Bernard Kilgore in 1941. He attained the role of CEO for the firm in 1945. By the end of his legendary leadership career, he had capped an inspiring twenty-five year tenure as leader of the *Journal.*

In this time, he became the chief architect of the iconic design for the front page, the "What's News" digest, and the publication's well-known national distribution policy that exponentially boosted the circulation of the newspaper from a more humble 33,000 in 1941 to an incredible 1.1 million by the time he died in 1967. The paper also claimed its very first Pulitzer Prize under his leadership in 1947 for the editorials that William Henry Grimes wrote.

Wall Street

Wall Street is a physical street that is seven blocks long and runs from Broadway to the New York East River. It lies to the south of the Manhattan borough of New York City. The street is incredibly significant because it has played host to a number of the most important financial entities in the United States.

The city originally got its name because of an earthen built wall that Dutch Settlers of the city erected in 1653 to ward off an anticipated invasion of the English. The street's importance grew so rapidly that before the Civil War in America this was already known as the nation's sole financial capital. In the district of Wall Street there are many important buildings and headquarters.

The street contains the Federal Reserve Bank, the New York Stock Exchange, the International Commodity, Cocoa, Sugar, Coffee, and Cotton Exchanges, and the NYSE Amex Equities. There are also numerous municipal and government bond dealers, investment banks, trust companies, and insurance and utilities' headquarters located here. A great number of the major American brokerage firms have their headquarters in this financial district.

Because of Wall Street, New York City is sometimes called the most important financial center in the world as well as the greatest and most powerful city economically. Investors find the two biggest stock exchanges in the world as measured by market capitalization here in the NASDAQ and the New York Stock Exchange. A few other significant exchanges also make or made their headquarters here. These are the New York Board of Trade, The New York Mercantile Exchange, and the one time American Stock Exchange.

In the 2000's there were seven major Wall Street firms here. These included Lehman Brothers, Merrill Lunch, Morgan Stanley, Goldman Sachs, Citigroup Inc, JP Morgan Chase, and Bear Stearns. Several of these companies failed outright or had to be sold at urgently distressed prices to rival financial companies in the Great Recession that ran from 2008-2010. Lehman Brothers had to file for bankruptcy in 2008. The U.S. government made JP Morgan Chase buy Bear Stearns. The Treasury and the Federal Reserve then forced Bank of America to purchase Merrill Lynch.

The catastrophic collapse of this many major financial firms dramatically downsized Wall Street with massive re-structuring. It proved to be especially severe for the economies of New York City and the surrounding states. This was because the financial industry in New York produced nearly a quarter of all income in the city. It also amounted to about 10% of all tax revenue for the city and 20% of taxes for the state of New York. City and state government revenues and budgets suffered dramatically from this loss of revenue for years. The Boston Consulting Group estimated in 2009 that as many as 65,000 jobs were permanently gone as a result of the financial crisis.

This city and financial center has grown to become a global symbol for investment and high finance. Movies have been made about it including two with the same title Wall Street and its sequel Wall Street: Money Never Sleeps. The financial district has become a part of modern mythology in many ways starting back in the 1800s.

The street emerged as a hated symbol of the greedy robber barons who took advantage of workers and farmers to the populists of the 19th century. When times were good it represented the way to get rich quick. Following such terrible stock market crashes as 1929 and 2008 the street looked like the home of financial manipulators who could crush major international companies and even derail the economies of entire nations.

Wash Sale

The Wash Sale refers to an IRS Internal Revenue Service code rule that outlaws any taxpayers from utilizing loss sales on securities in what they cleverly call a "wash sale." The rule essentially explains such a sale as any that occurs as the investor trades or sells securities at a loss within 30 days before or after this particular sale, buying a stock or other security that is deemed to be substantially identical, or otherwise obtaining an option to do the same. Such a sale will also occur when investors sell the security and their spouse or a company which they own subsequently purchases the same or substantially the same security back.

Where stocks are concerned at least, one company stock and another is never considered to be substantially the same to the IRS. They also do not count preferred stocks or bonds of one company and another as materially the same. Yet there are cases where the preferred and common stocks of a single company could be considered to be basically the same investment. This is especially true when the preferred stock can be freely converted into the company's common stock with no restrictions, or if they both possess voting rights, and if they trade for a price that is near the official conversion ratio of the preferred stock issue.

When such a loss becomes disavowed by the IRS thanks to the wash sale rule, it means that the taxpayer investor will be forced to add his loss back on to the cost of the newer stock. This would then be known as the cost basis on the new stock. Consider an example to help demystify what is at best a confusing topic. An investor might buy 100 shares of JP Morgan common stock at $35 per share, then sell them for $30 per share in a loss, and in less than 30 days later purchase another 100 shares of JPM common stock for $33. The $500 ultimate loss in this scenario would not be permitted for claiming by the IRS thanks to the wash sale rule. Yet it can be added back in to the $3,300 cost of the newer shares. The basis for the new cost then would be $3,800 as the 100 shares times $33 equals $3,300 plus the $500 loss on the prior trade equates to a total new cost basis position of $3,800.

In truth, the only silver lining to a stock or mutual fund trade that goes bad is that the capital loss can help to offset other more profitable investments elsewhere.

The ironic part is that there is no such wash rule for any investor who cashes out on profits on a trade then reenters the trade within 30 days. Tax professionals call this unfair scenario the "heads I win, tails you lose" IRS is the master rule. Options are similarly included under the wash rules which mean that you can also have your options loss disavowed if you repurchase the identical ones within 30 days.

Many investors will wonder where the IRS draws the lines on the ever popular newer index mutual funds such as the S&P 500 ones. The IRS throws sand in the eyes of the investor by stating that all circumstances have to be considered when evaluating if securities are in fact substantially identical. No one knows what this really means in point of fact. The general interpretation though is that no two mutual funds are "substantially the same" to each other. Yet selling a single S&P 500 index fund for a loss then purchasing another different S&P 500 index fund in 30 days or less would likely be disavowed by the tricky rule.

Wilshire 5000 Index

The Wilshire 5000 Index is also called the Total Stock Market Index. The reason for this impressive sounding name is that its ultimate goal is to track the aggregate returns of most ever publicly traded stock that is based in the United States and trades over one of the major American stock market exchanges. This index is not necessarily the most famous one in the investing universe though. The truth is that despite this fact, it remains the biggest market index on earth, when it is measured by actual market value.

The Wilshire 5000 Index is actually a misnomer. There are not only 5,000 firms within the index as many incorrectly suppose. Instead, there are over 6,700 individual companies' stocks within it. The number of firms actually changes all the time. When the Index was first created, it actually had only 5,000 composite companies. As more business have been created and traded publically on the major three U.S. exchanges since the Wilshire's inception, this has necessarily required that they add more net numbers of companies in order to keep up with their objective of representing all major American corporations.

In order to be a candidate for inclusion in the Wilshire 5000 Index, there are three criteria which the firms must meet. They have to be headquartered domestically within the United States. They must also trade actively over one of the significant stocks exchanges in America. Finally, their pricing data has to be easily accessible to both members of the general public and the American investing community.

The Wilshire index actually does not evenly weight all of its constituent members, as is typical with other market cap weighted indices as well. In fact, they provide a greater weighting to firms that are more highly valued and an underweighting to those companies which possess a lesser firm value. The ticker symbol for The Wilshire 5000 Index proves to be TMWX. The index is famous for its efforts to track the all around American stock markets' performance.

Some publically traded United States' based corporations are routinely excluded from any inclusion in The Wilshire 5000 Index. Among these are the stocks which trade over the OTC BB Over the Counter Bulletin Board platform and system. This includes the stocks from micro cap companies and those which are valued as penny stocks. All companies which trade on the NASDAQ, American Stock Exchanges, and NYSE New York Stock Exchanges are typically included. It is what makes the Wilshire index the most truly diverse of all American indices anywhere.

Those larger companies which are a part of the Wilshire index have a greater weighting and will thus have greater impact on the movements of the underlying index.

With the Wilshire 5000 Index, the 500 biggest firms command over 70 percent of the total value of the index. This actually means that it is an economic performance measurement of only American companies, the largest 500 of which dominate the up and down movement of the index.

It is important for investors to realize that the ETFs, index funds, and other mutual funds based on the Wilshire 5000 have a unique expense characteristic. The costs of maintaining a passive portfolio of over 6,700 different stocks which are constantly changing naturally will be higher than for a index fund that has only 30 or even 500 composite constituent corporations within it, as in the Dow Jones 30 companies' index or the S&P 500 composite index. Despite this fact, the fees do not amount to a much higher percentage wise difference for investments in the Wilshire 5000 Index.

XAU Precious Metals Index

The XAU precious metals index proves to be a stock shares index which trades on the United States' based Philadelphia Stock Exchange. This index is comprised of 29 different precious metals mining firms. Though there are 29 participants in the index, the index is heavily dominated by only the three largest of them. These three overwhelming players are mega-gold mining companies Barrack-Placer, Newmont Mining, and Anglo Gold Ashanti. Between the three of them, they represent over half of the entire index.

As of May 5, 2017, the 29 companies comprising the XAU precious metals index were as follows: Agnico Eagle Mines Limited, Anglo Gold Ashanti Limited, Barrick Gold Corporation, Coeur Mining Incorporated, Compania de Minas Buenaventura, El Dorado Gold Corporation, First Majestic Silver Corporation, Freeport-McMoran Incorporated, Gold Fields Limited, Gold Resource Corporation, Goldcorp Incorporated, Harmony Gold Mining Company Limited, Hecla Mining Company, Iamgold Corporation, Kinross Gold Corporation, McEwen Mining, New Gold Incorporated, Newmont Mining Corporation, Nova Gold Resources Incorporated, Pan American Silver Corporation, Primero Mining Corporation, Rand Gold Resources Limited, Royal Gold Incorporated, Sandstorm Gold Limited, Sea Bridge Gold, Silver Standard Resources Incorporated, Silver Wheaton Corporation, Still Water Mining, and Yamana Gold Incorporated.

Back in 2006, the Philadelphia Stock Exchange expanded its XAU precious metals index and grew the exposure beyond the traditional North American, British, South African, and Australian based miners to include significant exposure to Eastern Europe, South America, and Russia. They did this by adding in another four mid cap and small cap companies that had gold mining properties in those three parts of the world. At the same time, Placer Dome was acquired by Barrick Gold and became removed from the index.

The four new companies which they added to this important precious metals index were Royal Gold Incorporated, Rand Gold Resources Limited, Couer D' Alene Mines Corporation, and Bema Gold Corporation. Bema Gold Corporation was later acquired by Kinross Gold Corporation and subsequently became delisted from the XAU precious metals index. It is not terribly surprising that Canadian Bema Gold Corporation was taken over, as even in the heyday of rising gold prices back in 2005, Bema proved to be an anomaly in the gold mining world as it represented one of the only gold companies on earth to lose money in the booming gold price days of the mid 2000's.

The development of adding additional gold mining company exposure to Russia, Eastern Europe, South America, and Australia came about because of geographical leadership changes in both the gold and silver mining industries. The XAU precious metals index has long been the most closely studied and heavily watched bell weather of gold mining company shares. It outperformed the overall stock markets in the first five years of the new millennium, and managed to triple in market cap and overall share pricing from 2001 to 2005.

The Philadelphia Stock Exchange allows trading of the XAU precious metals index every Monday through Friday from 9:30am until 4pm local Philadelphia time. This index has only one serious rival in the world of gold mining companies' indices. This is the HUI Index listed as the AMEX Gold BUGS Index. The two indices represent the world's most closely followed precious metals composites.

There has occasionally been some confusion with the name XAU precious metals index. This is because XAU also denotes a single ounce of gold. Thanks to the ISO 4217 currency standard, the symbol became representative of the yellow metal itself.

Yield

In business and finance, yield is the word that states the quantity of cash that comes back to a security's owners. It is measured independently of variations in price. It proves to be a percentage of total return. It is used for measuring the return rates of fixed income investments, such as bonds, bills, strips, notes, and zero coupons; stocks, including common, convertible, and preferred; and various other insurance and investment hybrid products like annuities.

Yield can mean different things in varying situations. It is sometimes figured up as an IRR, or Internal Rate of Return, or alternatively as a ratio. Yield describes an investment owner's entire return or a part of the income.

The end result of the many differences in yield is that they can not be compared one against the other. This is because they are not all the same from one branch of finance and investments to another. You could see numerous different formulas for figuring up yield used by different investments and groups.

Bonds are a classic example of this. Nominal yield is also known as coupon yield. This proves to be the face value of a bond divided into the annual interest total. Current yield instead is those interest payments over the bond's price on the spot market.

A yield to maturity is the internal rate of return on the bond cash flow, including the bond principal when maturity arrives plus the interest received, and the purchase price. Finally, a bond's yield to call is the bond's cash flow internal rate of return if it is called in by the company at their earliest opportunity.

Bonds yields are unusual in that they vary inversely to the price of the bond. Should a bond price decline, then the yield will rise. If instead the rates of interest drop, then the bond's price will go up in general.

Some securities come with real yields. TIPS are a primary example of this. A real yield means that the face value of the instrument will be adjusted upwards compared to the CPI inflation index. It would then be set against this principal that is adjusted to make certain that an investor makes a better return than the rate of inflation.

This ensures that his or her purchasing power is protected. TIPS are one rare investment that will not allow investors to lose money if they purchased them in the auction and keep them until they mature, either as a result of deflation, meaning falling prices, or inflation, signifying rising prices over time.

Yield to Maturity (YTM)

Yield to Maturity is also widely known in investment and analyst circles by its acronym YTM, as well as by the phrases book yield and redemption yield. This represents the aggregate return which investors can expect to receive for a bond if they keep the security until the end of its actual life. This is why YTM is generally called a longer term bond yield even though it is still expressed as a rate per year. Another way of saying this is that this proves to be the investment's internal rate of return for the bond if the owner keeps it all the way through maturity. This assumes of course that the bond issuer makes all of its payments both on time and in the full amounts contracted.

In order to understand the Yield to Maturity calculations, it is critical to realize that the formula assumes all coupon payments the issuer makes will be exactly reinvested for the rate of the current yield of the bond. The formula similarly considers the bond's par value, current price on the market, term to maturity, and coupon interest rate. All of this makes the YTM a complicated yet good formula for determining the return of a bond. It allows investors to effectively compare and contrast those bonds which possess varying coupon rates and maturity dates.

There are several different ways to figure out the Yield to Maturity. It is a complicated formula so many investors simply fall back on pre-printed and -figured bond yield tables. Determining the exact YTM requires either a software program or the use of a financial or business calculator. This is because the value for a basis point drops as the price for a bond increases in an inverse manner. Many firms actually calculate YTM for six month time frames as well as on an annual basis. They do this because most coupon payments take place twice per year.

A significant difference between Yield to Maturity and the current yield lies in the fact that the YTM takes into account money's time value, while the simplified current yield computations will not. This is why investors often prefer to utilize the YTM instead of the current yield when they are crunching number on bond returns to compare and contrast with other bond issues and different types of investments.

There are a number of similar yet still variations on the classical Yield to Maturity figure. These should never be confused with the true YTM. Among these are the Yield to call (YTC), Yield to put (YTP), and the Yield to worst (YTW). Yields to call go with the assumption that the bond issuer will recall the bond by repurchasing it in advance of it reaching maturity. This assumes that the resulting cash flow period will be shortened. Yield to put is much like the YTC, only the seller is allowed to and may sell the bond back to its issuer on a specific date for a pre-determined price. Finally, Yield to worst means that the bonds in question can be put, called, or even exchanged. This is why YTW bonds usually have the smallest yields from the three variations on YTM and the YTM rate itself.

There are some important limitations to the utility of Yield to Maturity as a measurement for comparing and contrasting various bonds against other bonds and other forms of investment classes as well. With YTM, these calculations never take into account the actual taxes which investors will have to pay on the bonds. This is why YTM is sometimes called the gross redemption yield. These calculations for yield also do not factor in either selling or buying costs for the bonds themselves.

It is also important to keep in mind that YTM is limited by the fact that both it and current yields are estimate calculations. They can not ever be 100 percent accurate or reliable. The true returns will vary with the realized price of a bond when a holder sells it. The prices of such bonds can vary significantly as the market actually determines them (and not the issuer). Such variations in the value of a bond and the price for which it is sold may impact the YTM substantially. They more drastically impact the current yield calculations and measurement in the end.

Zombie Banks

Zombie banks prove to be financial institutions that in reality have literal economic net worths of less than zero. They still keep running because they are able to continue paying their debts using government's real or implied support for their credit and balance sheet. Although this term has come to be heavily used in the financial crises of 2007 to 2010, it did not originate there.

Instead, Edward Kane coined the phrase Zombie Banks back in 1987. He used it to refer to and relate the perils of allowing a great number of banks that were actually insolvent to continue operating. The phrase came to be utilized for the Japanese banking crisis that began in 1993. It once again arose in popularity during the financial crisis of the last few years where hundreds of banks have failed in single years.

Zombie banks have many problems. Among these are bank runs from frightened depositors who are uninsured for their full account values. They also suffer from margin calls from their counter parties in derivatives contracts.

Zombie banks can be deceptive, as on the surface they may look like they are actually healthy and have the necessary level of capital to run. As investors learn the fair value of their assets, then they are suddenly looked at as insolvent institutions. This is to say that Zombie Banks keep operating in a regular manner as if nothing is wrong with their balance sheets. Yet the truth is that they will likely be seized by the Feds when the word becomes wide spread that they do not have the assets and money that everyone believed.

Healthy banks are able to make loans to new borrowers at the same time that they honor their obligations to lenders and share holders. Insolvent banks, or Zombie Banks, are incapable of generating new loans, since they lack the money and capital to make such loans while still performing on their obligations to lenders and share holders.

Comprehending what constitutes a Zombie bank requires that you know the basics of a bank balance sheet. One side of a balance sheet actually contains a bank's assets. The other side is comprised of the bank's liabilities as well as the bank's equity. The two sides are supposed to equal out, which is expressed in the equation assets equal liabilities plus the bank equity.

Zombie banks manage to hide their problems since no one is able to determine how much their assets are really worth. Asset backed securities and collateralized debt obligations are examples of assets whose values can not clearly be determined at any given moment. They might be worth as much as seventy-five cents for every dollar, or they could be valued as low as twenty-five cents per dollar.

The problem comes when Zombie banks have over valued their assets. If they later are forced to revalue them to correct and more appropriate levels, they quickly discover that they no longer have the assets to cover their future liabilities. Admitting to this causes them to become Zombie banks. At this point, the bank share holders are typically wiped out, while the depositors are given their money back by the Federal Deposit Insurance Corporation.

Other Financial Books by Thomas Herold

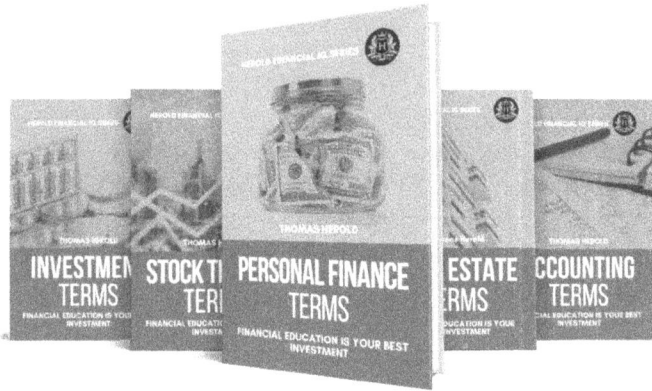

Herold Financial IQ Series
Financial Education Is Your Best Investment

Get Smart with the Financial IQ Series
The Herold Financial IQ series covers all major areas and aspects of the financial world. Starting with Personal Finance, Real Estate and Banking term. Covering Corporate Finance, Investment as well as Economics.

It also includes Retirement, Trading, and Accounting terms. In addition, you'll find Debt, Bankruptcy, Mortgage, Small Business, and Wall Street terminology explained. Not to forget Laws & Regulations as well as important acronyms and abbreviations.

Available on Amazon as Kindle, Paperback and Audio Edition
Go to Amazon.com and search for 'Herold Financial IQ' or copy and paste this link below.

http://bit.ly/herold-financial-iq

High Credit Score Secrets - The Smart Raise And Repair Guide to Excellent Credit

Poor Credit Score Could Cost You Hundreds of Thousands of Dollars
A recent financial statistic revealed that increasing your score from 'fair' to 'good' saves you an average of $86,200* over a lifetime. Imagine what you could do with that extra money?

Improve Your Credit Score in 45-60 Days or Even Less
This practical credit compendium starts off by demonstrating over 50 guaranteed methods of how you can almost immediately boost your credit score. Follow these simple, effective and proven strategies to improve your credit score from as low as 450 points to over 810.

Don't let bad credit hold you back from achieving financial freedom. Your credit score not only influences all your future choices, but it also can save you thousands of dollars.

Available on Amazon as Kindle, Paperback and Audio Edition
Go to Amazon.com and search for 'High Credit Score Secrets' or copy and paste this link below.

http://bit.ly/high-credit

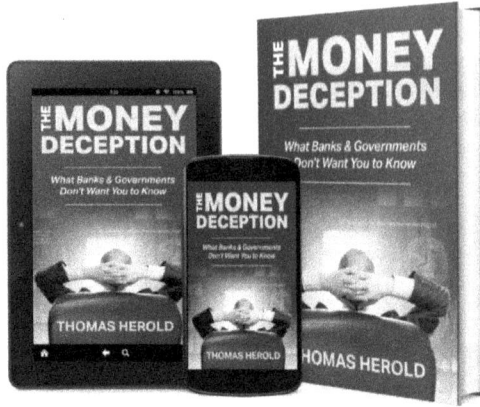

The Money Deception
What Banks & Governments Don't Want You to Know

„It is well enough that people of the nation do not understand our banking and monetary system, for if they did, I believe there would be a revolution before tomorrow morning." - Henry Ford

The Catastrophic Results of Money Manipulation
This money has been souped up by the 1% that now controls 50% of the world's wealth. The fastest and biggest wealth transfer in history is underway. Money evaporates from the middle class, leaving them struggling and without hope for retirement.

What's Happening to Your Money?
Going all the way down into the rabbit hole, it shows you the root of the problem and also lays the foundation for the future. It describes the most likely transition into a new worldwide crypto-based currency, which will become the new basis of our financial system.

Available on Amazon as Kindle, Paperback and Audio Edition
Go to Amazon.com and search for 'Money Deception' or copy and paste this link below.

http://bit.ly/money-deception

Other Books in the Herold Financial IQ Series

99 Financial Terms Every Beginner, Entrepreneur & Business Should Know

Personal Finance Terms

Real Estate Terms

Bank & Banking Terms

Corporate Finance Terms

Investment Terms

Economics Terms

Retirement Terms

Stock Trading Terms

Accounting Terms

Debt & Bankruptcy Terms

Mortgage Terms

Small Business Terms

Wall Street Terms

Laws & Regulations

Financial Acronyms

www.ingramcontent.com/pod-product-compliance
Lightning Source LLC
Chambersburg PA
CBHW071542210326

41597CB00019B/3089